HOW TO BE A
DOMESTIC GODDESS

Also by Nigella Lawson:

HOW TO EAT
THE PLEASURES AND PRINCIPLES OF GOOD FOOD

HOW TO BE A DOMESTIC GODDESS

BAKING AND THE ART OF
COMFORT COOKING

NIGELLA LAWSON

Photography by PETRINA TINSLAY

NEW YORK

FOR JOHN, GODDESS-MAKER

Library of Congress Cataloging-in-Publication Data

Lawson, Nigella, 1960–
    How to be a domestic goddess : baking and the art of comfort cooking / Nigella Lawson;
photography by Petrina Tinslay.
        p. cm.
    Includes bibliographical references and index.
    ISBN 0-7868-6797-3
    1. Baking. I. Title

TX763 .L37 2002
641.8'15—dc21

                                                                        2001024170

FIRST EDITION

10 9 8 7 6

CONTENTS

PREFACE

This is a book about baking, but not a baking book—not in the sense of being a manual or a comprehensive guide or a map of a land you do not inhabit. I neither want to confine you to the kitchen nor even suggest that it might be desirable. But I do think that many of us have become alienated from the domestic sphere, and that it can actually make us feel better to claim back some of that space, make it comforting rather than frightening. In a way, baking stands both as a useful metaphor for the familial warmth of the kitchen we fondly imagine used to exist, and as a way of reclaiming our lost Eden. This is hardly a culinary matter, of course; but cooking, we know, has a way of cutting through things, and to things, which have nothing to do with the kitchen. This is why it matters.

The trouble with much modern cooking is not that the food it produces isn't good, but that the mood it induces in the cook is one of skin-of-the-teeth efficiency, all briskness and little pleasure. Sometimes that's the best we can manage, but at other times we don't want to feel like a postmodern, postfeminist, overstretched woman but, rather, a domestic goddess, trailing nutmeggy fumes of baking pie in our languorous wake.

So what I'm talking about is not *being* a domestic goddess exactly, but *feeling* like one. One of the reasons making cakes is satisfying is that the effort required is so much less than the gratitude conferred. Everyone seems to think it's hard to make a cake (and no need to disillusion them), but it doesn't take more than 25 minutes to make and bake a tray of muffins or a sponge layer cake, and the returns are high: you feel disproportionately good about yourself afterwards. This is what baking, what all of this book, is about: feeling good, wafting along in the warm, sweet-smelling air, unwinding, no longer being entirely an office creature; and that's exactly what I mean by "comfort cooking."

Part of it too is about a fond, if ironic, dream: the unexpressed "I" that is a cross between Sophia Loren and Debbie Reynolds in pink cashmere cardigan and fetching gingham apron, a weekend alter ego winning adoring glances and endless approbation from anyone who has the good fortune to eat in her kitchen. The good thing is, we don't have to get ourselves up in Little Lady drag and we don't have to renounce the world and enter into a life of domestic drudgery. But we can bake a little—and a cake is just a cake, far easier than getting the timing right for even the most artlessly casual of midweek dinner parties.

This isn't a dream; what's more, it isn't even a nightmare.

A SHORT NOTE ON EQUIPMENT AND INGREDIENTS

You need neither a professionally appointed kitchen nor an expensively stocked pantry to bake. Your hands, a bowl, and a wooden spoon should see you through most of it, along with a couple of cake pans, one or two springform pans, a loaf pan, a muffin pan, a pie and tart pan, and a rolling pin. A food processor makes life easier for some jobs, but is hardly indispensable. If there is one piece of machinery that does make a baking life more pleasurable, it's a free-standing mixer; I now couldn't live without my KitchenAid mixer, or certainly wouldn't want to. The dough hook makes bread-making a far lighter task (though I would never suggest you give up completely the relaxing routine of kneading by hand), and the other attachments—paddle and whisk—mean that you can let the cake batter be mixed or egg whites whipped while you get on with other things. Unlike a processor, you don't feel excluded from the job at hand; it's thus a very good way of feeling that you're doing it all yourself but with the minimum of effort. Otherwise, a simple hand-held electric mixer is a cheaper alternative.

As for pans and molds, I've tried on the whole to use nothing that wouldn't be available at an average well-stocked kitchen shop or department store. Should you find difficulties locating any of the fancier pieces—the baby Bundt molds or nonstick ware—you should call Ecko Bakeware (540-988-7943) or Williams-Sonoma (800-541-1262) or check their Web sites.

None of the ingredients listed should prove troublesome, either. The instant royal icing and the paste colors I use to tint the icing are available from cake-decoration shops, as are gold leaf, other decorative items, and a huge range of cookie cutters. If you can't find what you need, try ordering from www.confectioneryhouse.com or www.wilton.com.

I often use self-rising cake flour in place of ordinary all-purpose flour. Don't use self-rising unless it's specified.

Eggs—organic, free-range for preference—are large unless stated otherwise in the text, and, likewise, butter is unsalted.

If you have any further inquiries, please email me at domesticgoddess@nigella.com.

HOW TO BE A
DOMESTIC GODDESS

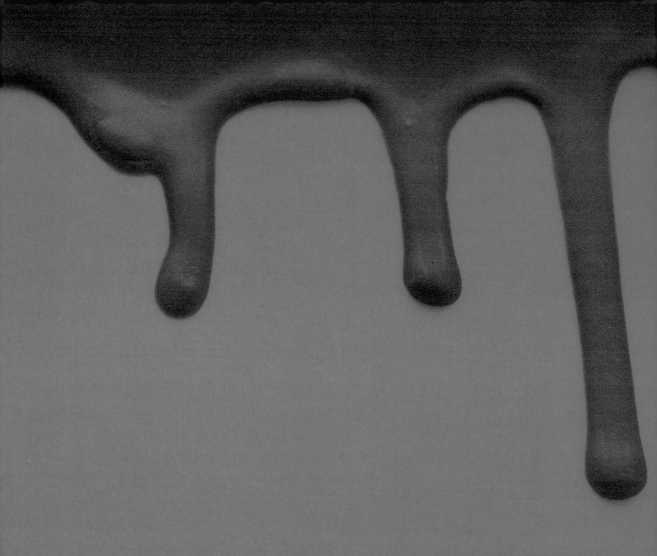

CAKES

CAKES

Cake baking has to be, however innocently, one of the great culinary scams: it implies effort, it implies domestic prowess; but believe me, it's easy. We've become so convinced that simple food comes out of simple cooking that we're happy to cook elaborate Tuscan suppers—which in reality demand much more than we could ever believe possible—but then balk at baking a cake, assuming that we don't have the time for all that, that we live a life that doesn't encompass those arcane culinary arts.

If that's how you think, then you're wrong. You know how you make a cake? You mix a few basic ingredients together, stick the mixture in a pan and bake it. And when I say mix, I don't mean mix it yourself, not if you don't want to: I mean process or beat with an electric mixer. How hard can that be?

Too much reassurance can, I know, be troubling in itself. If it's so easy to bake a cake, why is it that you can't? Be honest: I imagine the answer is that you don't often try, or haven't for years. Not all cakes come out perfectly or even the same each time, and not all cakes are equally easy to bake, but if you follow any one of the recipes below, you can be sure it will work. Of course there are always variants in cooking, some more controllable than others, but baking is somewhat different: it's chemistry first, poetry second. That's partly why I came to it late. When you're making a stew, well, you can go your own way, follow instinct, taste, convenience; you couldn't make a cake like this: a cake demands mathematical respect.

Some rules extend beyond the confines of the individual texts. You must remember three basic things: the first is that all ingredients should be at room temperature when you start; the second is that the oven should be at the required temperature when you put in the filled pan; finally, that pan should be of the dimensions specified. (If I'm honest, you can get away with some deviation here, but not too much—and anyway, why make things harder for yourself?)

I've said it's easy to make a cake, but this doesn't convey the depth of achievement you feel on making one. There's something about seeing such elemental change, that flour, butter, eggs, sugar could become this—and more, that you've made it happen—that's so satisfying. Such simple pleasures are not to be underestimated.

LOAF AND PLAIN CAKES

This is baking at its simplest and most elegant. There's no folderol or fancy footwork: you just feel humble and worthy and brimming with good things.

MY MOTHER-IN-LAW'S MADEIRA CAKE

I don't know if I ever ate Madeira cake as a child, but just the sight of this golden-yellow loaf with its long crack down the middle makes me feel satisfactorily nostalgic. This recipe, given to me by my mother-in-law Carrie, is the best of any version I've tried. It's just one of those plain cakes (no Madeira in the recipe!) you think you can't see the point of, until you start slicing and eating it.

1 cup softened unsalted butter	3 large eggs
3/4 cup sugar, plus extra for sprinkling	1 1/3 cups self-rising cake flour
grated zest and juice of 1 lemon	1/2 cup all-purpose flour
	9 x 5-inch loaf pan, buttered and lined with parchment or wax paper

Preheat the oven to 350°F.

Cream the butter and ¾ cup sugar, and add the lemon zest. Add the eggs one at a time with a tablespoon of the flour for each. Then gently mix in the rest of the flour and, finally, the lemon juice. Pour batter into prepared pan. Sprinkle with sugar (about 2 tablespoons should do it) as it goes into the oven, and bake for 1 hour or until a cake tester comes out clean. Remove to a wire rack, and let cool in the pan before turning out.

Makes 8–10 slices.

VARIATION

I love a good old-fashioned seed cake; if you do too, add a couple of teaspoons of caraway to this batter. For a lemon poppyseed cake, add the juice of another half lemon and a tablespoon or two of poppyseeds. And I once came across an expensive but tempting curiosity: tiny dried strawberries. I upped the liquid to the juice of 2 lemons and folded in about a cup of the strawberries. It was a wholly successful experiment.

EASY ALMOND CAKE

This cake isn't baked in a loaf pan but in a ring mold, preferably a patterned one; and it's a plain cake only in the sense that it isn't filled or iced (though feel free). It's densely almondy and eggily intense. And you know how you make it? You buy a block of ready-made marzipan and put it in the processor along with eggs, flour, sugar, butter and a sprinkle of extracts and blitz.

You could easily use a plain cake pan for this cake but I always use my spring-form tube pan (not hard to find) because the particular scent and delicacy of this cake make it perfect as a dinner-party dessert with a few raspberries in the middle, a few more scattered around the edge, and a light dusting of confectioners' sugar. When we cooked it for the picture opposite, we couldn't find the right pan (losing essential items is something of a specialty of mine), plus some of it stuck to the pan we did use. I could have made it again, but I didn't want to, because these things happen to all of us and I wanted to show it wasn't the end of the world. True, you don't see the molding as well as you might, if at all, but a quick bit of patching and some judicial sifting with sugar and it looked fine. Life isn't lived in a lab.

One gentle reminder here: you just will not get the marzipan to ooze into the cake batter if it starts off ice cold. In dire straits, I have cubed it and given it a quick whirl in the microwave. And if you wanted to replace the vanilla extract with the zest of an orange, I wouldn't mind in the slightest.

1 cup plus 2 tablespoons softened unsalted butter	**¼ teaspoon vanilla extract**
1 cup plus 2 tablespoons softened marzipan	**6 large eggs**
½ cup sugar	**1 cup self-rising cake flour**
¼ teaspoon almond extract	**10-inch springform tube pan or patterned ring mold, buttered and floured**

Preheat oven to 350°F. Chop the butter and marzipan to make them easier to break down, and put them in the bowl of the food processor, fitted with the metal blade, with the sugar. Process until combined and pretty well smooth. Add almond and vanilla extracts, process again, then break the eggs one at a time through the funnel, processing again each time. Mix the flour and tip down the funnel, processing yet again, and then pour the mixture into the prepared pan, scraping the sides and bottom of the bowl with a rubber spatula.

Bake for 50 minutes, but check from 40. Then, when the cake looks golden and cooked and a cake tester or fine skewer (or a piece of spaghetti) comes out cleanish, remove from the oven and leave to cool in the pan before turning out. (This is when you will be feeling grateful if it's the springform you're using.)

The fact that you could easily get 12 slices out of this cake is another reason why it comes in useful when you've got people coming for dinner. That it keeps for a good week is another point in its favor; you don't have to be fiddling around with all the courses just before liftoff. And if you don't want to eat raspberries with it, like the rosemary cake it's very good with apples. With this cake, I make a glorious pink apple purée. Either go for apples stewed in blood-orange juice (wonderful around February when the oranges are in), which gives a tenderly coral tint, adding a cinnamon stick or $1/2$–1 teaspoon of ground cinnamon, or use red-skinned eating apples and don't peel before cooking them. In fact, there's no need to core them either, just chop the apples roughly and put them in a pan with some butter, lemon juice, cinnamon or cloves and, if there's some around, a slug of Calvados. Strain the apples when they're cooked to an utterly yielding pulp, or push them through a food mill. If you want to smarten up the cake-plus-purée deal, then provide a bowl of crème fraîche (with or without Calvados and a little confectioners' sugar stirred in) with some toasted slivered almonds on top.

I am not someone who enjoys peeling and pithing oranges at great length, but sliced blood or ordinary oranges, with a syrup made by reducing equal volumes of juice and sugar to an almost-caramel, would partner an orange-zested version of this almond ring (the zest in place of vanilla) exquisitely.

Needless to say, I also love this cake with a bowl of new season's rhubarb on the side, cooked as if for the rhubarb tart (see page 107). And just one further suggestion . . . ice it with chocolate ganache (see page 22) or just top with it at the moment of serving so it's still warm and thickly runny, and serve with a bowl of vanilla ice cream with cooled, toasted, slivered almonds sprinkled over (and I suppose you could actually spoon the ice cream into the central cavity, before drizzling over the chocolate ganache and sprinkling over these almonds).

The point of these suggestions is not simply to be interfering and bossy, but to show how cake-baking can be brought to the service of contemporary eating. To call this book "Baking and the Dinner Party Solutions" would not to be too far-fetched. In fact, I will return to this theme later—and see page 39.

Serves 10–12.

ROSEMARY LOAF CAKE

In structure, this recipe is much the same as the Madeira cake, but it tastes very different. Don't be alarmed at the idea of using a herb usually associated with savory cooking: there is something muskily aromatic about it against the sweet vanilla egginess of the cake. And the cake itself works extraordinarily well as part of an elegantly austere dessert. I love it sliced thickly and eaten with cold, stewed apples. Peel, core and chop 3 or 4 large cooking apples, squeeze over the juice of a lemon and an orange, sprinkle with sugar to taste (I'd start off with 2 tablespoons per apple and be prepared to double it), and add a pat of butter. Cook till the fruit is pale and pulpy and leave to cool. If you want to point up the flavors, you could always chuck in a small sprig of rosemary, which you should remove when you're decanting the cold almost-purée to a bowl; but go steadily, we're aiming for subtlety here. I use my stash of rosemary sugar for sprinkling over this cake (just because it's there, really—and see page 336) but you can replace it with ordinary or granulated brown sugar without a second thought.

1 cup plus 2 tablespoons soft unsalted butter

3/4 cup sugar

3 large eggs

1 1/3 cups self-rising cake flour

1/2 cup all-purpose flour

1 teaspoon vanilla extract

needles from a 4-inch stalk of rosemary, chopped small, but not too fine (about 2 teaspoons)

4 tablespoons milk

1–2 tablespoons rosemary sugar or granulated brown or white sugar

9 x 5-inch loaf pan, buttered and lined with parchment or wax paper

Preheat the oven to 350°F. Now cream the butter, adding the sugar when it's really soft, and creaming both together till pale and smooth and light. Beat in the eggs one at a time, folding in a spoonful of the flour after each addition, then add the vanilla. Fold in the rest of the flour—I find a rubber spatula the best tool for the job—and finally the rosemary. Thin the batter with the milk—you're after a soft, dropping consistency—and pour, with some helpful prodding and scraping with your spatula, into the waiting pan. Sprinkle the top with a little sugar before putting it in the oven, and cook for 1 hour, or until a cake tester comes out clean. Leave to cool on a wire rack, in its pan, and when completely cold, unmold and wrap well in foil till you need to eat it. Like all these sorts of cakes, it keeps well.

Serves 8–10.

GATEAU BRETON

I came across this recipe for Brittany butter cake in the wonderful Anne Willan's *Real Food*, and as she says, it's really a cross between shortbread and pound cake. Rather like the crostata on page 105, it's hard to decide whether it's cake or pastry. I love a stubby slice of this any time, but it does make a perfect, chic ending to a dinner party, too, either with ice cream or fruit, or just with coffee.

Anne Willan suggests a kneading motion to bring this very sticky dough into shape; I use the dough hook on my free-standing mixer.

Use the best butter that you can find, for this is the plain cake at its simple best, and the taste of each of these few ingredients is crucial.

for the glaze:
**1 teaspoon egg yolk, from your 6
(see below)**
1 tablespoon water

for the cake:
1 1/2 cups cake flour
3/4 cup plus 1 tablespoon sugar
**1 cup plus 2 tablespoons unsalted
butter, cut into cubes**
6 large egg yolks
10-inch springform pan, buttered well

Preheat the oven to 375°F. Mix the glaze, and put aside while you get on with your cake.

Put the flour into a bowl, stir in the sugar, and add the butter and egg yolks.

With the dough-hook attachment of a mixer, slowly whirr till you've got a smooth, golden dough. (If you're making this by hand, make a mound of the flour on a worktop, then make a well in it and add the sugar, butter, and eggs and knead to mix.) Scoop this dough into the pan, and smooth the top with a floured hand: expect it to be very sticky; indeed, it should be.

Brush the cake with the glaze, and mark a lattice design on top with the prongs of a fork. For a reason I am not technically proficient enough to explain, sometimes the tine marks leave a firm, striated imprint (a bit like the scrapy lines that drive Gregory Peck mad in *Spellbound*); at others, as with the cake in the picture, they barely show once the cake's cooked. Bake for 15 minutes, then turn the oven down to 350°F. and give it another 25 minutes or so until it's golden on top and firm to the touch.

Let it cool completely in the pan before unmolding it. It'll keep well if you've got a reliably airtight tin. When you come to eat it, either cut it in traditional—though slightly narrower—cakelike wedges or, as I prefer if I'm eating it at the end of dinner, crisscross, making irregularly sized diamonds.

Serves 8–10.

DAMP LEMON AND ALMOND CAKE

I love lemon, I love almond, so this for me is cake nirvana. Perhaps it should be in the fruited cakes section, but the citrus element, though intense, just melds with the almonds to give a slab of damp, dense, sharp-toned meltiness. It is a plain cake, but gloriously plain.

If you can, leave this cake wrapped in a double layer of foil for a couple of days before eating it: both its sharpness and its melting dampness will increase in the waiting.

1 cup soft unsalted butter
3/4 cup sugar
4 large eggs
1/3 cup all-purpose flour
1 1/3 cups ground almonds

1/2 teaspoon almond extract
grated zest and juice of 2 lemons
**8-inch springform pan, lined on
    the bottom with parchment or
    wax paper**

Preheat the oven to 350°F.

Cream together the butter and sugar until almost white. Beat in the eggs, one at a time, adding a quarter of the flour after each addition. When all the eggs and flour have been incorporated, gently stir in the ground almonds, then the almond extract, lemon zest, and juice. Pour the mixture into the cake pan and bake for about 1 hour. I say "about" only because ovens seem to vary so violently. I've cooked this in one oven when it was finished after 50 minutes; in another when it needed 1 hour and 10 minutes. Whichever, after about 30 minutes you may well find you have to cover it loosely with foil; you don't want the top of the cake to burn. The cake is ready when the top is firm and a skewer, inserted, comes out cleanish: you want dampness, but no battery goo. Take the cake out and let it stand for 5 or so minutes in the pan. Then turn it out on a wire rack and leave till cool.

Then, preferably, wrap well in tin foil and leave it for a couple of days. Push some confectioners' sugar over the cake through a fine sieve or tea strainer when serving. I can't stop myself murmuring "raspberries" to you, either.

You could use this cake as the base for the lemon-raspberry plate trifle (page 153) in place of the lemon-syrup loaf cake that follows.

Serves 6–8.

LEMON-SYRUP LOAF CAKE

This isn't, strictly speaking, a plain cake since it has a form of icing, but I can't help feeling that its loafiness counts for a lot. Of course, you could bake this (for slightly less time) in a square, 8-inch pan, cutting the syrup-drenched sponge into smaller squares later.

for the cake:
¹/₂ cup unsalted butter
¹/₂ cup plus 1 tablespoon sugar
2 large eggs
zest of 1 lemon
1 cup plus 1 tablespoon self-rising cake flour
pinch of salt
4 tablespoons milk

9 x 5-inch loaf pan, buttered and lined with parchment or wax paper

for the syrup:
juice of 1¹/₂ lemons (about 4 tablespoons)
¹/₂ cup confectioners' sugar

Preheat the oven to 350°F, and butter and line your loaf pan well with parchment or wax paper. Make sure the lining comes an inch or so up the sides of the pan for easier unmolding later.

Cream together the butter and sugar, and add the eggs and lemon zest, beating them in well. Add the flour and salt, folding in gently but thoroughly, and then the milk. Spoon into the prepared loaf pan and put in the oven. While the cake is baking, get on with the syrup: put the lemon juice and sugar into a small saucepan and heat gently so that the sugar dissolves.

Bake the cake for 45 minutes, or until golden, risen in the middle (though it will sink a little on cooling), and an inserted cake tester comes out clean. As soon as the cake is out of the oven, puncture the top of the loaf all over with the cake tester or suitable implement. Pour over the syrup, trying to let the middle absorb it as well as the sides, then leave it to soak up the rest. Don't try to take the cake out of the pan until it is completely cold, as it will be sodden with syrup and might crumble.

Serves 8–10.

VARIATION

Double the ingredients for the syrup to make the base for the lemon-raspberry plate trifle (see page 153). And there's no reason why you couldn't spike the syrup with some of that glorious Italian liqueur, *Limoncello*. Otherwise, you can use whatever citrus fruit you like. I love Seville oranges, and I'd use them orange per lemon. If you want to evoke the bitter fragrance of this wonderful fruit beyond its short season, then mix the juice of ordinary sweet oranges with lime using, here, 1 smallish or medium-sweet orange and 1 lime, and the zest of both in the cake. See page 153 for the lime variant and, if the mood takes you, try a pink-grapefruit version, using the zest of half in the cake and the scant juice of 1 in the syrup.

FILLED AND ICED CAKES

I used to think that filled cakes were really not for eating as a dessert, that there really was something too nursery-teatime about them, but I am beginning to change my mind. After a summer lunch, a Victoria sponge filled with cream, fruit and maybe a little good jam, does work. It's a reminder that, when the ingredients are good and the cake tenderly fresh, this is one of the dreamiest combinations in the world. And I say that as someone without a particularly sweet tooth. But then, these cakes don't have to be cloyingly sweet.

Iced cakes, on the other hand, just are sweet, and to apologize for that would be to undermine the whole purpose of making them. And any iced cake is, of course, a birthday cake waiting to be called into service.

VICTORIA SPONGE

Traditionally, jam rather than fruit is used for this cake, but unless I've got some very good jam (and the one I do like using is the hands-free raspberry jam on page 346), I think adding just a few berries makes a crucial difference. I generally use raspberries with a little raspberry jam, and sometimes strawberries with their matching preserve. My other favorite (and my first choice for sponge drops, see below, page 43) is blackberries and blackberry jam, though ever since I found boysenberry jam regularly at the supermarket I often use that, again with either of those berries. At the bottom of the method, I've given yet more fruitful variations.

Although I've listed 1⅓ cups flour and 2 tablespoons cornstarch because I feel this makes for a lighter, more tender sponge, of course it's perfectly all right to replace these with the customary 1½ cups flour.

for the cake:

1 cup unsalted butter, very soft

¾ cup sugar

1 teaspoon vanilla extract

4 large eggs

1⅓ cups self-rising cake flour

2 tablespoons cornstarch

1 teaspoon baking powder (if using processor method)

3–4 tablespoons milk

2 8 x 2-inch cake pans (about 2 inches deep), buttered and lined with parchment or wax paper

for the filling:
**2–4 tablespoons raspberry or other
jam, depending on berries**
**½ pint raspberries or berries of
choice**

½ cup heavy cream

for the topping:
1–2 tablespoons sugar

Preheat the oven to 350°F.

I always make this basic sponge cake in the food processor, which involves putting in all the ingredients except the milk and processing till you've got a smooth batter. Then pulse, pouring the milk gradually through the funnel till your cake mixture's a soft, dropping consistency. Because I'm clumsy, I habitually make a too-runny mix, but it doesn't seem to matter. Likewise, if your ingredients are too cold you may end up with a batter that looks curdled: this doesn't seem to make any difference in the baking either (though it might get in the way of impressive rising).

If you want to make this the traditional way, cream the butter and sugar, add the vanilla and then the eggs, one at a time, adding a spoonful of flour between each. Fold in the rest of the flour and the cornstarch, adding no baking powder, and when all's incorporated, add a little milk as you need.

Pour and scrape the batter into the pans and bake for about 25 minutes, until the cakes are beginning to come away at the edges, are springy to the touch on top and a cake tester comes out clean. Leave the cakes in their pans on a wire rack for 10 minutes before turning out and leaving to cool completely.

When you're ready to eat the cake, put one layer on a plate, right-way up, spread with jam and scatter the fruit on top. Whip the cream till it's thickened but still soft and spread over the jammy fruit. Sit the other cake on top, and sprinkle over a tablespoon or so of sugar.

Serves 6–8.

VARIATIONS

One variation, which I think I make more often now than the original, is my lemon-mascarpone layer cake. I had an early and encouraging success with this at my daughter's first school party (and see pages 235–242 for other bakes for this event). It's very easy to make and the mascarpone brings contemporary tastes to a traditional cake. All you do is replace the vanilla with 1 teaspoon of Boyajian lemon oil (you can get this at selected supermarkets and specialty stores), adding it at the end, just before the milk. For the filling, soften 4 ounces mascarpone in a bowl before spreading it over the top of one of the cakes, and spread ½ cup of good bought lemon curd over that. Then sit the other cake on top and sprinkle over some sugar. If you can't find the lemon oil, just use the zest of 1 lemon and its juice, leaving out the milk, or using the scantest amount necessary.

There are another two fruity variants I play with. One is a rhubarb version, another a passionfruit one. In both cases, I use a teaspoonful of Boyajian orange oil in the cake. For the rhubarb filling, I stew about a pound of rhubarb, either using the poaching method (see page 107) or with about ½ cup of sugar and the juice of half an orange in a saucepan. Since I don't mind if this goes pulpy, I generally go for the stove-top method. Strain, reserving the juice. When the rhubarb is neither too soggy nor too warm, spread it over one of the cakes and add whipped cream. Reduce the rhubarb juice to an intense syrup, let it cool slightly, and drizzle over the cream. Then sit the second cake on top and sprinkle with sugar as usual.

With the passionfruit version, I make a passionfruit fool to lie softly in the middle of the sponge sandwich and a passionfruit glaze to dribble over the top. Mix the spooned-out pulp (seeds and all) of 4 passionfruit with the juice of a scant half lemon and a squeeze of orange, and set aside while you whisk about a scant ½ cup heavy cream with 2 tablespoons sifted confectioners' sugar till it's forming soft peaks. Just before serving, fold the passionfruit mixture into the cream and scrape it onto the top of one of the cakes. Lightly arrange the second cake over the filling and get on with the glaze. Push the pulp of another 4 passionfruit through a sieve and add to this aromatic liquid the juice of half an orange. Mix to a runny paste with sifted confectioners' sugar—start with 6 tablespoons and add more orange juice or more sugar as required. Pour over the waiting cake, letting it drip down the sides—I just drizzle it back and forth across the top, and let it run where it will.

For a coffee-flavored cake, keep the vanilla extract but add, too, 1 tablespoon of instant espresso powder to the flour in the cake batter. Fill with coffee buttercream (see page 210, but use espresso powder instead of vanilla) and if you really want to go to town, make double the buttercream, spread it slightly thinner for the filling and use the rest to coat the sides and top of the cake, covering the top, or indeed the whole thing, with walnut halves.

Other ideas you might want to bear in mind include the lemon variant of the sponge filled with poached dried apricots or baked plums and crème fraîche—though we're moving into Boston cream pie territory here—or the vanilla version filled with prunes that have been soaked then cooked in Armagnac, placed on one of the cakes, then covered with a crème patissière (see page 22) that has been flavored with brandy rather than vanilla. And when gooseberries are in brief season, stew ¼ pound or so with 1–2 tablespoons of sugar, 1 tablespoon of butter, and a couple of tablespoons of elderflower cordial (or, if you've got access to some, a couple of heads of elderflower, which you remove before mushing), then fork to a rough purée. When cool, fold into some softly whipped cream (you're making a gooseberry fool comparable to the passionfruit fool above) and fill a cake which you've made using a tablespoonful of elderflower cordial in place of vanilla. Strictly speaking, you should reduce the sugar to compensate for the sweetness of the cordial, but I like to leave the filling tart, so don't worry too much about the sugariness of the cake.

Boston cream pie

Butterscotch layer cake

Flora's famous zucchini cake

Victoria sponge

FLORA'S FAMOUS ZUCCHINI CAKE

This recipe was given to me by Flora Woods, who is now at Books for Cooks, a wonderful London bookshop. I love being given people's own or family recipes (and if that sounds like an invitation, it's meant to). I like to credit any recipe given to me, not only out of a sense of propriety, but because it's all the more interesting. Recipes don't, like Aphrodite, spring fully formed from their author's forehead: to give their provenance is a pleasure and more besides—it's where food and social history merge.

If zucchini cake sounds odd to you, think about carrot cake for a moment; this is just an adaptation of that (though if you feel it's safer, don't tell people it's made of zucchini until after they've eaten it). One warning: don't do what I did for the picture (page 17), which was to color the lime-curd filling green. I don't know what got into me, but I got out my color paste and my probe (a broken instant-read thermometer I use for mixing colors when I ice) and proved in one characteristically rash act that food is better left to its own devices. I decided we could just about live with the menacing green: things do go wrong in cooking and, generally, you can live with them. Still, I've learned my lesson here, for all of us.

for the cake:

¼ cup raisins, optional

12 ounces zucchini (2–3), weighed before grating

2 large eggs

½ cup vegetable oil

½ cup plus 1 tablespoon sugar

1½ cups self-rising cake flour

½ teaspoon baking soda

½ teaspoon baking powder

2 8 x 2-inch cake pans, greased and lined with parchment or wax paper

for the filling:

lime curd (page 344)

for the icing:

7 ounces cream cheese

½ cup confectioners' sugar, sifted

juice of 1 lime, or more to taste

2–3 tablespoons chopped pistachio nuts

Preheat the oven to 350ºF.

If you're using raisins, put them in a bowl and cover with warm water to plump them up.

Wipe the zucchini with a kitchen towel (but don't peel them), then grate. The coarse side of an ordinary box grater is the best thing to use: anything too fine or too quick can turn them to a wet mush. When you've grated them, put them in a sieve over the sink to drain.

Put the eggs, oil, and sugar in a bowl and beat them until creamy. Sift in the flour, baking soda, and baking powder and continue to beat until well combined. Now stir in the grated zucchini and add the drained raisins. Pour the mixture into the pans, and bake for 30 minutes until slightly browned and firm to the touch. Leave in their pans on a rack for 5–10 minutes, then turn out and let cool on the rack until your filling and icing are ready.

If you don't want to make the lime curd for the filling, then just buy a good lemon or lime curd and sharpen with some freshly squeezed lime juice. To make the cream-cheese icing for the top, beat the cream cheese in a bowl until smooth, add the confectioners' sugar, beating well to combine, and then stir in the lime juice to taste. Now get your cakes ready for assembling. Put one cake on the plate and spread with completely cooled lime curd. Put on the top cake and smear it thickly with the cream-cheese icing. If you feel the icings need firming up a little, put the cake in the refrigerator for a while. Just before serving, scatter chopped pistachios over the top.

Serves 8.

VARIATION

As an alternative, cook the same mixture in those large (sometimes called "Texas") muffin pans. When they're cooked and cooled, cut them in half and put the cream-cheese icing in the middle. Pour hot curd over the top, covering each little cake. Refrigerate the cakes until cold and sift confectioners' sugar on top just before serving.

Makes 12.

BUTTERSCOTCH LAYER CAKE

This is the sort of cake that people label "very rich" but then go on to have three slices with languorous ease. Yes, it is rich, but the gorgeousness is never palate cluttering or cloying. It makes a comforting dessert after a wintry kitchen supper of something like meatballs or roast chicken and leeks.

To make a coffee-butterscotch cake—as heavenly as it sounds—add a tablespoonful of instant espresso powder to the flour. And it occurs to me as I write this that, for fruit lovers, this cake, in its regular, uncoffeed state, would be even more seductive with a few sliced, perfectly ripe bananas in with the filling. But I have to say it does it for me as it is.

for the icing:

1 cup sugar

1/2 cup cold water

1 1/4 cups heavy cream

14 ounces (1 3/4 cups) cream cheese at room temperature

for the cake layers:

1 cup unsalted butter, very soft

7 tablespoons softened brown sugar

1/2 cup sugar

4 large eggs

1 1/2 cups self-rising cake flour

2–4 tablespoons heavy cream

2 8 x 2-inch cake pans, greased and lined with parchment or wax paper

Preheat the oven to 375°F and then get on with the icing. I do this first, since you need to make some caramel and then let it cool. Dissolve the sugar in the water over a low heat, remembering not to stir at all as it will crystallize if you do. When it seems dissolved, turn up the heat and boil until it turns a dark golden color. This will probably take 10–15 minutes. And try not to be faint-hearted: caramel has to be near burning; it wouldn't be caramel otherwise.

When you've reached that exciting stage, take the pan off the heat and slowly whisk in the cream. It may go a little lumpy but don't panic, it will smooth out. When all the cream's in, put the pan back on the heat for a further minute, whisking until smooth and combined. I find one of those little curly wire whisks the best tool for the job. Cool, and then refrigerate until you need it.

The easiest way to make the cake is to put all the ingredients except the cream into the bowl of the food processor and blitz till smooth. (It's for this reason the butter must be very soft before you start.) Scrape down the sides of the bowl, then process again, adding a couple of tablespoons of cream down the funnel with the motor running. Stop and check the consistency of the batter: if it's on the runny (though not liquid) side then stop here; otherwise, add another 1–2 tablespoons of cream to achieve this dropping consistency. If you want to make it by hand, follow the method for the Victoria sponge (page 14).

Divide the batter between the prepared pans and bake for about 25 minutes; the cake layers are ready when they're beginning to shrink away from the sides of the pan and when a cake tester or skewer comes out clean. Leave on a wire rack for 10 minutes, then turn out and leave on the rack until completely cooled.

Now for the assembly. Pour the thoroughly cooled caramel into a glass cup measure with a spout. (You'll be using some if not all of the rest to dribble over the iced cake later.) Beat the cream cheese until softened and smooth, then add the cupful of caramel and beat gently to combine.

Put one cake layer on a plate. Using a rubber spatula or an ordinary blunt knife, roughly spread just under half of the icing over the top of the waiting cake. Place the other cake on top and then roughly ice the top of that cake with what remains in the bowl. Don't feel constrained to use up every last scrap of icing: it tastes almost at its best straight out of a finger-wiped bowl. Using a teaspoon, drizzle some of the reserved caramel over the cake: think Jackson Pollock.

Serves 8.

BOSTON CREAM PIE

This is not a pie at all but a cake, and apparently the focus of much heated debate by the culinarily concerned, and although I make the cake as I do for a Victoria sponge, there are enough differing factors overall to make me feel this deserves its own entry. The story is that, in 1850, the pastry chef at Boston's Parker House Hotel (a gastronomic hotbed, obviously, since Parker House rolls evidently emanate from here too) had the brainwave of adding a bitter chocolate glaze to a "Boston pie"—a custardy layer-cake affair—and for some reason the addition of chocolate brought the word "cream" into play.

I made this cake once with the addition of a few halved strawberries in the middle, folded into the crème patissière, and some more dotted about the edge on the plate, and although I prefer it without, I have to report that I was in the minority. And for Valentine's Day, consider going into full-on kitsch mode by making the strawberry version, using cakes baked in a couple of heart-shaped tins.

The idea of making crème patissière might seem daunting if you've not done it before, but it really isn't hard—and remember the flour does stabilize it, so it's nowhere near as tension inducing as custard.

for the cake:

**1 batch Victoria sponge recipe
(see page 14)**

2 8 x 2-inch round cake pans, buttered

for the ganache:

**1/2 cup plus 2 tablespoons heavy
cream**

1 teaspoon vanilla extract

1 teaspoon unsalted butter

5 ounces bittersweet chocolate

for the crème patissière:

1/2 cup milk

1/2 cup heavy cream

**1 vanilla bean or 1 teaspoon vanilla
extract**

3 large egg yolks

2 tablespoons sugar

1 tablespoon all-purpose flour

Preheat the oven to 350°F and make the cakes following the recipe on page 14. Then pour into the prepared pans and bake for about 25 minutes, as before, while you make the crème patissière.

Warm the milk and cream in a saucepan along with the vanilla pod split lengthwise. Bring to the boil, then remove from the heat, cover, and let stand to infuse for 10 minutes. If you're not using the bean, add the vanilla extract later, when you've combined all the ingredients. In a large bowl, whisk the yolks and sugar until creamy, and then beat in the flour. With the point of a small, sharp knife, scrape the seeds out of the vanilla bean into the milk, and add this warm milk to the egg mixture and whisk until smooth. Pour back into the saucepan and stir or whisk gently over low heat until the custard thickens. Remove from the heat and let the custard cool by pouring it into a wide bowl and tearing off some wax paper, wetting it, then covering the bowl with it. This stops the custard from forming a skin. Don't put this in the refrigerator: something goes horribly wrong with the texture if you do, and you want utter, smooth voluptuousness here.

When the cakes are done, sit them in their pans on a wire rack for 5–10 minutes, then turn out and cool directly on the rack. When the cakes and the crème patissière are cool, you can make the chocolate ganache with which you're going to ice this pileup of gorgeousness. Warm the cream, vanilla extract, and butter with the chocolate, chopped into small pieces, and bring to the boil in a thick-bottomed saucepan (I find a nonstick pan the best for this), by which time the chocolate should have melted. Remove from the heat and whisk till smooth and thickened. Let cool a little before using, but you want it still runny enough to ice with. Tear off four strips of wax paper or baking parchment, about 3 inches wide, and arrange in a square on the plate on which you're serving the cake. Sit one of the cakes on top and spread with cooled crème patissière, then top with the second cake. Dollop spoonfuls of the chocolate icing on top, letting it spread and drip down the sides of the cake.

When the entire confection is cool and set, and you're about to bring it to the table, remove the strips of paper to reveal—aha!—a drip-free plate.

Serves 8.

COCONUT CAKE

I may have an exaggerated sense of camp or kitsch, but a highlight of this recipe from my point of view is that it uses coconut rum. Actually, this is quite useful for baking, since it's hard to come by coconut extract or essence worthy of the name.

But this is also a beautiful cake, pale gold and white and delicately flavored.

for the cake:
1 cup unsalted butter, softened
3/4 cup sugar
1/2 teaspoon vanilla extract
4 large eggs
1 1/3 cups self-rising cake flour
2 tablespoons cornstarch
1/2 teaspoon baking powder
scant 1/4 cup grated coconut soaked
 in 1/2 cup plus 2 tablespoons
 boiling water
2 8-inch round cake pans, buttered

and lined with parchment or
wax paper

for the filling:
2 tablespoons grated coconut
6 tablespoons soft unsalted butter
1 cup confectioners' sugar, sifted
1 tablespoon coconut rum

for the icing:
2–4 tablespoons coconut rum
1/2 cup plus 1 tablespoon instant royal
 icing

Preheat the oven to 350°F and make the cake by putting all the ingredients in the food processor and blitzing till you have a soft batter. If you want to make it by hand, then proceed as for the Victoria sponge (page 14), adding the coconut at the end and leaving out the baking powder. Pour into the prepared pans and cook for about 25 minutes or until ready: not so springy on top as a plain sponge, but still coming away from the edges; a cake tester, inserted, should come out cleanish.

To make the buttercream icing for the middle of the cake, toast the coconut in a dry frying pan, shaking every now and again, till it's fragrant and golden. Remove to a waiting plate and let cool. Cream together the butter and confectioners' sugar and when you've got a light, smooth paste, beat in the coconut rum and then the cold, toasted coconut.

Spread the filling between the two layers, and get on with the icing for the top. Using either a free-standing mixer with the flat paddle, or an ordinary bowl and an electric hand-held mixer, beat together 2 tablespoons of coconut rum and the royal icing powder (in other words, just follow the packet instructions, replacing the water with coconut rum). You may need to add another 1–2 tablespoons of coconut rum, but see how it goes. When you've got a smooth, runny but not liquid paste that will ice the top well, pour over the very center of the cake and let ooze out toward the edge and drip slightly down the sides. Leave to set before cutting and eating.

Serves 8.

AUTUMNAL BIRTHDAY CAKE

There is no reason on earth why this, adapted from the *Magnolia Bakery Cookbook* by Jennifer Appel and Allysa Torey, has to be a birthday cake, but since the first two times I made it were for my sister-in-law's and a friend's birthdays in late October and early November, that's how I think of it. In both cases, I put just one (gold) candle on top: better on any number of counts. I know that adorning plates with autumn leaves is not my usual aesthetic, but that's another benefit of using this as a birthday cake: you can allow yourself a little ironic leeway.

for the cake:

3/4 cup butter, softened

1/3 cup sugar

3 large eggs

1 1/2 cups maple syrup

3 1/3 cups self-rising cake flour

3/4 cup hot water

**2 8-inch round cake pans, buttered and
    lined with parchment or wax paper**

for the icing:

2 large egg whites

1/2 cup maple syrup

7 tablespoons sugar

1/4 teaspoon cream of tartar

1/4 teaspoon salt

1 teaspoon vanilla extract

1/4 teaspoon maple extract, optional

1/2 cup or 4 ounces pecans

Preheat the oven to 350°F. Beat together the butter and sugar until very pale and fluffy. Add the eggs one at a time, beating in well after each addition, then gradually add the maple syrup to make a smooth mixture. Finally, spoon in the flour alternately with the hot water, beating gently until smooth again. Divide the batter between the two pans, and cook for 40 minutes. A cake tester, inserted, should come out clean when they're cooked. Let the cakes cool in their pans on a rack for 10 minutes before unmolding them, then leave them to get cold before you get on with the icing.

Put everything except the extracts and pecans into a glass or metal bowl that fits over a saucepan to form a double boiler. Fill the saucepan with enough water to come just below—but not touching—the bowl when it sits on top. Bring the water to the boil, set the bowl on top, and using an electric hand-held whisk, beat the mixture vigorously for 5–7 minutes. It should stand up in peaks like a meringue mixture. Take the bowl off the saucepan, away from the heat, and add the extracts, beating them in for another minute.

Cut out 4 strips of baking parchment and use to line the cake plate, as explained on page 22. Using your dreamy, ivory-colored meringue, ice the middle, sides and top of the cake. Give the icing a swirly effect rather than smooth, letting the top have small peaks. Chop most of the pecans finely, leaving some pieces larger. Sprinkle over the top of the cake, and throw at the sides. This cake is best eaten the day it's made. Serves 8.

BABY BUNDTS

At a blackboard-walled vegetarian café in New York once, I ate a little yogurty lemony ring-molded cake and wanted to whip up something similar immediately on my return. I've given you this version not simply because it reminds me of the original inspirational one I ate but because it's the simplest to make. Melting the butter and then proceeding simply by stirring wet ingredients into dry (rather than rubbing butter into flour and so forth) won it for me.

It's getting easier and easier to buy what might once have been recherché baking materials, so I don't feel guilty about suggesting a recipe that requires a tray of mini-Bundt molds.

for the cakes:
1/2 cup plain yogurt
6 tablespoons butter, melted
2 large eggs
zest of 1 lemon
1 cup all-purpose flour
1/2 teaspoon baking soda
pinch of salt

7 tablespoons sugar
1 mini-Bundt pan with 6 molds,
approximately 4 x 2 inches each,
buttered or oiled well

for the icing:
1 1/3 cup confectioners' sugar
juice of 1 lemon

Preheat the oven to 325°F.

In a measuring cup, mix the yogurt, melted butter, eggs, and lemon zest. Put the flour, baking soda, salt, and sugar into a large bowl. Mix the wet ingredients into the bowl, folding everything in well, then fill the mini-Bundt molds with the mixture, and cook for 25–30 minutes. When they come out of the oven, leave them to cool a little before turning them out, otherwise they'll break—but don't let them get too cold either, as they will stick. Let them cool on a rack, flat-side down.

To make the icing, sift the confectioners' sugar into a bowl, and add enough lemon juice to make an icing thick enough to ice the tops and drizzle down like snow-capped peaks.

Makes 6.

VARIATION

As with all citrus recipes, you can be fairly free with substitutions. Lime is an obvious and beckoning proposition. And you could use orange either as an alternative or along with the lemon (say the zest and juice of a half of each for the cakes and icing, respectively) to make a St. Clement's version.

FRUITED CAKES

I haven't gone all quaint and ye olde. I use the word *fruited* simply to make it clear that what follows is not just fruitcakes—in fact, there's only one here—but all sorts of cakes with fruit in them. For the rest of the more traditional fruitcakes, turn to the Christmas chapter.

CHERRY-ALMOND LOAF CAKE

I have a nostalgic fondness for this yellow slab punctured by waxy halves of scarlet cherries—the cake we called station cake at home—but this is best with those dark and glossy natural-colored glacé cherries.

1 cup natural-colored glacé cherries	**2–3 drops almond extract**
1²/₃ cups self-rising cake flour	**¹/₂ cup ground almonds**
1 cup butter, softened	**6 tablespoons milk**
¹/₂ cup plus 1 tablespoon sugar	**9 x 5-inch loaf pan, lined and buttered**
3 large eggs, beaten	

Preheat the oven to 325°F. Halve the cherries, wash them in a colander under cold water, then pat them dry, toss them in some flour, and shake well to get rid of excess.

Cream the butter and sugar until light and fluffy. Gradually add the beaten eggs and almond extract, then gently fold in the remaining flour and ground almonds. Fold in the cherries and then the milk and spoon the thick mixture into the loaf pan and bake for ³/₄–1 hour, or until a cake tester comes out clean.

As with all of these sorts of cakes, leave in the pan on a wire rack until completely cooled.

Makes 8–10 slices.

RHUBARB CORNMEAL CAKE

You can never have too many rhubarb recipes in my book and this cake clamors to be made. It is definitely better in the early days of the rhubarb season just because the breathtaking pink of that first, forced fruit (and, yes, I know it's a vegetable really) makes for a prettier cake. The cornmeal (or polenta, and a few years back no doubt I'd have called this rhubarb polenta cake) helps absorb some of the rhubarb's juices.

The point, too, about this cake is that it is surprisingly versatile. Eat it at room temperature as an orthodox teatime cake, or slightly warm for a dessert after lunch or dinner. For a Sunday-lunch dessert, make a bowl of custard (page 134) to go with it, to be eaten cold or at room temperature; to turn this into a dinner-party sweet, whip up a bowl of divine muscat-mascarpone cream, and serve some more honeyed-grape muscat.

1 pound 2 ounces rhubarb	2 large eggs
1 cup sugar	1 teaspoon vanilla extract
1 cup all-purpose flour	1/2 cup unsalted butter, soft
1 teaspoon baking soda	1 cup plus 2 tablespoons plain yogurt
1/4 teaspoon salt	9-inch springform pan, buttered and
1 teaspoon ground cinnamon	lined with parchment or wax paper
1/2 cup plus 2 tablespoons fine cornmeal (polenta)	

Preheat oven to 350°F.

Wash and dry the rhubarb if necessary (which I rarely find it to be), and then trim, removing any stringy bits, and cut into 1/2 inch slices. Put into a glass or china bowl and cover with 1/3 cup of the sugar, while you get on with the rest of the cake. Don't let the rhubarb stand for more than half an hour or the sugar will make too much liquid seep out.

Mix the flour, baking soda, salt, cinnamon, and cornmeal together. With a fork, beat the eggs with the vanilla in a measuring cup or small bowl. In a large bowl, cream the butter and the rest of the sugar, then gradually add the egg and vanilla mixture, beating while you do so. Then add the flour-cornmeal mixture alternately with the yogurt. They just need to be combined: don't overmix.

Finally, add the rhubarb together with its sugary, pink juices, folding in to mix, and then pour the speckled batter into the prepared pan. Put in the preheated oven and bake for about 1 hour or until springy to the touch. You may need to cover it with foil after about 40 minutes so that the top doesn't scorch. Let cool in the pan on a wire rack for a while before unmolding.

Serves 8–10.

MUSCAT-MASCARPONE CREAM

I made this expressly to go with the rhubarb and cornmeal cake, but it is a useful way of giving a little chic spin to any basic cake. It would also be wonderful with Christmas pudding or mince pies.

2 large eggs, separated
1/2 cup or 4 ounces muscat

1 cup plus 2 tablespoons or 9 ounces mascarpone
1/3 cup confectioners' sugar, sifted

Whisk the egg whites until stiff but not dry and put aside for a moment. Beat the yolks with the muscat and, when smoothly combined, beat in the mascarpone and confectioners' sugar. Whisk well and then, when you've got a voluptuous, thickening cream in front of you, fold in the egg whites. You can keep this in the refrigerator, covered, for a day before using it.

Serves 8–10.

VARIATION
If you wanted to serve this as a dessert in itself, then use 3 eggs, $^{1}/_{2}$ cup muscat, $^{1}/_{4}$ cup sugar and boost the mascarpone to $1^{3}/_{4}$ cups (about 14 ounces) this should be enough for 4 alpine glasses' worth. Don't forget to put out cookies for dipping, too.

Serves 4.

BANANA BREAD

This is the first recipe anyone hesitant about baking should try: it's fabulously easy and fills the kitchen with that aromatic fug which is the natural atmospheric setting for the domestic goddess. There are countless recipes for banana bread: this one is adapted from one of my favorite books, the one I read lying on the sofa to recover from yet another long, modern, stressed-out day, Jim Fobel's *Old-Fashioned Baking Book: Recipes from an American Childhood*. If you're thinking about giving this cake to children, don't worry, the alcohol doesn't pervade: you just end up with stickily, aromatically swollen fruit.

scant 1/2 cup golden raisins

6 tablespoons or 3 ounces bourbon
or dark rum

1 cup plus 2 tablespoons all-purpose
flour

2 teaspoons baking powder

1/2 teaspoon baking soda

1/2 teaspoon salt

1/2 cup unsalted butter, melted

1/2 cup sugar

2 large eggs

4 small, very ripe bananas, mashed

1/4 cup chopped walnuts

1 teaspoon vanilla extract

9 x 5-inch loaf pan, buttered and
floured or with a paper insert

Put the golden raisins and rum or bourbon in a smallish saucepan and bring to the boil. Remove from the heat, cover, and leave for an hour if you can, or until the raisins have absorbed most of the liquid, then drain.

Preheat the oven to 325°F and get started on the rest. Put the flour, baking powder, baking soda, and salt in a medium-sized bowl and, using your hands or a wooden spoon, combine well. In a large bowl, mix the melted butter and sugar and beat until blended. Beat in the eggs one at a time, then the mashed bananas. Then, with your wooden spoon, stir in the walnuts, drained raisins, and vanilla extract. Add the flour mixture, a third at a time, stirring well after each bit. Scrape into the loaf pan and bake in the middle of the oven for 1–1¼ hours. When it's ready, an inserted toothpick or fine skewer should come out cleanish. Leave in the pan on a rack to cool, and eat thickly or thinly sliced, as you prefer.

Makes 8–10 slices.

VARIATION

I haven't done a tremendous amount of fiddling with this recipe, but I did once make it, for friends who are more chocolate-crazed than I am, by replacing 2 tablespoons of the flour with good cocoa powder and adding 4 ounces of bittersweet chocolate, cut up into smallish chunks. And you could just as easily use the chocolate chips sold in the baking aisle of supermarkets.

MARZIPAN FRUIT CAKE

This may be the only proper fruitcake in this section, but it is my favorite one in the entire world. This is in the first place because it contains marzipan (which I love) and in the second because it doesn't contain any candied peel (which I hate, or do in its normal, bitter, store-bought state). Moreover, the dried pears which I've thrown in as well have a fudgy graininess which melds perfectly with the marzipan.

You do have to start this the night before you're baking, but all that means is the marzipan needs chopping and freezing and the fruits need soaking in advance.

1/2 cup plus 2 tablespoons golden raisins

scant 1/2 cup natural-colored glacé cherries, halved

5 ounces dried pears, chopped

1/3 cup plus 1 tablespoon white rum

9 ounces marzipan

1/4 cup ground almonds

zest of 1 lemon

1 cup plus 2 tablespoons all-purpose flour

1/3 cup sugar

scant 1/2 cup butter

2 large eggs

1 teaspoon orange-flower water

8-inch springform pan, buttered and lined bottom and sides, so that the parchment paper comes a good 4 inches above the rim

So, the night before, mix the raisins, glacé cherries, and pears in a large bowl and cover with the rum. Dice the marzipan and put in the freezer. Leave both to soak and freeze overnight.

When you come to make the cake the next day, preheat the oven to 250°F. Beat together the almonds, lemon zest, flour, sugar, butter, and eggs. Add the drained fruit, orange-flower water, and the frozen marzipan. Put the cake mixture into the pan, leveling the surface and making a slight indent in the middle to get an even surface when baked. Bake for 2–2½ hours or until a cake tester comes out clean. Don't overcook, as it will continue to cook in its own warmth as it cools. Nor should you worry too much about it: there's enough fruit and marzipanny squidge to make sure this golden cake doesn't easily turn dry.

Allow the cake to cool in the pan before unmolding and rewrapping in parchment and foil to store for about a week. Feed with a little more rum before you wrap for a richer taste if you want (just puncture the top of the cake a few times and slowly dribble a few spoons of rum over). You should also be aware that the wrap-and-keep advice is a counsel of perfection. Last time I made this, two days was the longest I was able to leave it before greedily unwrapping and slicing into it.

Serves 8–10.

APPLE AND WALNUT CAKE

I got the idea for making this cake from a conflation of two things: the first was reading Anna del Conte's recipe, in her *Secrets from an Italian Kitchen*, for an apple cake made with olive oil; the second was the reproachful remainder of a bottle of walnut oil bought to make some walnut dressing and then left on the shelf with seemingly no further purpose in life. So I thought I'd try making a cake with what I had left, and it worked— well, more than worked.

Since I can't be the only person to have been in this predicament, I pass on the recipe, but with one proviso. The cake is lovely, but in an unfancy, *cucina rustica* kind of a way; walnut oil is expensive: I don't advise you to buy it specially for this cake.

I've marked the walnuts as optional just because the first time I made it I didn't use any—I wanted to eat it as pared down as possible to see how I felt about the walnut oil. If you leave out the walnuts and replace the walnut oil with olive oil (not extra virgin), and the rum with water, you have Anna's delicious *torta di mele*.

scant **1/2 cup golden raisins**	**1/2 teaspoon cream of tartar**
6 tablespoons or 3 ounces rum	**1/2 teaspoon salt**
1/2 cup plus 2 tablespoons walnut oil	**1 pound tart eating apples, peeled,**
3/4 cup sugar	**cored, and cut into small cubes**
2 large eggs	**zest of 1 lemon**
2 1/4 cups self-rising cake flour	**scant 3/4 cup walnuts, optional**
1 teaspoon cinnamon	8-inch springform pan, buttered
1 1/2 teaspoons baking soda	and floured

Put the golden raisins and rum (or water) into a saucepan and bring to the boil, then remove from the heat, letting the raisins plump up aromatically. Now, preheat the oven to 350°F.

Beat the oil and sugar together in a bowl, and add the eggs one at a time, beating until it looks like a light mayonnaise. I'd use an electric mixer of some sort here. Add the dry ingredients to the egg mixture, folding with a metal spoon. Then stir in the apples, lemon zest, drained raisins, and walnuts if using. Smooth what will be a fairly stiff batter into the pan and bake for 1 hour, poking into it with a cake tester or toothpick to check if it's done.

Let the cake stand for 10 minutes in the pan on a wire rack, then turn out and leave to cool. Anna advises leaving the cake a day before eating it (I'd wrap it well, once completely cool, in foil first), but I have to admit I love eating it with the warm breath of the oven still faintly upon it.

Serves 6.

WINTER PLUM CAKE

This is "winter" cake in the sense of "out-of-season," or "store-cupboard." To be frank, I'd had a can of red plums in the cupboard for so long I felt I had either to find a way of using it or chuck it out. I'm glad to say that this was the outcome.

for the cake:

20-ounce can red plums

3/4 cup self-rising cake flour

1/2 teaspoon baking powder

1/3 cup ground almonds

1/2 cup butter, softened

1 cup plus 1 tablespoon light brown sugar

2 large eggs

1 scant teaspoon almond extract

8-inch springform pan, buttered and lined with parchment or wax paper

for the icing:

1 cup confectioners' sugar

1–2 tablespoons hot water

Preheat the oven to 325°F.

Drain the plums, then chop and leave them in a sieve to drain once more. Mix the flour, baking powder, and ground almonds. Cream the butter and sugar, then beat in the eggs, adding a tablespoon of the flour mixture after each one. Beat in the almond extract, then fold in the rest of the flour mixture and the drained, chopped plums. Turn into the prepared pan and bake for about 1¼ hours, though check at 1 hour. When it's ready, that's to say beginning to come away at the sides and so forth, take it out of the oven, leave it in its pan on a wire rack for about 10 minutes, then turn out onto the rack.

When cool, coat with icing, which you make simply by mixing the sifted confectioners' sugar with water till you have a shiny paste. Pour over the top of the cake to cover thinly, not necessarily uniformly, and leave to drip, here and there, down the sides.

If you want to turn this into a Sunday-lunch dessert, serve warm and without icing and make a pitcher of custard to pour over (see page 134).

Serves 6–8.

CUPCAKES

Now this really is "Baking and the Dinner Party Solution."

At about the time I started getting into top cupcake mode, ostensibly for children, I noticed that the people who really seemed to get excited by them were the children's parents. I think it's not till you hit 30 that nostalgia is even a remotely comforting option. Since then, I've decided that cupcakes and fairy cakes—by which I mean the plain-bottomed prettily iced cupcakes—are the perfect things to make for dinner. And by this I mean not some shiny tabled, silver-laid grand dinner party but those evenings when you have friends for supper in the kitchen (the only kind of dinner party I know). Give people cheese instead of dessert (or nothing at all: it ain't obligatory) and wheel out these dinky numbers with the coffee and tea. You can make the cakes a day in advance, keep them in an airtight container and ice them later—although since the icing helps keep them fresh you may as well, if you're using a water rather than a butter icing, ice them a day before too and then you'll have nothing to do on the day itself.

I don't normally like teensy-weensy individually portioned things, but cupcakes seem to hit some pre-rational spot and I succumb. But then everyone always does. What follows is not all there is: see also espresso and cappuccino cupcakes on pages 198–199, chocolate-cherry cupcakes on page 196, dolly-mixture fairy cakes on page 215, butterfly cakes on page 217, Halloween cupcakes on page 216, and Christmas cupcakes on page 267.

FAIRY CAKES

These are so quick both to make and to bake that it really is possible to whip some up for after dinner when you get home from work. On the whole, I leave my fairy cakes plain and unadorned beneath; it's above, when I get to play with colors and flowers and sugar decorations, that a little imagination and artistry comes into play. Not that I can claim much credit, certainly not for the latter: I buy rice-paper roses and sugar daisies and pansies rather than make them. But I like the playing part—choosing the colors, the detail. You can see by the cover of this book that my weak spot is the white-on-white look. (In fact, I've told Hettie, my savior and right-hand, who's worked with me since this book's inception, that when she gets married she has to let me make her a stacked pyramid of these. Luckily, she's up for it.)

My other favorite—and then I really will leave you to your own devices—is the fifties pistachio-green version with the pale-pink rice-paper rose atop.

1/2 cup unsalted butter, softened

7 tablespoons sugar

2 large eggs

3/4 cup self-rising cake flour

1/2 teaspoon vanilla extract

2–3 tablespoons milk

18-ounce package instant royal icing

12-cup muffin pan lined with 12 paper baking cups

Preheat the oven to 400°F.

It couldn't be simpler to make fairy cakes: just put all the ingredients except for the milk in the food processor and then blitz till smooth. Pulse while adding milk down the funnel, to make for a soft, dropping consistency. (If you do want to make by hand, just follow the method for the Victoria sponge, page 14.) I know it looks as if you'll never make this scant mixture fit 12 cupcake cups, but you will, so just spoon and scrape the stuff in, trying to fill each cup equally. Put in the oven and bake for 15–20 minutes or until the fairy cakes are cooked and golden on top. As soon as bearable, take the fairy cakes in their paper cups out of the pan and let cool on a wire rack. I like my cherry-topped fairies to have a little pointy top, but for all floral and other artistic effects, darling, you need to start with a level base, so once they're cool, cut off any mounded peaks so that you've got a flat surface for icing.

I've specified a whole package of instant royal icing because the more colors you go in for the more you use, though really 9 ounces should be enough. I make up a big, uncolored batch, and then remove a few spoonfuls at a time to a cereal bowl and add, with my probe (a broken thermometer, but a skewer is just as good), small dots of colors from the paste tubs, stirring with a teaspoon and then adding more coloring, very slowly, very cautiously until I've got the color I want (pastel works best here, whatever your everyday aesthetic). I then get another spoon to spread the icing on each cake (it's important to use a different spoon for icing than for mixing or you'll end up with crumbs in the bowl of icing) and then I leave it a moment to dry only slightly on the surface before sticking on my rose, daisy, or whole bouquet of either.

Makes 12.

VARIATION

To make lavender cupcakes, follow the basic recipe above, but reduce the vanilla to a few drops, about 1/4 teaspoon if you feel like measuring. Half an hour before making up the mixture, put 1/2 cup of milk into a little saucepan with 6–8 sprigs of lavender. Bring to the boil, but just before it starts boiling remove from the heat, cover with foil, and leave for 20 minutes. Then strain into a cup and leave for another 10 minutes. Make up the batter as above, using a few tablespoonfuls of lavender milk at the end to loosen the mixture in place of the usual plain milk. Cook as normal and when cool, make up a fairly thick icing by mixing 1 2/3 cups confectioners' sugar, sifted, with more of the lavender milk. Tint it ivory with the color paste "Caramel" and place a sprig of lavender on top.

BURNT-BUTTER BROWN-SUGAR CUPCAKES

It's difficult to explain the wonderful resonant taste that burnt butter has, but think of it as a kind of mouth-filling nuttiness.

for the cupcakes:

1/2 cup plus 2 tablespoons unsalted butter

3/4 cup self-rising cake flour

3 tablespoons sugar

5 tablespoons light brown sugar

2 large eggs

1 teaspoon vanilla extract

1 teaspoon baking powder

2–3 tablespoons milk

12-cup muffin pan lined with 12 paper baking cups

for the icing:

1/2 cup plus 2 tablespoons unsalted butter

1 2/3 to 2 cups confectioners' sugar, sifted

1 teaspoon vanilla extract

2–3 tablespoons milk

Preheat the oven to 400°F and then get on with burning your butter. Put it in a small saucepan on medium heat, stirring all the time until it turns a dark golden color. Take the pan off the heat and strain the butter into a bowl or cup, as it will have made a sediment. In other words, this is like clarified butter, but with a smoky note. Let the butter solidify again but don't put it in the refrigerator; you need it to remain soft for the cupcakes. This shouldn't take long, except in hot weather, in which case leave the preheating of the oven till after the butter's been burnt.

When the butter is solid but still soft, put all the cake ingredients except the milk in a food processor and blitz to a smooth batter. As normal, add the milk down the funnel, pulsing sparingly to form a soft, dropping mixture. And, again, if you want to make them by hand, follow the Victoria sponge method (page 14).

Divide among the paper cups, and cook for 15–20 minutes. While the cupcakes are baking, get on with the icing. It's the same procedure for the butter—burn, strain, solidify—then beat it with half the sugar or enough to make it stiff. Add tablespoons of milk and the remaining sugar alternately to reach a good consistency, and finally the vanilla.

While the icing's still soft, smear messily over the cooled and waiting cupcakes. Makes 12.

CARROT CUPCAKES WITH CREAM CHEESE ICING

I wanted to have some sort of carrot cake here and felt that this cupcake version was the right one. I know carrot muffins have long been in existence but I wanted something luscious and sweet and treaty: a cake not a breakfast scourge. For a reason I cannot quite fathom, these seem to go down particularly well if I bring them out after serving fish.

for the cupcakes:
scant 1/2 cup light brown sugar
3/4 cup sunflower oil
2 large eggs
1 1/2 cups all-purpose flour
3/4 teaspoon baking soda
1 teaspoon cinnamon
pinch of salt
zest of 1/2 lemon
zest of 1/2 orange
2 medium carrots, grated

scant 1/2 cup or 4 ounces walnuts,
chopped
12-cup muffin pan lined with 12 paper
baking cups

for the icing:
generous 4 ounces or 1/2 cup
cream cheese
1 2/3 cups confectioners' sugar, sifted
1–2 teaspoons lime juice
12 walnut halves

Preheat the oven to 400°F.

Beat the sugar and oil together, then add the eggs one at a time. Add the flour, baking soda, cinnamon, salt, and zests, then fold in the grated carrot and walnuts. Spoon the mixture evenly into the muffin cups, and bake for 20 minutes. Cool on a rack while you get on with the icing.

Beat the cream cheese in a bowl till smooth and softened somewhat, and then beat in the sifted confectioners' sugar. Squeeze in the lime juice to taste.

When the cupcakes are cool, just smear the icing on top. I find using an ordinary blunt knife works well, and I like to see the knife marks in the icing: these are not meant to be smooth, elegant concoctions. Stick a walnut half in the center of each iced cupcake.

Makes 12.

SPONGE DROPS

Sponge drops are not so much cupcakes as saucer-cakes. You make up a very light batter and drop spoonfuls on a baking sheet. Bake them, cool them, and sandwich them together with cream, jam and a few berries and you have mouthfuls of heaven. These taste so much better than their school-night-supper name evokes: the lightness of the sponge together with the cool fatness of the cream and the juicy sweetness of the berries, and all in such small quantities (and I never thought I'd be grateful for that), make these completely seductive.

for the sponge drops:

2 large eggs

¼ cup sugar

⅓ cup self-rising flour

2 tablespoons cornstarch

½ teaspoon baking powder

2 baking sheets, greased or lined with wax or parchment paper

for the filling:

½ cup plus 2 tablespoons heavy cream, whipped

5–6 tablespoons blackberry (or other) jam

½ pint blackberries (or other berries)

Preheat the oven to 400°F.

Lightly whisk the eggs, then add the sugar and whisk again until the mixture becomes pale, creamy, and voluminous; I'd use an electric mixer of some sort here. Sift in the flour, cornstarch, and baking powder, and fold the dry ingredients in with a metal spoon. Spoon scant dessert-spoon-sized drops onto the baking sheets, leaving room between them so that they can spread. Cook for 5 minutes, them remove them with a metal spatula to cool on a rack.

When they are cool, sandwich them with whipped cream, jam, and softly crushed berries.

Makes 8–9 cakes.

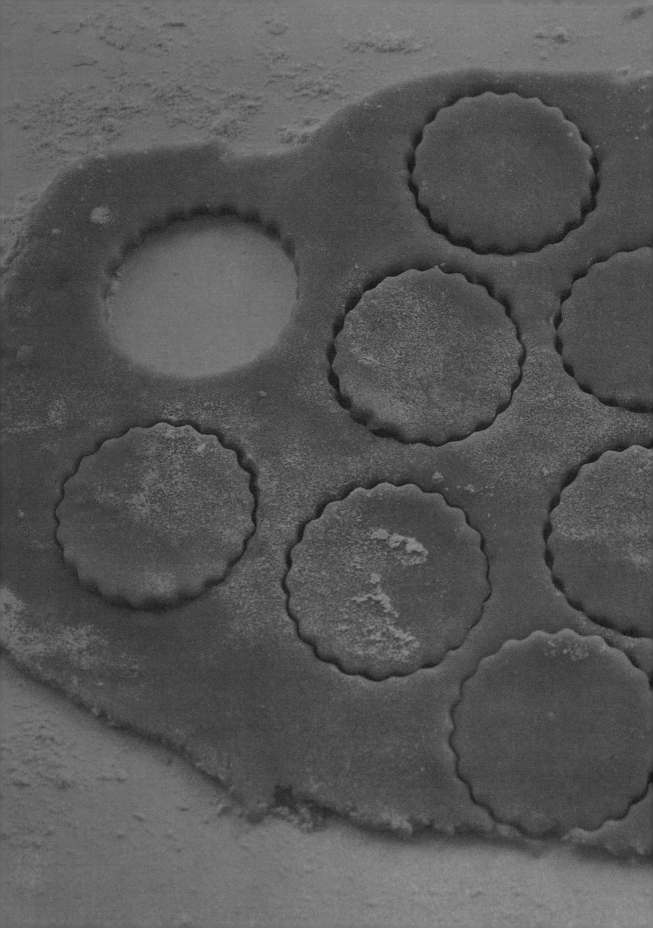

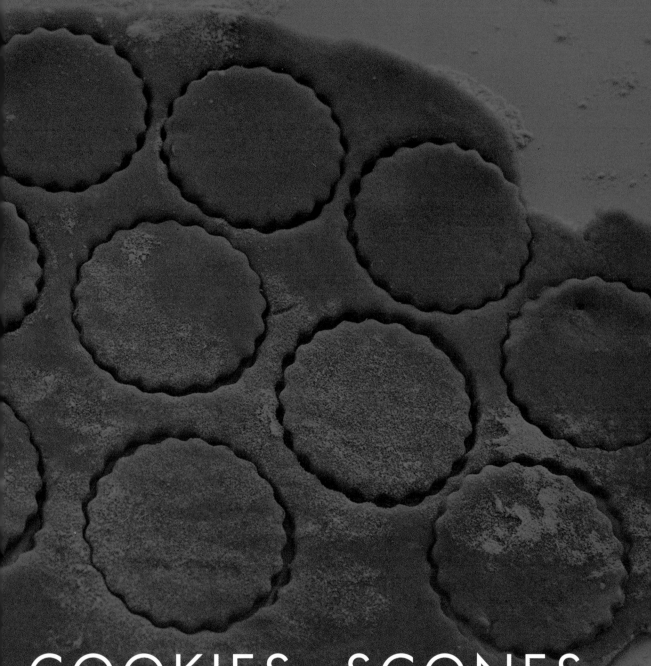

COOKIES, SCONES, AND MUFFINS

COOKIES, SCONES, AND MUFFINS
Including Pancakes and Small Things

Cookies are one of the first things we learn to cook when we're little—or at least roll and stamp out, get the feel of, which is just as important—and there seems to be a sense in which we're recapturing some remembered, no doubt idealized, past whenever we make them in adulthood; they still feel like playing. When I want to cook but have no fixed idea of what, and have no actual meal to prepare to justify fiddling about in the kitchen, I often convince myself that there are cookies that need to be made.

The cookies here are mostly of the free-form kind: you either spoon them onto a baking sheet or roll them into balls between your hands to shape them. There are exceptions, as you'll see, but the blueprint recipe for cutter-shaped cookies is in the children's chapter. Their need, I felt, was greater than ours. (And, of course, for chocolate cookies, see the chocolate chapter.)

I know cookie-baking may seem like a quaintly archaic practice now, but it can make a modern life very much easier. A lot of the recipes that follow can be made to augment a carton of good, bought ice cream to ridiculously great effect. And much easier than making the ice cream and buying the cookies.

ROSEBUD MADELEINES

It was the curled-in smallness of these tender sponge cookies, as well as the fact that they're flavored with rosewater, that made me name them as I have. I like them with coffee after dinner, but eat them with whatever and however you want. The dried rosebuds in the picture are obviously not an obligatory ingredient: for me, it's just a *Citizen Kane* kinda thing.

**scant ¼ cup unsalted butter, plus
    1 tablespoon for greasing
1 large egg
scant 2 tablespoons sugar
pinch of salt**

**⅓ cup all-purpose flour
1 tablespoon rosewater
2 mini-madeleine molds, for
    24 madeleines
confectioners' sugar for dusting**

Melt all the butter over a low heat, then leave to cool. Beat the egg, sugar, and salt in a bowl for about 5 minutes, preferably with an electric mixer of some sort, until it's as thick as mayonnaise. Then sprinkle in the flour; I hold a sieve above the egg and sugar mixture, put the flour in, and shake it through. Fold in the flour with a wooden spoon and then set aside a scant tablespoon of the cold, melted butter for greasing the pans and fold in the rest along with the rosewater. Mix well, but not too vigorously. Leave to rest in the refrigerator for 1 hour, then take out and leave at room temperature for half an hour. Preheat the oven to 425°F.

Generously brush the insides of the madeleine molds with the tablespoon of butter (melting more if you feel you need it) before filling them with half the cake mixture (this amount does 2 batches). About 1 teaspoonful in each should do: don't worry about covering the molded indentations; in the heat of the oven the mixture will spread before it rises. Bake for 5 minutes, though check after 3. Turn out and let cool on a rack, then arrange on a plate and dust with confectioners' sugar. Repeat with the remaining half of the mixture.

Makes 48.

COCONUT MACAROONS

These are a very English kind of macaroon, the sort you always used to see displayed in bakers' shops alongside the madeleines (those sponge castles dipped in luminous strawberry jam and dredged in throat-catching grated coconut, and so very different from those that inflamed the memory of Marcel Proust). The difference with coconut macaroons is that you need neither to be ironic nor self-consciously retro-cool to enjoy them.

One bit of retail bossiness here: buy shredded, not grated, coconut, otherwise the sugary, fragrant dampness—which is, after all, the whole point—will be lost.

2 large egg whites
1/4 teaspoon cream of tartar
1/3 cup sugar
2 tablespoons ground almonds
pinch of salt

1 teaspoon vanilla extract
(or coconut extract, should such be
available)
1 cup plus 2 tablespoons shredded
coconut
1 baking sheet, lined with parchment
or wax paper

Preheat the oven to 325°F.

Beat the egg whites until frothy—no more—then add the cream of tartar and carry on beating, Missus, until soft peaks are formed. Add the sugar a teaspoon at a time and whisk until the peaks can hold their shape and are shiny. Fold in the almonds, salt, vanilla, and coconut. The mixture will be sticky but should, all the same, hold its shape when clumped together.

Form into clementine-sized domes, 2 to 3 inches in diameter. Don't make them too flat; they look best if you keep them nicely rounded, but this is really just a matter of personal taste, so follow your own.

Cook for 20 minutes or until they're just beginning to turn golden in parts.

Makes 8 large macaroons.

PISTACHIO MACAROONS

These are the world's most elegant macaroons. The color alone, that waxy pale jade, perfectly matches the aromatic delicacy of their taste; and their nutty chewiness melts into the fragrant, soft paste with which they're paired. Of all the recipes in this book, this is the one of which I think I'm most proud: cookie bliss.

These are perfect at the end of dinner alongside some confectioners'-sugar-dusted raspberries; or alone with coffee, gracefully piled on a plate or cake stand.

for the macaroons:
¹/3 cup or 3 ounces pistachios
³/4 cup confectioners' sugar
2 large egg whites
1 tablespoon sugar

for the buttercream:
¹/4 cup or 2 ounces pistachios
1²/3 cups confectioners' sugar
¹/2 cup unsalted butter, softened
2 baking sheets, lined with parchment or wax paper

Preheat the oven to 350°F.

Grind the pistachios in a food processor along with the confectioners' sugar (this stops them turning into an oily mess), until as fine as dust. Whisk the egg whites until fairly stiff, but not dry, sprinkle the sugar over and whisk until very stiff. Fold the whites into the pistachio-sugar dust, and combine gently. Pipe small rounds onto your lined baking sheet, using a plain ½-inch nozzle. Let them sit for about 10 minutes to form a skin. Then put in the oven and cook for 10–12 minutes: they should be set, but not dried out.

Remove from the oven and let cool, still on their sheets, while you get on with the filling. This is simple work: grind the nuts and confectioners' sugar in the processor as before; then cream the butter and continue creaming as you add the nut dust. Make sure you have a well-combined soft buttercream. Then simply sandwich the macaroons together.

Makes 20 sandwiches.

SPANISH MACAROONS

I'm not sure I would spend a whole lot of time trying to persuade a Spaniard of the origin of these cookies, but I call them Spanish because they seem so instantly redolent of that aroma of oranges, almonds, and the faintest warm breath of cinnamon that I associate with Spain. Indeed, I have a vague taste-memory of eating macaroons like this when I was in Seville once, and I suppose it was those that I was trying to recreate. I know in my heart of hearts they would be better with blanched almonds which you then grind yourself when you want them, but since I made these with ready-ground nuts and was pleased with them as they were, it seemed honest to leave it that way. If you decide to buy whole almonds to grind, get a bit more than a pound: they're oilier than the ready-ground, so you need more to get the right consistency.

1 ³/₄ cups plus 2 tablespoons ground or 2 ¹/₄ cup or 18 ounces whole blanched almonds, ground
1 ²/₃ cups confectioners' sugar, sifted
zest of 2 oranges

¹/₂ teaspoon almond extract
¹/₂ teaspoon cinnamon
1 large egg, plus 3 large egg whites
2 baking trays, lined with parchment or wax paper

Preheat the oven to 350°F.

Mix together the almonds, sugar, orange zest, almond extract, and cinnamon. In a separate bowl, or wide-mouthed measuring cup, beat the whole egg together with the egg whites. Make a well in the center of your dry ingredients, then pour and mix in the egg. The mixture will be very sticky, I know, but that's fine.

Form walnut-sized balls by rolling the torn-off pieces of dough between your palms, and place on the prepared baking sheets. It will help if you wet your hands under a cold tap and go back to the sink for degunging and rewetting every now and again as you go along. Apart from making the whole operation less messy, it will make for smoother cookies.

Cook for 20 minutes, by which time the cookies should look lightly browned on the surface but won't have lost their sweet and tender chewiness underneath. Cool on a rack.

Makes about 30.

SWEET AND SALTY PEANUT COOKIES

If greed alone were the spur and measure, these would be my favorite cookies. There's something about the contrast between salt and sweet and their crumbly lightness that makes them instantly addictive. They make a seductive partnership with vanilla ice cream: you can do this the elegant grown-up way with bowls of ice cream and a plate of the cookies; or, my weakness, made up into sandwiches, the nubbly discs clasped round the soft, cold cream.

Two requests: don't use jumbo peanuts and don't use all butter. You need that vegetable shortening: quite apart from its trailer-trash charm, it's what makes them light.

⅓ cup light brown sugar, plus more for dipping later

scant ½ cup unsalted butter

scant ¼ cup vegetable shortening

1 large egg

1 teaspoon vanilla extract

1 cup plus 2 tablespoons self-rising flour

½ cup plus 1 tablespoon or 4½ ounces salted peanuts

2 baking sheets, lined with parchment or wax paper

Preheat the oven to 375°F.

In a large bowl, mix together the sugar, butter, shortening, egg, and vanilla. Just beat it together, no ceremony, to combine well. You may find this easiest to do with an electric mixer. Stir in the flour and then the peanuts—and that's your dough done. Now, drop the dough in rounded teaspoons about 2 inches apart onto the prepared baking sheets. Oil the bottom of a glass, or brush with melted butter, and dip it into some more light brown sugar and then press gently on the cookies to flatten them.

Bake for 8–10 minutes, by which time they should be cooked through (though remember that cookies always continue to cook for a while out of the oven), then remove to a wire rack to cool.

Makes about 30.

RICCIARELLI

I love these beautiful, bone-white Sienese macaroons. They're like soft, chewy, almond lozenges. I know it sounds odd to say use ¾ pound ready-ground almonds or about 1 pound blanched almonds which you then grind yourself, but as with the Spanish maca-roons, the drier ready-ground ones absorb more liquid, so you need less. However, these are definitely better when you grind the nuts yourself—and I'm not asking you to do it by hand, but in a food processor for God's sake—so if you can, get them whole and blanched.

You have to start these macaroons the day before you want to eat them—not because any drastic action is required, but just because you need to let them dry out before baking them.

2 large egg whites
pinch of salt
¾ cup sugar
zest of 1 lemon
½ teaspoon vanilla extract
1 teaspoon almond extract

1⅓ cups ground almonds or
    2¼ cups or 18 ounces whole
    blanched almonds, ground
confectioners' sugar for dusting
2 baking sheets, lined with parchment
    or wax paper

Whisk the egg whites and salt until they're stiff and dry, then gradually whisk in the sugar until you reach a marshmallowy consistency. Now add the lemon zest, vanilla extract, and almond extract along with the ground almonds; mix to quite a hard paste.

Shape into small diamonds, dusting confectioners' sugar over your hands to help you form the lozenge-shaped ovals if the mixture's a little sticky. Lay on the baking sheets and leave to dry out overnight or for equivalent hours.

Heat the oven to 250°F. and cook the ricciarelli for about 30 minutes, by which time they should be pale and slightly cracked. When cool, dust with confectioners' sugar and serve.

These keep well in an airtight container.

Makes about 34.

SNICKERDOODLES

You can't help wanting to cook a cookie with a name like this. Luckily, these live up to it. They're verging on cakes, but only in the sense that they're neither crisp nor flat; what they taste like, in fact, are oven-baked doughnuts—small, cinnamony, with a drier crumb than the dunkin' sort.

I love these as part of a dessert, with a bowl of warm, spicy, poached or stewed plums and a bowl of cold crème fraîche.

1²/₃ cups all-purpose flour

1/2 teaspoon ground nutmeg

3/4 teaspoon baking powder

1/2 teaspoon salt

1/2 cup butter, at room temperature

1/3 cup plus 2 tablespoons sugar

1 large egg

1 teaspoon vanilla extract

1 tablespoon cinnamon

2 baking sheets, lined with parchment or wax paper or greased

Preheat oven to 350°F.

Combine the flour, nutmeg, baking powder, and salt, and set aside for a moment. In a large bowl, cream the butter with the ⅓ cup of sugar until light in texture and pale in color, then beat in the egg and vanilla. Now stir in the dry ingredients until you have a smooth, coherent mixture. Spoon out the remaining sugar and the cinnamon onto a plate. Then, with your fingers, squeeze out pieces of dough and roll between the palms of your hands into walnut-sized balls. Roll each ball in the cinnamon-sugar mixture and arrange on your prepared baking sheets.

Bake for about 15 minutes, by which time they should be turning golden brown. Take out of the oven and leave to rest on the baking sheets for 1 minute before transferring to a wire rack to cool.

Makes about 32.

VARIATION

Replace 2 tablespoons of the flour with cocoa to make what we call at home—naturally enough—chocodoodles.

MAPLE-PECAN COOKIES

I made these in a flush of excited inspiration with the maple extract I'd bought at the super-deli Dean & Deluca in New York City.

1 cup plus 2 tablespoons unsalted butter, softened
1/2 cup plus 1 tablespoon light brown sugar
1 teaspoon maple extract

2 1/4 cups self-rising cake flour
35 (approximately 1/2 cup) pecan halves
2 baking sheets, lined with parchment or wax paper or greased

Preheat the oven to 325°F.

Cream the butter and sugar. When you've got a soft, supple mass, add the maple extract and work in the sifted flour. Roll into walnut-sized balls, and press with the base of a glass that you've lightly oiled (and if you've got some in the house, you could use walnut oil) or brushed with melted butter. Press gently onto the lined baking sheets—leaving a 2-inch space round each as they'll spread—and stud each with a pecan half.

Cook for 15 minutes. They start off golden so it's hard to tell if they're cooked just by sight, but lift one up to check it's no longer doughy on the bottom. Remove from the oven, leave for a minute or two on the trays, and then transfer to a wire rack to cool.

Makes about 35.

VARIATION

You can always substitute walnut halves for the pecans, but if you leave them completely nut-free, these are wonderful as cheese biscuits. Yes, they're sweet, but in the same way as digestive biscuits are strangely good with both creamy and hard cheese, so these can pair with a pungent blue cheese quite wonderfully.

Lemon gems, Granny Boyd's cookies (page 204), and sweet and salty peanut cookies (page 55)

LEMON GEMS

My children call these fried-egg cookies and if you look at the photo you'll see why. But that doesn't convey the desirably acid intensity of their lemoniness. Of course, they are also sweet, but if you use good lemon curd (or make your own), they won't be too sweet: you will get that necesssary contrast between sharp, shining jellied curd, and buttery, sugared dough.

½ cup vegetable shortening

½ cup unsalted butter, softened

¼ cup sugar

1 large egg yolk

1 tablespoon lemon juice

zest of 1 lemon

¼ teaspoon salt

1¾ cups all-purpose flour

scant ¼ cup ground almonds

2 tablespoons cornstarch

6–7 tablespoons lemon curd

2 baking sheets, lined with parchment
    or wax paper

Preheat the oven to 350°F.

In a large bowl, beat the shortening, butter, and sugar together, then add the egg yolk, lemon juice, zest, and salt. Gently fold in the flour in two additions, then the ground almonds and cornstarch. Take care not to be too heavy-handed, as rigorous blending will make the dough very sticky. It veers toward that anyway, so when all's combined, put the dough in the refrigerator to chill for at least an hour.

Form into balls the size of cherry tomatoes and place the balls 1 inch apart on your prepared baking sheets. Make an indentation with your thumb in each biscuit, and then cook for 20–25 minutes. They should appear golden and firm.

As soon as they come out of the oven, fill each cookie with a scant ½ teaspoon of lemon curd. When they're all filled, transfer them to wire racks to cool.

Makes about 40.

COFFEE AND WALNUT SPLODGE COOKIES

These are American-style cookies; in other words, just dropped onto the baking sheet free-form. Try to use the instant espresso powder if you can: real coffee or instant coffee granules made up with water change the texture of the dough, and you end up with a slightly too cakey texture (or else a too weak taste). There is an element of cakiness here, but an entirely desirable one.

1²/3 cups all-purpose flour

1 teaspoon baking powder

¹/2 teaspoon salt

³/4 cup plus 2 tablespoons unsalted butter, softened

¹/4 cup sugar

¹/4 cup light brown sugar

2 tablespoons instant espresso powder

2 large eggs, beaten

generous ³/4 cup or 7 ounces walnut pieces

2 baking sheets, lined with parchment or wax paper

Preheat the oven to 350°F.

Mix flour, baking powder, and salt together. In another bowl, cream the butter with the sugars. Add the espresso powder, then, when combined, add the eggs. Stir in the flour mixture and walnut pieces, but don't overmix.

Line a couple of baking sheets with parchment and, using a tablespoon or a relatively small ice-cream scoop, drop mounds onto them, leaving about 2 inches between each as they will spread as they cook.

Bake for 12 minutes, by which time they should be goldenish on top and just firm to the touch.

Cool on a wire rack.

Makes 30.

ITALIAN COOKIES

This is a rather sweeping description of those shortbready swirls punctuated by glacé cherries that you see everywhere in Italy, mostly sold by weight. Actually, when you do buy them, they can tend toward challenging dryness and sweetness: these are buttery, light, and modestly sugared. Don't be put off by using a pastry bag: piping out this kind of dough is extraordinarily satisfying.

1 cup unsalted butter, softened
1/2 cup sugar
1 large egg
zest of 1/2 lemon
2 1/4 cups all-purpose flour

1/2 teaspoon baking powder
pinch of salt
approximately 20 natural-colored
   glacé cherries
2–3 baking sheets, lined with
   parchment and wax paper

Preheat the oven to 350ºF.

Cream the butter and sugar together until very light, almost mousse-like (I use my electric mixer for this). When you're happy with the consistency, after about 5 minutes maybe, beat in the egg and lemon zest. Now add the flour, baking powder, and salt: this is still easiest in a mixer (using paddle attachment) but not hard by hand. Just go gradually but confidently: you want everything smoothly combined but not beaten within an inch of its life. Remember that it won't be a firm dough; if it were, you wouldn't be able to squeeze it through the pastry tip.

Fix a star tip into a piping bag and then fill the bag with the mixture and start piping rosettes or, as the Italians often do, rosettes with a tail; this gives you licence to pipe them any way, really, and not to worry about neatness of form. Just leave a good 2 inches between each cookie. Stick a cherry half into the center of each rosette or at one end of your squiggles, and bake for about 12 minutes. The edges will be just turning gold, but the cookies overall will still be pale. Transfer to wire racks to cool.

Makes about 40.

VARIATION
Use a teaspoon of vanilla extract or a few drops of almond extract in place of the lemon zest and—a very un-Italian move, this—use M&Ms instead of cherry halves.

SAVORY CRACKERS

IRISH BLUE CRACKERS

You don't need to use Irish cheese—though Cashel Blue does go particularly well here—nor do you need to worry about getting blue cornmeal if it eludes you (though I did find mine at the supermarket): these crackers are delicious enough made with all flour and with any robust but crumbly, creamy cheese, blue or otherwise.

3/4 cup Cashel Blue or other blue cheese, crumbled
scant 1/2 cup unsalted butter, softened
1 large egg yolk
3/4 cup all-purpose flour

1/4 cup blue cornmeal
pinch of salt (depending on saltiness of cheese)
1 beaten egg for glazing (optional)
2 baking sheets, lined with parchment or wax paper

Preheat the oven to 400°F.

Mix the cheese, butter, and egg yolk together and then work in the flour, cornmeal and the salt if you're using, just enough to form a soft dough. Shape the dough into a fat disc, wrap it in plastic wrap, and put in the refrigerator for 30 minutes or so to rest before it's rolled out. Dust a surface with flour (and sprinkle a little blue cornmeal onto it if you'd like) and roll out your cheese pastry to a thickness of about a quarter inch. Cut into whatever shapes you like; I quite like them squarish, but half-moons might be good, given the ingredients. If you're going to eat these by themselves, brush with the egg glaze before putting in the oven; if they're to be served with cheese (and they do go so well with the Cashel Blue of which they're partly made) leave them plain.

Cook for 10–15 minutes, by which time they'll be crisp at the edges and puffy in the middle. Remove to a wire rack to cool.

Makes about 30.

HOT DISCS

Think of these as a cross between tortilla chips and mini-poppadoms, the sort of crackers that are perfect for dipping into salsa, hummus, or guacamole. Leave the seasonings out (bar the salt) and you have nineteenth-century Mereworth biscuits, to be eaten with soft cheese or the creamiest unsalted butter.

Irish blue biscuits

1 2/3 cups all-purpose flour

1 heaping teaspoon salt

1/2 teaspoon cayenne pepper

1/4 teaspoon ground cumin

1/4 teaspoon ground coriander

scant 2 tablespoons cold unsalted butter, diced

zest of 1 lime, very finely grated

7 tablespoons hot milk

2 1/2-inch plain round cutter

2–3 baking sheets, buttered

Preheat the oven to 425°F. Put the flour, salt, cayenne, cumin, and coriander in a bowl and rub in the butter as you would for biscuits. Add the zest and then gradually pour in the milk until you've got a firm but soft dough. Roll out one half of this as thin as you can: it should look almost transparent and feel like fine cloth. Stamp out as many rounds as you can, transfer them to your baking sheets and cook for 5 minutes, though check after 3½. When cooked they will be tinged with brown and wonderfully puffed up. Remove to a wire rack to cool and repeat with the rest of the dough.

Makes about 75.

OATCAKES

There's something very satisfying about making such good, plain fare as oatcakes—as if you're doing something sober and basic and not entertaining yourself with fripperies.

If you can bring yourself to use lard, please do. Did you know that it is a less saturated fat than butter?

1 cup plus 2 tablespoons quick-cooking oats

pinch of salt

1/4 teaspoon baking soda

1 tablespoon lard or butter, melted

6–14 tablespoons very hot water

1 baking sheet

3-inch round biscuit cutter (optional)

Preheat the oven to 400°F.

Put the oats in a bowl and add the salt and baking soda. Make a well, pour in the fat and, stirring with a wooden spoon, enough hot water to mix to a stiff dough. Knead it for a while to make it come smoothly together, then roll out as thinly as you can. Cut into triangles or rounds, and bake on the ungreased sheet for 15–20 minutes, or until the edges are turning golden brown and the oatcakes themselves are firm (they'll crisp up on cooling). Remove to a wire rack to cool.

Makes 15–20.

SCONES AND MUFFINS

LILY'S SCONES

These are the best scones I've ever eaten, which is quite how it should be since they emanate from one of those old-fashioned cooks who starts a batch the minute the doorbell rings at teatime. Yes, I know they look as if they've got cellulite (see page 71)—it's the cream of tartar, which is also why, despite their apparent solidity, they have that dreamy lightness.

3¹⁄₃ cups all-purpose flour

1 teaspoon salt

2 teaspoons baking soda

4¹⁄₂ teaspoons cream of tartar

¹⁄₄ cup cold unsalted butter, diced

2 tablespoons vegetable shortening,
   in teaspooned lumps

1¹⁄₃ cups milk

1 large egg, beaten, for egg-wash

2¹⁄₂-inch crinkle-edged round cutter

1 baking pan, lightly greased

Preheat the oven to 425°F.

Sift the flour, salt, baking soda, and cream of tartar into a large bowl. Rub in the fats till the mixture goes like damp sand. Add the milk all at once, mix briefly—briefly being the operative word—and then turn out onto a floured surface and knead lightly to form a dough.

Roll out to about 1 to 1¼ inch thickness. Dip the cutter into some flour, then stamp out at least 10 scones. You get 12 in all from this, but may need to reroll for the last 2. Place on the baking sheet very close together—the idea is that they bulge and stick together on cooking—then brush the tops with the egg wash. Put in the oven and cook for 10 minutes or until risen and golden.

Always eat freshly baked, preferably still warm from the oven, with clotted cream and jam or, my favorite, Thunder and Lightning, which is (as in the picture) clotted cream and molasses.

Makes 12.

VARIATION

Add 3 ounces of raisins or golden raisins for fruit scones, or, something I'm keen on, use the same amount of dried sour cherries, with or without the finely grated zest of ¹⁄₂ an orange. To make cheese scones, add 3 ounces of sharp Cheddar, grated.

STRAWBERRY SHORTCAKES

I've long been fascinated by this American dessert, which isn't really a scone so much as a tender, buttery sponge with scone-like properties, split and crammed with strawberries. There's so much dispute, as there always is with traditional recipes, over the right method to make them, serve them, eat them: should they be individual-sized or one huge fat disc? should butter be spread on the tender cut sides while still warm, before the fruit and cream are dolloped on?

I don't intend to enter into the debate—don't feel qualified to anyway—but since I'm a great fan of the methodical-to-the-point-of-obsessive American food magazine *Cook's Illustrated*, I got guidance from its executive editor Pam Anderson's book, *The Perfect Recipe*. I sometimes veer away from it, by using crème fraîche instead of whipped cream, or by using light cream in place of half-and-half (which we don't anyway have here) and I do like to sprinkle a little balsamic vinegar on the crushed strawberries, but in all respects that matter, this is her recipe.

This is what you want to bring out to people by the plateful on a summer's day after lunch in the garden.

for the shortcakes:

2 cups plus 2 tablespoons all-purpose flour

1/2 teaspoon salt

1 tablespoon baking powder

5 tablespoons sugar

1/2 cup unsalted butter, frozen

1 large egg, beaten

1/2 cup light cream

1 large egg white, lightly beaten

1 baking sheet, greased or lined with parchment or wax paper

21/2-inch round cutter

for the filling:

approximately 11 ounces strawberries

1 tablespoon sugar

few drops balsamic vinegar (optional)

1 cup heavy cream, whipped, or crème fraîche

Preheat the oven to 425°F.

Mix the flour, salt, baking powder, and 3 tablespoons of the sugar in a bowl. Grate the butter into these dry ingredients and use your fingertips to finish crumbling the butter into the flour. Whisk the egg into the cream, and pour into the flour mixture a little at a time, using a fork to mix. You may not need all of the eggy cream to make the dough come together, so go cautiously.

Turn the dough out onto a lightly floured surface, and roll gently to a thickness of about ¾ inch. Dip the cutter in flour and cut out as many rounds as you can. Work the scraps back into a dough, re-roll and finish cutting out—you should get 8 in all. Place the shortcakes about 1 inch apart on the baking sheet, brush the tops with the egg white, and sprinkle them with the remaining 2 tablespoons of sugar. If it helps with the rest of your cooking, or life in general, you can cover and refrigerate them now for up to 2 hours.

Bake for 10–15 minutes, until golden brown, and let them cool for a short while on a wire rack. Meanwhile, crush half the strawberries with the spoonful of sugar and the few drops of balsamic vinegar if using, and halve or quarter the remaining strawberries, depending on their size. Whip the heavy cream, if you're using.

The shortcakes should be eaten while still warm, so split each one across the middle and cover with a spoonful of the crushed strawberry mixture, a few halved or quartered strawberries, then dollop some whipped cream or crème fraîche on top, and set the top back on.

Makes 8.

VARIATION

I love these American-style with passionfruit in place of the strawberries, though if you're going along with this, don't use crème fraîche; you need velvety-smooth, whipped heavy cream, unpasteurized if possible.

Lily's scones (page 67)

BLUEBERRY MUFFINS

I had always thought that muffins were a lot of fuss about a disappointing nothing. But that, I found, was because they were the industrially produced ones. When you make them yourself—and they are the easiest things in the world to make, which is why you'll find a couple of recipes for them in the children's chapter—they're nothing like as tall and puffy as the ones you see in shops and cafés, and you'll also notice that they've got some interest about them. That dry mass of aerated wodge in cellophane isn't the sort of muffin you want for your breakfast; these are.

If it helps, you can weigh out all the dry ingredients, leave them in a plastic wrap–covered bowl overnight, and measure out the liquids into a pitcher which you can keep covered in the refrigerator. That way, you could do all the measuring and close work before you go to bed, then, on getting up, melt the butter, preheat the oven, mix the wet with the dry ingredients, fold in the fruit and dollop them in their pans. In a quarter of an hour, give or take, you will have a kitchen full of baking smells and a plateful of muffins on the table.

6 tablespoons unsalted butter
1 1/3 cup all-purpose flour
1/2 teaspoon baking soda
2 teaspoons baking powder
1/4 cup sugar
pinch of salt

3/4 cup plus 2 tablespoons buttermilk
**   (or 1/2 cup plain yogurt and**
**   7 tablespoons low-fat milk)**
1 large egg
7 ounces blueberries
12-cup muffin pan lined with 12 paper
**   baking cups**

Melt the butter, and set it aside to cool for a little. Preheat the oven to 400°F.

Combine all the dry ingredients in a bowl, and in a measuring cup beat together the buttermilk (or yogurt and milk), egg, and melted butter. Using a wooden spoon and a light hand, pour the wet ingredients into the dry and mix gently to combine. Don't worry about lumps: the important thing with muffins is that the mixture isn't overworked. Fold in the blueberries, again keeping mixing to a minimum. You could also add orange zest at this point if you wanted. Spoon into the muffin cups—I use an ice-cream scoop and a small rubber spatula for this—and bake for 20 minutes, by which time the muffins should be risen and golden and firm on top. Eat warm or cooled as you like; I like warm, broken with fingers and smeared, mouthful by mouthful, with good unsalted butter and blueberry jam.

Makes 12.

BAKLAVA MUFFINS

I know this sounds like a mad idea, but I came across it in a ringbound book I bought off the Net in the middle of the night called *The Joy of Muffins*. Joy indeed, for what do you know, these taste so good: gooey, crunchy, soft and filling; sticky buns for the slapdash cook.

for the filling:
scant 1/2 cup chopped walnuts
1/3 cup sugar
1 1/2 teaspoons cinnamon
3 tablespoons butter, melted

for the muffins:
1 cup plus 7 tablespoons all-purpose flour
2 teaspoons baking powder
1/2 teaspoon baking soda

1/4 cup sugar
1 large egg
3 tablespoons unsalted butter, melted
1 cup plus 2 tablespoons buttermilk (or 3/4 cup plain yogurt and 1/3 cup low-fat milk)
12-cup muffin pan lined with 12 paper baking cups

for the topping:
about 1/2 cup honey

Preheat the oven to 400ºF.

Mix all the filling ingredients together in a small bowl, and then get on with the muffins. In a large bowl, mix together the flour, baking powder, baking soda, and sugar. In a wide-mouthed measuring cup, whisk the egg, melted butter, and buttermilk (or yogurt-milk mix). Make a well in the dry ingredients, pour in the liquid, and mix lightly and gently, remembering to keep it bumpy rather than going all-out for smooth: anything more than the gentlest handling makes for heavy muffins. Fill the muffin cups one-third full, add a scant tablespoon of filling, then cover with more muffin mixture until two-thirds full. Sprinkle any remaining filling on top of the muffins.

Bake for 15 minutes, by which time they should be golden brown and ready. Put the muffins, still in their paper cups, onto a rack and drizzle with honey. You may find it easier to warm the honey a little before pouring.

Makes 12.

LEMON-RASPBERRY MUFFINS

I think of these more as teatime muffins than breakfast ones, but please don't feel constrained by my prejudices (and it's not often you'll hear me say that).

¼ cup butter

1 ⅓ cups all-purpose flour

2 teaspoons baking powder

½ teaspoon baking soda

½ cup sugar

¼ teaspoon salt

juice and finely chopped zest of
   1 lemon

approximately ½ cup milk

1 large egg

5 ounces raspberries

12-cup muffin pan lined with 12
   paper baking cups

Preheat the oven to 400°F.

Melt the butter and set it aside to cool. Stir together, in a largish bowl, the flour, baking powder, baking soda, sugar, salt, and zest. In a measuring cup, pour in the lemon juice, then enough milk to come up nearly to the 1 cup mark (and it will curdle, but that's just fine), then beat in the egg and melted butter. Pour into the dry ingredients and stir briefly; the batter should scarcely be combined. Fold in the raspberries, spoon this lumpy mixture into the muffin cups and bake for about 25 minutes. When cooked, the tops should spring back to your touch. Leave in the pan for 5 minutes to cool slightly, then sit them on a rack to cool for a further 10–15 minutes.

Makes 12.

PANCAKES

There is something about a pancake, a breakfast pancake, that has domestic goddess stamped all over it.

JONNYCAKES

Jonnycakes are pancakes—or griddlecakes, really—made with the addition of cornmeal, one of the great indigenous American ingredients. I love these eaten sweet with maple syrup or as part of a brunch with sausages, bacon, and eggs.

1/2 cup plus 2 tablespoons fine
   cornmeal or polenta
1/2 cup all-purpose flour
4 teaspoons baking powder
2 teaspoons sugar

1/2 teaspoon salt
2 large eggs
1 1/3 cups milk
2 tablespoons butter, melted

Stir together the dry ingredients in one bowl; in another (big) bowl, whisk the eggs and milk. Then gradually beat in the dry ingredients and when combined stir in the melted butter. Heat an oiled griddle or pan and drop, one by one, tablespoonfuls of the batter on the hot surface to make little pancakes about 2½ inches in diameter.

    After 1–2 minutes, the top of each yellow pool of batter will begin to bubble. Turn over briskly and give a minute or so on the other side before removing to a hot cupboard or moderate-to-low oven to keep warm.

    This amount makes 30–35 pancakes. This sounds like a lot, but be warned: my two-year-old eats five for breakfast, easily.

WELSHCAKES

These are somewhere between pancakes and cookies, and much as I think I don't like dried fruit enormously, I can wolf down plates of these. This recipe comes from the grandmother of a Welsh girl, Heulwen, who helped with my children after my second baby was born. And these were an immensely comforting part of that time.

1/2 cup cold unsalted butter, diced
1 2/3 cups self-rising cake flour
1/4 cup sugar, plus more for sprinkling
1/4 teaspoon ground allspice

scant 1/2 cup golden raisins
1 large egg, beaten
3-inch crinkled round cutter
smooth griddle or cast-iron frying pan

Rub the butter into the flour as you would if making biscuits, then stir in the sugar, spice, and dried fruit. Add the egg to make a soft but not sticky dough. Form a disc, cover with plastic wrap, and leave in the refrigerator for a minimum of 20 minutes.

    Roll out on a floured surface to a thickness of about ¼ inch, and cut out your little cakes; you will need to re-roll and so forth but that shouldn't be problematic. Preheat your unoiled griddle or cast-iron frying pan and cook the cakes for about 3 minutes each side, until golden brown. Remove to a cold plate and sprinkle with sugar.

    Makes about 20.

AMERICAN BREAKFAST PANCAKES

These are those thick, spongy American pancakes that are often eaten with warm maple syrup and crisp fried bacon. I love them with the syrup alone, but if you do want bacon, you want a crisp salty ribbon of it here. You can easily cook these pancakes by dolloping the batter onto a hot griddle (smooth, not ridged, side) or cast-iron pan, but I use a blini pan, one of my pet implements.

1 1/2 cups all-purpose flour
1 tablespoon baking powder
pinch of salt
1 teaspoon sugar

2 large eggs, beaten
2 tablespoons butter, melted and
** cooled**
1 1/3 cups milk
butter for frying

The easiest way to make these is to put all the ingredients into a blender and blitz. But if you do mix up the batter by hand in a bowl, make a well in the flour, baking powder, salt, and sugar, beat in the eggs, melted butter, and milk, and transfer to a pitcher: it's much easier to pour the batter into the pan than to spoon it. I like to leave the batter for 20 minutes before using it; and you may then want to add more milk to the mixture if you're frying in the blini pan, so that it runs right to the edges.

When you cook the pancakes, all you need to remember is that when the upper side of the pancake is blistering and bubbling it's time to cook the second side, and this needs only about 1 minute, if that.

I get 11 blini-pan-sized pancakes out of this, maybe 16 silver-dollar-sized ones on the griddle.

VARIATION
Sprinkle blueberries onto the uncooked side of the pancake just after you've poured the batter into the pan.

PIES

PIES

A pie is just what we all know should be emanating from the kitchen of a domestic goddess. Not simply because it is the traditional fare of the kitchen *Koenigin*, but because few things approach it when it comes to inducing that warm, bolstering sense of honorable satisfaction.

The truth is, however, that the less familiar pastry-making becomes, the harder we believe it to be; but all you have to do is make some and then you'll realize that it doesn't require expertise or dexterity beyond your capabilities. And I write as someone who is a clumsy and impatient cook. There is nothing like becoming competent at some hitherto terrifying activity to make one confident. And in cooking, as in everything else, confidence (and competence) breeds confidence. To learn how to make pastry, all I did was make some, and make it again. Then, some time later, again. Suddenly, I found I could do it, more or less without thinking about it. I'd never before considered myself a baker, and so it was particularly satisfying to become this person who turned out pastry and made pies and beautiful tarts.

But like the first kiss, it's the first pie that counts: as soon as I'd whipped it out of the oven and sprinkled sugar over it, I felt suffused with heady satisfaction. This was a real pie: the sort that I thought only women with sensible hands habitually wiped briskly on aprons could make. It changed my culinary self-image instantly. And that's why I am so evangelical now.

Perhaps the greatest joy of pastry-making is that it's mud-pie time; you get floury, sticky, wholly involved. I don't mean by this that you shouldn't use any equipment: I use my free-standing mixer, or processor.

(I need to, indeed, because I nearly always freeze the butter and flour together before combining as this helps you get a more feathery, flaky pastry.) I also suggest rolling the pastry between two sheets of plastic wrap for easy handling. But you still need to use your hands for that last crucial combining, the rolling, and draping into the pan, and the piecing together of your pie.

Just do it.

Blackberry and apple pie (page 118)

BASIC SHORTCRUST

The basic rule for pastry is that you use half the weight of fat to flour (and I nearly always prefer to make up that fat with equal amounts of butter and shortening and use all-purpose flour) and use a liquid—egg yolk, orange juice, whatever—to bind it. Throughout this chapter, though, and wherever necessary, I give precise ingredients for the particular recipe, so I give just my method here. What's more, it's foolproof; I was once that fool.

Put the flour in a shallow bowl, add the cold, diced fats and stir gently to coat. Put in the deep freeze—no need to cover—for 10 minutes. As you do so, put your liquid in a bowl or cup with a pinch of salt and transfer to the fridge. Either in a processor or—for choice—in a free-standing mixer with flat paddle, blend the fats and flour until you have a mixture that resembles sandy porridge. Then, gradually process or paddle in the liquid until the pastry is almost coming together. Use your hands now to form it into a disc or couple of discs, wrap in plastic wrap, and let it rest in the refrigerator for 20 minutes before rolling out.

PROCESSOR PUFF-PASTRY

Having discovered the world's most wonderful and hysterically easy Danish pastry (see page 327), it occurred to me that the principle would surely apply to the un-yeasted version, that is to say, puff pastry. I tried it: it worked.

1²/3 cups bread flour
pinch of salt
1 cup plus 2 tablespoons cold unsalted
   butter, cut into ¹/4-inch slices

squeeze of lemon juice
5–6 tablespoons ice water

Pulse the flour and salt together in the food processor, then add the cold butter and pulse 3–4 times; the pieces of butter should still be visible. Turn out into a large bowl and add a squeeze of lemon juice and enough ice water to bind the pastry. Wrap in plastic wrap and rest in the refrigerator for half an hour.

Dust a surface with flour, roll the pastry out into a long rectangle, and fold in three like a business letter. Now turn the folded pastry so that if it were a book the spine would be on your left. Repeat twice more, turning every time.

Wrap again and rest in the refrigerator for another half-hour before you use it.

This makes enough for two 8- to 10-inch pie bases.

SAVORY PIES

SUPPER ONION PIE

This is just what I want to eat for supper when it's dark early and I'm tired. It is a pie, yes, but not one with pastry that needs rolling out: you just make a cheese-scone dough and then press it over some onions, already softened and aromatic, in the pan.

for the filling/topping:
4 medium red onions
1 tablespoon olive oil
1 heaping tablespoon butter
salt and pepper to taste
3–4 sprigs of thyme, de-stalked, or
**   ¹/₂ teaspoon dried thyme**
¹/₂ cup plus 2 tablespoons or 5 ounces
**   sharp Cheddar cheese or Gruyère,**
**   grated**

for the scone dough:
1²/₃ cups all-purpose flour
1 scant teaspoon baking powder
1 teaspoon salt
scant ¹/₂ cup milk
3 tablespoons butter, melted
1 scant teaspoon dry English mustard
1 large egg, beaten
8- to 10-inch cast-iron skillet or 9-inch
**   pie plate, buttered**

Preheat the oven to 400°F. Peel the onions, halve them, then cut each half into 4 segments each. Heat the oil and butter in the pan, then add the onions and cook over a medium heat, stirring regularly, for about 30 minutes; they should be soft and tinged with color. Season with salt and pepper, and add the thyme. Turn into a pie dish, and scatter 2 ounces of the cheese over the waiting onions. Leave while you get on with the dough topping.

Put the flour, baking powder, and salt together in a bowl with the remaining cheese. Pour the milk into a measuring cup, add the melted butter, mustard, and egg, mix well and then pour onto the flour mixture in the bowl. Mix to a dough using a fork, a wooden spoon, or your hands; it should be quite sticky. Then tip it out onto a work surface and press into a circle about the size of the pie dish. Transfer it to the dish, pressing it to seal the edges.

Put it in the oven for 15 minutes, then turn down to 350°F. and give it another 10 minutes, by which time the dough should be golden and crisp on top. Let it stand for a couple of minutes, then cover with a large plate and turn upside-down so the plate's beneath and the pie dish on top. Place on a flat surface and remove the dish.

I love this with brown sauce, either homemade (see the domestic goddess's pantry, page 362) or bought.

Makes 6 generous slices.

PIZZA RUSTICA

Pizza rustica is not a pizza in the way that we've come to understand it, though anyone who's spent time in Italy might well have come across it. The word *pizza* simply means pie, and this term denotes a deep, pastry-encased creation, stuffed with relatively unfancy ingredients. For a non-Italian, however, these ingredients are at the upper end of the economic scale, and hardly rustica at all, and it's for this reason I thought up my pizza rustica *all'inglese* (see page 89), though any Italian deli should be able to supply you with the wherewithal easily enough, and increasingly the supermarkets stock what you'll need too. The wonderful Anna del Conte gave me this recipe—from her magnum opus, *The Gastronomy of Italy*. Using a springform pan rather than pie dish makes the building-up of the pie easy, and the finished, unmolded creation looks a miracle of proud, golden accomplishment.

for the pastry:

1²/3 cups all-purpose flour

¹/2 cup cold unsalted butter, cut into
 ¹/2-inch cubes

2 egg yolks

2 tablespoons ice water

1 heaping teaspoon salt

1 tablespoon sugar

8-inch springform pan, buttered

for the filling:

2 ounces luganega or other mild pure
 pork sausage, skinned

1 tablespoon olive oil

generous 8 ounces ricotta

2 ounces smoked provolone, diced

4 ounces Italian mozzarella, crumbled

¹/4 cup freshly grated parmesan

¹/2 clove garlic, chopped

2 tablespoons chopped flat-leaf
 parsley

2 pinches chili powder or crushed
 dried red chilies

4 ounces prosciutto, cut into small
 pieces

4 ounces mortadella, cut into small
 pieces

2 eggs, lightly beaten

black pepper

1 heaping tablespoon dried bread
 crumbs

for the glaze:

1 egg yolk

2 tablespoons milk

pinch of salt

Put the flour and butter in a dish, and put this dish in the freezer for 10 minutes. Stir together the yolks, water, and salt in a cup, and put this cup in the refrigerator. Then, when time's up, tip the flour and butter into the bowl of the food processor, add the sugar and pulse to combine: you want a soft crumbly mass, somewhere between sand and por-ridge oats. Bind with the egg yolks, water, and salt, and when it looks like it's on the verge of coming together (you have to stop slightly short of this actually happening), tip the

pastry out and press it together with your hands. Don't worry, though, if the pastry is a little too damp: I find one of the miracles of this pre-freezing pastry technique is that it makes it more foolproof on every level. It always seems to roll out well.

Divide into two discs, one somewhat larger than the other, and put both into the refrigerator to rest wrapped in plastic wrap.

Preheat the oven to 400°F, put in a baking sheet, and get on with the filling. Fry the sausage in the oil for about 5 minutes, breaking it up with a wooden spoon as it cooks, then transfer it to a bowl and let it cool. At which time, add all the other ingredients except the bread crumbs and mix thoroughly.

Roll out the larger disc of pastry between plastic wrap so it's large enough to cover the bottom and sides of the pan, leaving a few inches' overhang. Sprinkle the bottom of the now pastry-lined pan with bread crumbs, and then fill with the hammy, eggy mixture waiting in its bowl. Roll out the smaller disc between plastic wrap to make the lid, place it on top of the filled pie, turn over the edges of the overhang to form a border and press down with the tines of a fork.

Just before baking, glaze the pie by brushing over the milky, salty egg, stab it here and there with the prongs of a fork to make steam holes, and place it on the baking sheet in the preheated oven. Give it 10 minutes at this temperature, then turn it down to 350°F and bake for a further 45 minutes.

Leave the pie to cool for at least 10 minutes before serving it, but it's at its best after about 25. It's still wonderful at room temperature, though, and I long for leftovers too, eaten standing by the fridge's open door the next day.

Makes 8–10 good-sized slices.

PIZZA RUSTICA ALL'INGLESE

This recipe comes second, but not in terms of taste or success. To say it's an anglicization of the very Italian pie above isn't quite to describe it, but I did want to preserve the idea of the original, only taking into consideration ingredients that were as easily accessible and familiar to us as the ones in the filling above would be to Italians.

This version makes for a slightly less deep pie, but it's still a comfortingly chunky number. And as with the pie above, it's wonderful cold and can be happily put back in its pan once it is, so it is very easily transportable. Well, picnics don't exist just in the books of Enid Blyton, and this would be so good eaten on a scratchy blanket with bottles of soda pop.

Since the pastry and method for its preparation and cooking remain the same, as do all other governing injunctions, I'm just giving you the ingredients and method for the filling. By all means use eight ounces of a sharp Cheddar in place of the mild Cheddar and Lancashire below if you want; indeed, make up your own mixture freely to suit yourself, as I did.

7 ounces lean pork

7 ounces bacon

bacon fat or 2 tablespoons vegetable oil

4 ounces mild Cheddar

4 ounces Lancashire cheese

1 cup plus 2 tablespoons cottage cheese, drained in a strainer and processed

2 big or 4 small spring onions

1 clove garlic

2 tablespoons chopped parsley

2 eggs, lightly beaten

freshly ground black pepper

1 heaping tablespoon dried bread crumbs

Mince the pork and bacon in a food processor. Fry the minced pork and bacon for about 5 minutes in the fat rendered from the bacon, or use vegetable oil. Transfer to a bowl and let it cool slightly, and then add all the other ingredients except the bread crumbs. Proceed as for pizza rustica on page 86.

Makes 8–10 slices.

SAUSAGE AND SPINACH PIE

Once I had got into making these golden discs, enthused by the springformed shape and firmness, I wanted to experiment with a number of fillings. This one turned into one of our favorite lunches. Try it: you'll see why.

for the pastry:
as for pizza rustica (page 86)
8-inch springform pan, greased and lined with parchment or wax paper

for the filling:
2 medium onions, puréed in a food processor
3–4 young sage leaves, chopped
2 tablespoons olive oil
1 pound, 2 ounces Cumberland or other mild sausage, skinned
2–3 tablespoons chopped parsley

2 pounds spinach, washed, cooked, chopped, and drained very well (or 2 10-ounce packages frozen, defrosted)
1 tablespoon freshly grated parmesan
1 large egg, beaten
1 heaping tablespoon bread crumbs

for the glaze:
1 large egg yolk
2 tablespoons milk
pinch of salt

Preheat the oven to 375°F, and make up the pastry as for the pizza rustica. Fry the processor-puréed onion and the sage in the olive oil for 5–10 minutes on a medium heat. Add the sausage meat, mashing it with a fork to mix in with the onion, and cook for a further 5 minutes. Take the pan off the heat and add the chopped parsley and spinach and the parmesan. Season with salt and pepper, and add the egg, mixing well.

Now roll out the pastry between plastic wrap to line the pan as before, then sprinkle with bread crumbs, add the filling, cover with pastry, and so on. Curl the pastry edges over to form a neat border around the tin and press the edge with the prongs of a fork. Make a steam hole in the middle and glaze. Cook for about 40 minutes, or until the pie is golden and firm.

Remove from the oven and let stand for at least 10 minutes before cutting into it. Because of the spinach, which tends to continue to ooze liquid when cooling, this pie, as with the one that follows, isn't so good cold. But, in an emergency . . .

Serves 6–8.

SPINACH, RICOTTA, AND BULGUR WHEAT PIE

This started off life as a vegetarian version of the sausage and spinach pie above, though it is in no way an inadequate substitute for the carnivore's version, but rather an entirely seductive alternative in its own right.

for the pastry:
as for pizza rustica
8-inch springform pan, greased and
   lined with parchment or wax paper

for the filling:
scant 1/2 cup bulgur wheat
1 teaspoon vegetable stock granules
1 pound fresh spinach, washed,
   cooked, chopped, and drained very

well (or 1 10-ounce package frozen,
   defrosted)
2 cups or 1 pound ricotta
3 green onions, finely chopped
zest of 1 lemon
pinch of cayenne pepper
pinch of dried thyme
2 large eggs
2 tablespoons parmesan, grated
2 tablespoons dried bread crumbs

Make the pastry following the method for the pizza rustica, and preheat the oven to 400°F, slipping in a baking sheet as you do so.

Put the bulgur and stock granules in a bowl and cover with boiling water. Place foil over the bowl and let the bulgur soak for 10–15 minutes. Give the spinach another press against the colander to squeeze out any further wateriness. Mash the ricotta with a fork, and add the spring onions, lemon zest, cayenne, thyme, and spinach. Stir in the eggs, parmesan, and soaked bulgur (draining first if necessary) and season with salt and pepper.

Roll out the pastry as above, adding bread crumbs, filling, and top; sealing edges, making steam vents, and so forth, and bake the pie for 10 minutes before turning the temperature down to 350°F and cooking it for a further 45.

I like this pie best when it has stood for 25 minutes after coming out of the oven. Serves 6–8.

ZUCCHINI AND CHICKPEA FILO PIE

We're still in the realm of the springform here, but it is, nevertheless, a different sort of pie. Quite simply, it's a pie for those of you who don't want to make pastry. I know that you can buy shortcrust not only ready-made but ready-rolled, but that never seems a happy choice to me; buying ready-made filo dough, on the other hand, is quite simply what you do. (Though, until recently, I was far more frightened of taking the filo sheets from the box than I was of making my own basic pastry.) Correspondingly, I use canned chickpeas, though please feel free to soak and cook the dried ones if you prefer.

I can't claim this as an Iranian creation, but I certainly had the tastes and fragrances of some Iranian dishes in mind.

¹/₂ teaspoon cumin seeds

1 small onion or ¹/₂ large onion, finely diced

2 tablespoons olive oil

¹/₂ teaspoon turmeric

1 teaspoon ground coriander

3 plump zucchini

generous ¹/₂ cup basmati rice

2¹/₄ cups vegetable stock, or chicken if you prefer

2 15-ounce cans of chickpeas, drained

scant ¹/₂ cup melted butter

7 ounces filo pastry dough

8-inch springform pan

Preheat the oven to 400°F and put in a baking sheet.

Gently fry the cumin seeds and onion in the olive oil until the onion's soft. Add the turmeric and coriander. Dice the zucchini (unpeeled), add them to the onion mixture, and cook on a fairly high heat to prevent the zucchini becoming watery. When they are soft but still holding their shape, add the rice and stir well, letting the rice become well coated in the oil. Add the stock ¹/₂ cup at a time, stirring while you do so. When all the liquid has been absorbed the rice should be cooked, so take it off the heat, stir in the chickpeas, and check the seasoning.

Brush the insides of the springform pan with some of the melted butter. Line the bottom and sides of the pan with ³/₄ of the filo, buttering each piece as you layer. Leave a little filo overlapping the sides, and keep 3–4 layers for the top. Carefully put in your slightly cooled filling, and then fold in the overlaps. Butter the last layers of filo and scrunch on top of the pie as a covering. Brush with a final coat of butter, and put in the oven for about 20 minutes, or until the filo is golden and the middle hot. Check this by inserting a slim, sharp-bladed knife (or cake tester). If, when you remove it, it feels hot when you press it against your wrist, the pie's ready.

Serves 6–8.

STEAK AND KIDNEY PUDDING

You may think that a steak and kidney pudding made with a thick shortening crust is not the sort of food you eat. All I can say is cook it and you'll change your mind. When we made this for the photographic shoot, we, to a woman, wolfed it down with what I can only describe as besotted greed.

Contrary to most people's preconceptions, shortening gives the crust an almost ethereal lightness. True, this is only the case if it's eaten immediately—any standing around and it seems to seize up and gain thick-set density—but eat fast and it'll still be delicious when you get around to second helpings. I always use vegetable shortening, as I don't like eating meat products whose derivation I do not know. The only thing I'd add is that while shortening crust is very easy to make, you must make it at the last minute.

As for equipment: life is very much easier if you buy a plastic pudding basin with a fitted lid than if you use a traditional basin and make a pleated foil lid and string handles. You don't need to steam the pudding: you can simply immerse it in a large pan of boiling water.

I often double the quantities for the meat filling, then freeze half, so I'm only a defrost away from another pudding. Traditionally, oysters were added to steak and kidney pud; I thought a little oyster sauce might be an appropriate contemporary adaptation, and it was, rewardingly so. And I happened to find some beer called Oyster Stout which seemed entirely right for it too, but it's hardly essential: any stout in a storm. . . .

I always cook the meat filling a day or two in advance: the flavors deepen wonderfully and the whole thing seems less of a performance.

for the filling:
2 tablespoons all-purpose flour
1/2 teaspoon English dry mustard
18 ounces top round or chuck beef, cut into 3/4 inch pieces
9 ounces lambs' kidney, cut into chunks
2 tablespoons butter
2 tablespoons olive oil
1 medium onion, chopped
5 ounces portobello mushrooms (i.e., 2 medium-sized), peeled and roughly chunked

1/2 cup plus 2 tablespoons beef stock
1/2 cup plus 2 tablespoons stout or dark ale
1 scant tablespoon oyster sauce

for the shortening crust:
2 1/4 cups self-rising flour
1/2 teaspoon salt
3/4 cup vegetable shortening
1/2 teaspoon dry English mustard
3-quart plastic pudding basin with lid, both well buttered

The 2 hours of steaming—which involves little activity on your part—seems less of a consideration when separated from the pudding's preparation. So, preheat the oven to 250°F, season the 2 tablespoons of flour with salt, pepper, and the dry mustard, and put it into a plastic bag along with the steak and kidney. Seal it, and toss everything around to get an even coating of flour.

Warm the butter and oil in a casserole and brown the meat (including the kidney) in batches, removing each to a dish. Fry the onion in the pan, then add the mushrooms and fry them briefly, adding more oil if you need it. Put all the meat back into the casserole and over a medium heat add the stock, stout, and oyster sauce. Bring it to the boil, scraping any floury bits off the bottom. Cover with a lid and cook in the preheated oven for 1½ hours. When it's cooked, check the seasoning and put aside to cool.

About 2½–3 hours before you want to eat, fill a large saucepan with water and bring to the boil. When it begins to boil, start making the pastry, and not before. Mix the flour, salt, shortening, and dry mustard in a large bowl; then, stirring with a wooden spoon, add enough cold water to make a firm dough. Roll out on a floured surface into a large circle, approximately ⅜ inch thick, and cut away a quarter segment from the circle to use later as the lid. Ease the three-quarter circle of pastry into your buttered pudding basin; there should be about an inch of overhang. Spoon the cold filling in, not letting it come up higher than about ¾ inch below the rim.

Roll out the quarter segment into a small circle to fit the top and seal it with the overhanging edges. Clip on the basin's buttered lid, immerse it in water or place it in a steamer over water and leave it there for 2 hours, remembering to check water levels occasionally.

Turn the pudding out onto a plate with a good rim, or some sort of shallow bowl: there is a wonderful moment when, like a bulldozed building, your pudding begins to crack and crumple and then cascades downward; you need to make sure every thick oozy bit of stout, beefy liquid is safely contained.

Serves 6 generously.

SMALL PIES

I know I have never been much of a friend to the small-portioned, but these are, for all that, lunchtime favorites at my house.

CORNISH PASTIES

The best Cornish pasties I've ever had were bought from the shop/post office in Helford, England, and then taken, with some fries, cold beer, and a jar of spiced apple chutney (see page 357), to be eaten lying on the beach further up the Helford River. We made these shortly after coming back. I really do think you need to use lard, not butter: apart from anything else, Cornish pasties are not fancy French baked goods meant to exude the flavor of expensive butter, and lard gives you the fluttery lightness you need.

for the pastry:
1 cup or 8 ounces lard
3 1/3 cups self-rising flour
pinch of salt
ice water to bind
1 baking sheet, lined with parchment
or wax paper

for the filling:
1 small–medium onion, chopped
**1 large potato, peeled, quartered,
and sliced thinly**

**4 ounces rutabaga or turnip, peeled,
quartered, and sliced thinly**
1 tablespoon lard
**18 ounces top round or chuck beef,
diced fairly small**
1/4 teaspoon mace
1/4 teaspoon dry English mustard

for the glaze:
1 large egg, beaten

First make the pastry following the usual method (see page 83).

Preheat the oven to 400°F and get on with the filling. Cook the onion, potato, and rutabaga in the lard. Add the beef and cook on a medium heat, moving it around to brown the meat evenly. Turn the heat down a little, season with the mace, mustard, and salt and pepper, and cook for about 30 minutes until everything is tender.

Divide the pastry into 4 pieces, and roll each one out between plastic wrap into a rough circle about the size of a small dinner plate (9 inches); these are going to be fat daddies. Make all the circles before you start filling so that the filled pasties don't go soggy hanging around. Put a quarter of the filling into one side of the circle, brush beaten egg around the edge and fold over to seal the pasty. Curl the edges inward and then crimp them in a pastylike fashion. Repeat with the other pasties.

Place the pasties on the baking sheet and brush with beaten egg. Cook for 15 minutes, then turn the oven down to 350°F and give them a further 15 minutes.

Eat as soon as you can without burning your tongue (though I love them warm, 15–20 minutes after they've come out of the oven) with apple chutney or brown sauce, or anything else you damn well please.

Serves 4 generously.

CHEESE, ONION, AND POTATO PIES

This is the picnic food of fondest imagination, although actually we eat these for ordinary supper in the kitchen fairly often. I say "we": that's to say I make them for the children, then snaffle down a couple myself. I love them as much cold as warm, which is why I've suggested you make eight.

The trick, if trick it be, is to use green onions, which have all the flavor but none of the BO-ey breath of the usual onion, as in cheese & onion, component.

I use Yorkshire pudding pans, with their wide, shallow indentations, for these, and prefer that more English, even rustic, look. But if you wanted to use individual tart or popover pans, of course you could.

for the pastry:
2 large egg yolks
1 heaping teaspoon salt
2 tablespoons cold water
1²/3 cups all-purpose flour
2 tablespoons vegetable shortening, teaspooned out
7 tablespoons cold unsalted butter, diced
2 4-cup popover pans

for the filling:
2 large potatoes (boiling not baking)
scant ¹/2 cup finely chopped green onions (about 6)
4–5 ounces sharp Cheddar: ¹/3 cup grated, ¹/4 cup diced
2 tablespoons grated parmesan
¹/4 cup Red Leicester cheese, grated
2 tablespoons chopped parsley
4 tablespoons crème fraîche to bind
salt and pepper to taste

Make the pastry by the usual method (see page 83), then halve it, form each half into a disc, wrap in plastic wrap, and leave in the refrigerator for 20 minutes.

Preheat the oven to 400°F.

Meanwhile, peel and dice the potatoes, put them in a saucepan with plenty of cold water, and bring to the boil. Boil gently for 5–10 minutes, or until the cubes are cooked but still retain their shape. Drain and leave to cool.

In a large bowl, combine the green onions, cheeses, slightly cooled potato, and parsley. Bind with the crème fraîche and season with salt and pepper. Roll out one of the pastry discs, cut 8 rough circles slightly larger than the indents and push 4 into the first tray to make the bases. Fill each with an eighth of the mixture and put the remaining 4 circles on as lids. Seal the pie edges with the back of a knife, making a little hole in each one. Repeat for the second tray with the other disc and the remaining half of the filling.

Cook for 20 minutes, by which time the pastry should be firm, beginning to turn gold, but still pale, and let the pies stand a little out of the oven in their trays before easing them out of the molds.

Makes 8.

SMALL TOMATO TARTS

These, which are so much lighter and fresher than you could ever hope for, are just what I want for lunch when it's warm enough to eat outside, but they'd make an equally good starter for a dinner party. I make the pastry with cornmeal for crispness and to prevent sogginess, but this kind of pastry is quite fragile, so I wouldn't want to make a larger tart to cut into wedges—hence my willingness to live with the individual portions. But old prejudices die hard: I'd arrange them all on one large oval dish for people to help themselves rather than plate them up singly in advance.

for the pastry:

3/4 cup all-purpose flour

1/4 cup fine cornmeal or polenta

1 tablespoon sugar

1/2 teaspoon salt

1/2 cup butter

scant 2 tablespoons vegetable shortening

3–4 tablespoons ice water, or enough to bind

8 individual tart pans
(4³/4 inches x ³/4 inches)

for the filling:

2¹/4 cups or 18 ounces chopped canned tomatoes

salt and pepper to taste

pinch sugar

2 ounces pecorino cheese sliced into thin slivers with a potato peeler

1 small handful basil, finely shredded

32 cherry tomatoes, halved around the equator

32 black olives in oil, halved

First make the pastry: pulse the dry ingredients in the food processor, then add the butter and shortening, diced into small pieces. Pulse briefly until the mixture resembles coarse bread crumbs, then add enough ice water to form a dough, pulsing with the gentlest touch to combine. Form into two discs, wrap with plastic wrap and refrigerate for 30 minutes.

Roll out one of the pastry discs between plastic wrap into a rough square. Cut into 4 squares (each piece should be big enough to fill the small tart pan) and drape into the pans, folding the edges inward. Repeat with the other disc of pastry and the 4 remaining pans, and put them back in the refrigerator for 15 minutes. Preheat the oven to 400°F, putting in a couple of baking sheets as you do so.

Meanwhile, empty the tomatoes into a bowl, and season well with salt, pepper, and a pinch of sugar. To arrange the tarts, put a thin layer of tomato mix, then 3 slices of pecorino cheese on top, then a sprinkling of basil, then 8 tomato halves with 8 olive halves in rows, and finally a grind of pepper.

Cook for 20 minutes on the baking sheets and let the tarts stand a bit, on a rack out of the oven, before you take them out of their tins.

Makes 8.

SMALL MUSHROOM TARTS

Heady with the success of the tomato tarts, and interested in the custardless quiche, though such, of course, is a contradiction in terms, I started playing with the idea of a mushroom version. There's something rather magnificent in the way these cream-glazed long-sliced flat mushrooms look like silvery sardines as they lie in their polenta pastry shell, and something utterly glorious in the intense woodiness of their taste.

for the pastry:
see the tomato tart polenta pastry, above
8 individual tart pans
   (4³/4 inches x ³/4 inches)

for the filling:
¹/2 ounce dried porcini, soaked in warm water
2¹/2 cups or 20 ounces mixed mushrooms, or button mushrooms if that's all that's available

6 tablespoons butter
2 cloves garlic, chopped
8 large wild mushrooms, such as shiitake or cremini
juice of 1 lemon
salt and pepper to taste
¹/3 cup or 3 ounces parmesan cut into slivers with a potato peeler
4–6 tablespoons chopped parsley
8 heaping teaspoons crème fraîche

Make up the pastry as before, and preheat the oven to 400°F, putting in 2 baking sheets. Drain the porcini and wipe dry before chopping small. Dice the mixed or button mushrooms and fry in half the butter, adding the chopped garlic and porcini. Fry until the mushrooms have softened, then transfer to a bowl.

Slice the wild mushrooms ¼ inch thick and fry in the remaining butter for just enough time to soften them. Add the lemon juice and season with salt and pepper. Cook off some of the liquid, then take them off the heat.

Roll out the pastry and line the pans as for the tomato tarts. To arrange the tarts, put a couple of tablespoons of the diced mushroom mixture into each tart, then 2 slices of parmesan, then distribute the wild mushrooms on top before adding a sprinkle of parsley and a teaspoon of crème fraîche.

Cook for 25 minutes or until the pastry is golden brown and the cream has melted. Leave to stand for a few minutes before unmolding.

Makes 8.

SWEET PIES AND TARTS

It hadn't quite struck me how varied pudding, pies, and tarts were until I embarked on all this; I've got a wonderful gingham-print American book called *Pie Every Day* and sometimes I did feel tempted. But in order not to bombard you with suggestions, I've curtailed my selection here: these are my absolute favorites (for now, at least). Anyway, the whole point is that once you've played around with some of the ideas in this chapter, you will find it easy enough to make substitutions and changes of your own.

(KEY) LIME PIE

What follows are two versions of key lime pie, although there is little chance of using fresh key limes. You can use bottled key lime juice (or so it's claimed), but I tend to use ordinary limes.

A note on crusts: it's traditional to use graham crackers, but I wanted to make a chocolate-based one as well, I suppose in memory of the chocolate lime sweets I ate as a child. If you use chocolate graham crackers, it's hard to cut the tart once it's been refrigerated, so I suggest you use ordinary graham crackers but with a teaspoonful of cocoa added when you mix them with the butter. I also love using coconut cookies.

And as far as the filling goes, don't expect a lime pie to be green. It's yellow—though the first pie is slightly greener because of the zest. A really green pie is a dyed pie.

The following seems to be the basic model for a key lime pie; and it's the one in Jane Grigson's monumentally absorbing *Fruit Book*. Don't be put off by the idea of condensed milk. It's essential, and the sourness of the limes totally sets off its temple-aching sugariness.

for the crust:
3/4 cup plus 2 tablespoons or
  7 ounces graham crackers
scant 1/4 cup softened, unsalted
  butter
9-inch springform pan

for the filling:
5 large egg yolks
14-ounce can sweetened condensed
  milk
zest of 3 limes
1/2 cup plus 2 tablespoons lime juice
  (of 4–5 limes)
3 large egg whites

Preheat the oven to 325°F and put in a baking sheet.

Put the graham crackers and butter into the food processor and blitz till all's reduced to oily crumbs. Press these into the pan, lining the bottom and going a little way up the sides, and chill while you get on with the rest.

You need an electric mixer for this. I always use my KitchenAid, but a hand-held one is fine. Beat the egg yolks until thick, add the can of condensed milk, grated zest, and the lime juice. Whisk the egg whites separately until soft peaks form, then fold gently into the yolk mixture. Pour into the lined pan and cook for 25 minutes, when the filling should be firm. It may puff up and then, on cooling, fall, but that's the deal.

Leave to cool on a rack before unmolding, and chill well.

Serves 6–8.

VARIATION

This version comes from a friend of Hettie (who works with me), who in turn works for the Nestlé home economics team. Here, cream is used in place of the eggs, and it's not cooked. In some ways, I suppose, it's more like a light, limey cheesecake—and extraordinarily easy to make.

for the crust:
as above

for the filling:
juice and zest of 4 limes
14-ounce can sweetened condensed milk
1¹⁄₃ cups heavy cream

Make your base and chill it as above, then make the filling. You do this simply by (electrically) whisking all the ingredients together in a large bowl till thick and creamy. Pour into the lined pan and chill for a further 30 minutes or until set.

CROSTATA

This is another recipe from my lovely Anna. I always use blackberry jam and mostly my own homemade stuff (see page 348), which is a doddle to make when you just use a half pint of berries, out of which you'll get the exact right amount for the tart below. But, obviously, substitute the jam of your choice.

This is a spongy kind of a pastry, a cake more than a tart. And, as authentically Italian as it is, it is deeply wonderful with a pitcher of proper English custard (hot for me). It cheers me up just thinking of it.

6 tablespoons soft unsalted butter
1/2 cup sugar
2 large eggs
1 1/3 cup cake flour
pinch of salt

1 teaspoon baking powder
zest of 1 lemon
3/4 cup plus 2 tablespoons
  blackberry jam
8-inch deep fluted tart pan

Preheat the oven to 350°F and put in a baking sheet.

Cream the butter and sugar. Beat in the eggs one at a time until the volume has increased. Sift the flour, salt, and baking powder, and fold into the egg and butter mixture. Finally, add the lemon zest.

Spoon into the pan, spreading it out to leave a thicker edge of about 1 inch all around. Spoon the jam into the center, leaving the edge clear. Cook for 35–45 minutes, by which time the pastry/cake will be golden and bouncy-firm. Let it cool in the pan before unmolding.

Serves 6–8.

VARIATION

Obviously, as I've said above, the jams can be varied to suit taste and season, but one variation I love is to replace the jam with marmalade and add the zest of an orange along with the lemon. I think a finer rather than coarser cut marmalade is better here; if, as is often the case, it's sweeter than it should ideally be, mix it up first with the juice of half a lime (better than lemon because you get more sharpness for less liquid).

RHUBARB TART

This is perfect for January, when the new season's forced rhubarb is just in, rosy and budding with its rhubarbiness. It's made all the more dazzling by the contrast with the snowy whiteness of the filling beneath. And I like the neatness of this, in shopping terms at least: you need the cream cheese for the pastry, so why not use it as well for the smooth and voluptuous interior? I know it looks as if there's a lot of fat per flour for the pastry, but go with it.

for the filling:
About 2 pounds fresh rhubarb (untrimmed weight)
1 cup sugar

for the pastry:
1 cup all-purpose flour
1 tablespoon sugar
1/4 teaspoon salt
7 scant tablespoons cold unsalted butter, diced
7 scant tablespoons cold cream cheese, diced

2–3 tablespoons cold heavy cream to bind
1 deep 8-inch flan pan or shallow 10-inch pan

for the glaze:
6 tablespoons rhubarb juice, reserved from stewing

for the cream-cheese filling:
7 ounces cream cheese
3/4 cup plus 2 tablespoons heavy cream
2 tablespoons sugar
4 tablespoons muscat or rum

Heat the oven to 375°F.

Trim and cut the rhubarb into ¾ inch pieces, place in a shallow ovenproof dish (I use a Pyrex dish of about 8 inches x 12 inches), pour the sugar over the rhubarb and toss it all together so the sugar's well dispersed. Cover with foil and cook for about 45 minutes, or until tender. When you take the rhubarb out, slip in a baking sheet. When the rhubarb's cool, strain it and reserve the juice.

Meanwhile, get on with making the pastry. Using a food processor, mix the dry ingredients, then add the butter and cheese and pulse to make a crumbly mixture. Bind with the cream, pulsing sparingly. Let the pastry rest in the refrigerator for at least 20 minutes before lining your tart pan. After you've rolled the pastry out between plastic wrap and lined the pan with it, put it back in the refrigerator for another 20 minutes.

Remove from the refrigerator and line with foil. Fill the pastry shell with baking beans (though you could just as well use any dried beans) and put on the sheet in the oven for 15 minutes. Gingerly remove the beans and foil—bearing in mind their heat—and cook for a further 5 minutes or until it's turning golden brown and is cooked through. Leave to cool on a wire rack.

When you want to assemble the tart (and you can do the steps above a good couple of days in advance, though keep the cooked and cooled flan case in an airtight container), reduce about 6 tablespoons of the juice to a syrup by boiling it robustly in a small saucepan. Don't leave the pan unattended, though, as the juices will become thickly syrupy in a matter of minutes.

Now for the filling: using a whisk, soften the cream cheese, then add the cream, whipping until it has mixed well and thickened slightly. Take care not to overbeat—this must be voluptuous and undulating. Add the sugar and muscat (which is lovely to drink with it, too) or rum, stir to a soft mascarpone consistency, then fill the pastry shell with it. Top with the strained rhubarb pieces, then drizzle over your puce-pink glaze. Stand back and admire—then eat.

Makes about 8 slices.

VARIATION

In late summer, I do a caramelized plum variant of this with about 2 pounds or so of plums, halved then roasted for about 15 minutes in a hot oven with a teaspoon each of butter and sugar in every dimpled cavity. When they're cool, I spread them on the creamy filling, boil down the buttery plummy juices that were left behind and pour those over the tart.

BITTER-ORANGE AND BLUEBERRY TART

Ideally, this should be made with bitter Seville oranges, but since they are available for only one month of the year and ordinary oranges are around all the time, it seems reasonable to have sweet eating oranges as the first choice, adding the juice of a lime in order to reproduce as closely as possible the fragrant bitterness of Sevilles.

I find this easiest to do over a few days; one, because the taste is so much better when the juice and cream and so forth are left to deepen in the fridge for a couple of days, and, two, because then one splits what could be quite an undertaking into a series of small tasks, no one activity taking more than a few minutes.

This is the perfectly balanced tart: the tangily sharp smooth pale cream offset by the sweet, purple-black beadiness of the berries on top.

for the filling:

juice (3/4 cup plus 2 tablespoons) and zest of 1 eating orange and 1 lime or of 2–3 Seville oranges

3/4 cup plus 1 tablespoon sugar

1 1/3 cups heavy cream

6 large eggs

for the pastry:

7 tablespoons soft unsalted butter

1/4 cup sugar

3 large egg yolks

1 cup plus 2 tablespoons all-purpose flour

9 x 2 inch fluted tart pan

for the glaze:

1 tablespoon arrowroot

2 tablespoons sugar

2 scant teaspoons orange juice

1/2 cup water

9 ounces blueberries

Start with the filling, a couple of days in advance if this suits. In a large bowl or, better still, a wide-mouthed measuring cup, mix the juice with the sugar, add the zest, heavy cream, and eggs, and stir to combine. Cover and chill for 2–3 days in the refrigerator or leave for a few hours at room temperature.

You can make the pastry at the same time as you mix up the juices and cream or a day or two later. Cream the butter and the sugar together, then add the yolks one at a time. Stir in the flour to form a soft dough, then form into a fat disc, wrap in plastic wrap and rest in the refrigerator for half an hour. Preheat the oven to 350°F and put in a baking sheet. Roll out the pastry between plastic wrap to fit the pan and line, pushing gently down so that it lies flat at the bottom, leaving a little overhang. Put back in the refrigerator for a further 20 minutes to rest again.

Roll a rolling pin over the top of the pastry shell to cut off excess pastry neatly. Line the pan with foil or crumpled baking parchment and fill with baking beans. Put the pan in the oven for 15 minutes, then remove beans and foil or parchment and give it another 5–10 minutes, until the bottom has dried out. Transfer to a wire rack to cool a little and turn the oven down to 325°F.

Strain the liquid mixture into the pastry shell to remove the zest, put back on the sheet in the oven and cook for 45 minutes. (You may find this easier—if more long-winded—if you strain the mixture into a pitcher and pour from this into the pastry shell already on the sheet in the oven with the rack pulled out.)

When the tart's cooked—and it should be firm on top but with a hint of a wobble underneath—remove to a wire rack and let cool. Unmold and transfer to the serving plate.

To make the glazed blueberry topping, combine the arrowroot and sugar in a small saucepan, then stir in the juice and water. Put the pan on the heat and bring to the boil, stirring all the time: it should turn clear pretty soon. Take it off the heat and add the blueberries, then spoon the now-glossy berries over the waiting tart. Leave to set for about 10 minutes.

Serves 8.

BAKED SUMMER-FRUIT TART

I keep the word *baked* in the title simply to distinguish it from a fruit tart, which comprises a squidgy filling of crème patissière with fresh berries on top. Here, you make a custard, pour it into a partially cooked pastry shell, tumble fruit on top, and put it in the oven for a few minutes to set into a harmonious whole. I've used crème fraîche for the custard because I wanted an edgy note to counterbalance the sweetness of the glazed fruits.

for the pastry:
3/4 cup soft unsalted butter
1/2 cup sugar
6 large egg yolks
2 1/4 cups all-purpose flour
1 deep 10-inch tart pan

for the custard:
8 large egg yolks
7 tablespoons sugar

2 1/2 cups crème fraîche
zest of 1 orange

for the glazed fruits:
1 cup summer fruits—blackberries, raspberries, red currants, and blueberries
4 tablespoons of blackberry jam
2 tablespoons water

Make the pastry up a few days in advance if you're the sort of person who's soothed by this strategy. Cream the butter and sugar, and then add the yolks one by one, beating after each addition. Fold in the flour gently until the dough comes together. Form into a disc, wrap in plastic wrap, and put in the refrigerator for at least 2 hours.

Preheat oven to 375°F and put in a baking sheet. Roll out the pastry between plastic wrap and line the tart pan, leaving an overhang of about 1¼ inches. Rest again in the refrigerator or freezer for 20 minutes, then roll your rolling pin over the top of the tart pan to cut off excess pastry. Bake blind—that's to say, lined with foil and filled with dried beans—for 15–20 minutes. Then remove foil and beans and bake for another few minutes to dry the base out. Half fill a sink with cold water (for salvaging nearly splitting custard later, in the unlikely event it may be necessary). Whisk together the yolks and sugar until they are pale and creamy. Warm the crème fraîche in a saucepan, and then whisk it into the yolks and sugar, adding the orange zest. Put everything back into the saucepan, and return to the heat, stirring constantly until it becomes thick. This will only happen gradually, so be patient and keep the heat quite low. Pour the custard into the cooked pastry shell, and top with the mixture of summer fruits. Put the tart back into the oven, lightly covered with foil, for 10 minutes. Uncover the tart and cook for a further 5 minutes.

Put the jam and water into a small saucepan and warm. Using a pastry brush, lightly coat the summer fruits with the glaze. Leave to cool for a little. Whichever way you cut it, this is *good*.

Serves 8–10.

BLACK AND WHITE TART

I apologize for the slightly eighties ring to the title, but I can't help myself. You could use any berries here, but I made this to wallow in the sheer beauty of the blackberries and white currants of the last summer of the last century. This is one of the easiest tarts you could make: a cheesecake base, the filling a mascarpone cream, and the berries dropped like gleaming gems—jet and moonstone—on top.

for the crust:

1 cup plus 2 tablespoons or 9 ounces graham crackers, roughly broken

6 tablespoons unsalted butter, melted

10-inch fluted tart pan, 1 1/2 inches deep

for the filling and topping:

1 large egg, separated

1/4 cup sugar

2 1/4 cups or 18 ounces mascarpone

squeeze of lime or lemon (to taste)

1 tablespoon tequila or white rum, optional

14 ounces blackberries

4 ounces white currants

Put the graham crackers in the food processor and blitz to crumbs. Then, motor running, add the melted butter down the funnel. Tip into the tart pan and, using your fingers, press onto the base and up the sides. Put in the refrigerator while you get on with the creamy filling-cum-topping.

Whisk the egg white until stiff but not dry and set aside for a moment. Beat the yolk with the sugar until thick and pale; you may think there's too much sugar to make a paste, but persist: it happens. Add the mascarpone, beating till smooth, then the lime or lemon juice and the rum, if using. Fold in the egg white and pile and smooth this mixture into the prepared tart pan. Arrange the blackberries and white currants on top, but loosely. You should, for ease of eating, remove most of the stalks and stems, but I like to leave some still on for beauty's sake.

Serves 8.

VARIATION

You can alter the fruit as you like, and certainly don't feel constrained to stick with berries. The best and freshest peaches are wonderful, as are figs, and in winter you could soak and cook dried figs or apricots, arrange the fruit on the cream, then drizzle over some reduced cooking liquid.

BLACKBERRY GALETTE

This is really a free-form pizza-like tart, which I made for the first time while we were doing the photography for this book. We happened to have some polenta pastry left over and some spare blackberries in the fridge and I, suddenly rebelling against the planning and rule-following necessary to get all the food photographed, played around. This was the result. And really, you could use any fruit. I'd stick with the polenta or cornmeal pastry only because nothing soaks up the fruit's juices better without going soggy.

for the pastry:

1/3 cup all-purpose flour

2 tablespoons polenta or fine cornmeal

1 scant tablespoon sugar

1/4 teaspoon salt

scant 1/4 cup cold butter

1 tablespoon vegetable shortening

1–3 tablespoons ice water or enough to bind

1 baking sheet, lined with parchment or wax paper

for the filling:

1/2 pint blackberries

approximately 3 tablespoons sugar

3 heaping tablespoons crème fraîche, plus more to serve

In a food processor, pulse the dry ingredients, then add the butter and shortening diced into small pieces. Pulse briefly until it resembles coarse bread crumbs, then add enough ice water to form a dough, pulsing gently to mix. Form it into a disc, wrap in plastic wrap and put in the refrigerator to rest for about 30 minutes.

Preheat the oven to 375°F. Roll the pastry out into a rough circle, transfer to the baking sheet and scatter blackberries on top, leaving a good 3-inch margin round the edge. Sprinkle with 1–2 tablespoons sugar, to taste, then dollop with crème fraîche. Sprinkle a further tablespoonful of sugar over, dampen the edges with water, then wrap them over themselves to form a knobbly, ramshackle rim and put in the oven for about 20 minutes or until the pastry is cooked through.

Serves 6.

DOUBLE APPLE PIE

I don't want to nominate favorites, but even so, I have to say this is a pie I am ecstatic about—perhaps because it's so far removed from what I've spent my life cooking.

The notion of putting Cheddar in the pastry of an apple pie is not a new one but I was pleased all the same to see how well it worked. I've used a springform pan (learning a lesson from the pizza rustica, above), which makes this a good, hefty, sliceable pie.

The double-apple element—Cortlands to hold their shape, McIntoshes to make for an appley-velvet background—does entail quite a bit of work, but it isn't difficult work, just moderately time-consuming. Anyone who's hanging about the house claiming to want to help should be handed a vegetable peeler and an apple corer without delay.

for the pastry:

4 tablespoons cold unsalted butter, diced

4 tablespoons vegetable shortening

1 2/3 cups self-rising cake flour

scant 1/4 cup finely grated Cheddar

1 large egg

ice water to bind

pinch of salt

8-inch springform pan

for the filling:

about 1 1/2 pounds McIntosh apples (about 3 large), peeled and cored

about 2 1/4 pounds Cortland apples, peeled, cored, and cut into eighths

6 tablespoons unsalted butter

pinch of ground cloves

good grating of nutmeg

2 large eggs, beaten

1/3 cup sugar plus extra for sprinkling

Make the pastry in a food processor as normal: pulse the butter and shortening into the flour until it looks like crumbs. Leaving the mixture in the bowl, put the grating blade in and process the cheese into the crumb mixture. Replace the normal blade, and add the egg, ice water, and salt to bind. Turn the pastry out and press it into two discs, one slightly smaller than the other. Wrap each in plastic wrap and put them in the refrigerator to rest for at least 20 minutes.

Preheat the oven to 400°F, putting in a baking sheet. Slice the McIntoshes into small chunks and fry in half the butter until they become soft and begin to lose their shape. Add the cloves and nutmeg. Tip the apple mush into the food processor, and purée, pulsing so as not to make it too like baby food. Add about three-quarters of the beaten egg and all of the sugar and pulse again to mix. Fry the Cortlands in the other half of the butter and cover them to help them cook a little. Cook for about 10 minutes: they should be tender but still holding their shape.

Roll out the larger disc of pastry between plastic wrap and line the pan with it, letting it hang over the sides. Pour in the puréed mixture, and then push the Cortland pieces into the purée to coat them. Roll out the smaller disc of pastry between plastic wrap to form the top. Lay over the pie, and curl the edges inward, crimping them to seal. Decorate with any leftover pastry if you wish, and brush with the remaining egg as a glaze. Cook for 15 minutes, then turn the oven down to 350°F for a further 30 minutes. Sprinkle with sugar when it comes out of the oven.

Let it cool a little before unmolding (it will, anyway, slice better when it's not piping hot). And although it tastes like the sort of pie that should be eaten cold, don't leave it hanging around too long or the wonderful pastry will start to sog and wilt.

Serves 8.

BLACKBERRY AND APPLE PIE

This otherwise traditional English pie also uses cornmeal in the pastry, to soak up the liquid given off by the blackberries when cooking. Otherwise I love this pretty much uninterfered with. The apples come from the tree in my garden and I use the leaves as a template for the decoration on top.

I like a pitcher of cream with this, but ice cream seems to be everyone else's favorite whenever I've made it. Traditionally, though, it should be eaten with some creamy, vanilla-scented, eggy custard.

for the pastry:

4 tablespoons cold unsalted butter, diced
4 tablespoons vegetable shortening, teaspooned out
1 1/3 cups self-rising cake flour
scant 1/4 cup fine cornmeal
2–4 tablespoons salted ice water or enough to bind
squeeze of lemon juice as needed
8-inch shallow pie plate

for the filling:

about 1 1/2 pounds Golden Delicious or other cooking apples (2 medium)
1/4 cup unsalted butter
7 tablespoons sugar
1 tablespoon rosewater
1/2 teaspoon ground cinnamon
3 scant tablespoons cornstarch
12 ounces blackberries

for the glaze/topping:

1–2 tablespoons milk
1–2 tablespoons sugar

Make the pastry according to the usual method (see page 83) then form into two discs, one slightly smaller than the other. Cover with plastic wrap and rest the pastry in the refrigerator.

Preheat the oven to 375°F, remembering to put a baking sheet in at the same time. Peel, core, and slice the apples. In a saucepan, melt the butter and add the sugar, rosewater, and cinnamon, then cook the apples in the pan for about 3 minutes; remove them to a dish with a spatula. Pour the caramelly juices into a measuring cup and whisk in the cornstarch to form a paste.

Line the bottom and sides of the pie dish with the bigger disc of pastry, and put the apples and blackberries into the pie. Pour over the cornstarch-butter mixture, stirring gingerly to cover all of the fruit without tearing the pastry. Roll out the smaller disc of pastry, dampen the edges of the pie with water, and put the pie lid on top. Crimp the edges, either by hand or using a fork, to seal. Decorate the top with any pastry scraps, made artistically into leaves, or stamped out into miniature apple shapes with cutters, or whatever takes your fancy.

Glaze with milk and cook for 30 minutes, by which time the still slightly knobbly top should be golden. Sprinkle with sugar when it comes out of the oven, and leave for about 15 minutes before cutting into it.

Serves 6.

PEACH CREAM PIE

This is one of the first pies I made in my early baking days: it's plain, but with just enough goo to make one feel that in some way it's a stolen treat—and a way of letting daylight into those long, cold, fruitless wintry days.

For this filling—fragrant and eggy—I use an ordinary packet of dried peaches, which I soak and then cook to ensure honeyed tenderness (though you can leave out the soaking and just cook for a bit longer if you really haven't got time). They are then bound with a light, creamy custard.

for the pastry:

pinch of salt

juice of 1 orange

1²/3 cups self-rising cake flour

1/2 cup cold unsalted butter, diced

yolk of 1 large egg

ice water to bind

milk to glaze

1–2 tablespoons sugar for sprinkling

9-inch pie plate

for the filling:

9 ounces dried peaches, soaked for at least 6 hours in 2¹/4 cups water

6 tablespoons light cream

1 tablespoon honey

1 large egg, beaten

I like self-rising flour for fruit pies, but all-purpose works just as well. If you're making the pastry in advance you may as well use all-purpose flour, as the leavening agent in the self-rising will have fizzled out by the time you use it. Dissolve the salt in the orange juice and set aside in the fridge. Put the flour and the diced butter in a bowl and put this bowl in the freezer for 10 minutes. I am assuming you're using a food processor to make the pastry, in which case after the 10 minutes are up, put the very chilled flour and butter in the bowl of the mixer and process until you have a mixture that resembles the flat crumbliness of oats. Add the egg yolk, give a quick whizz, and then add the salted juice and whizz further. If the pastry hasn't come together, add ice-cold water, teaspoon by teaspoon, till it does. The minute it starts to clump, take it out of the machine, divide in half, and press into a couple of discs. Cover with plastic wrap and put in the refrigerator for 10 minutes.

Put a metal sheet in the oven and preheat to 400°F. Put the soaked peaches, with their water, in a saucepan, cover, and bring to the boil. Let boil for 5 minutes, and then drain, reserving the liquid. Set the peaches aside, pour the liquid back into the pan, boiling it down until you have about 3 tablespoons of syrupy peach juice. Then cut each peach slice in half lengthways.

Roll out one of the pastry discs between plastic wrap and use it to line a 9-inch pie plate (not a dish, which would be too deep). Dampen the edges with water, but don't cut off the overhang yet. Fill with drained peach slices, mounding slightly in the center. Stir the cream and the honey into the peach juice, add to the beaten egg and pour the mixture over the fruit. Roll out the other disc of pastry and cover the pie. Cut off the overhang, and pinch all along the rim with your finger and thumb to crimp. Using a sharp knife, cut four slashes in the center of the pie to let steam escape. Dab some milk over to glaze and put on the sheet in the oven.

After 20 minutes, turn down to 350°F and cook for another 30–35 minutes. You may need to cover loosely with foil about halfway through to prevent it burning, but remove the foil for the last 5 minutes.

Take the pie out of the oven, put on a rack, and sprinkle with a tablespoon or two of sugar. Leave for about an hour before eating.

Serves 6–8.

RED CURRANT MERINGUE PIE

There is just something about the fragrant acerbity and sweet, crispy-tipped soft meringue of this pie that makes you realize what an oven is for. Strangely, red currants are not used much in cooking, but their intense sourness allied to that rounded exaggeration of flavor is just what you need to stop even the joyfully sweet from cloying. I've made a hazelnut crust because this nut and this fruit were born to be together.

for the pastry:

½ cup all-purpose flour

2 tablespoons ground hazelnuts

1 tablespoon sugar

6 tablespoons softened unsalted butter

1 large egg yolk

1 tablespoon ice water or more to bind

8-inch, deep fluted tart pan

for the filling:

9 ounces red currants

2 tablespoons unsalted butter

⅓ cup sugar

3 tablespoons orange juice

2 large egg yolks, beaten

3 tablespoons cornstarch

for the topping:

2 large egg whites

7 tablespoons sugar, plus 1 teaspoon for sprinkling

¼ teaspoon cream of tartar

Make the pastry in a food processor, in the usual way (see page 83), then wrap and rest in the refrigerator for 20 minutes. Roll out between plastic wrap and line the tart pan, making the sides come just a little way over the edge of the pan. Rest again in the refrigerator until the filling is ready. Preheat the oven to 375°F, putting in a baking sheet at the same time.

Heat the red currants, butter, sugar, and orange juice in a saucepan for 3–5 minutes; it should become syrupy but the fruit should remain whole. Take off the heat and add the beaten yolks and cornstarch. Put the fruit mixture into the cold, uncooked tart pan. Place in the oven on the ready-heated baking tray and cook for 20 minutes.

Meanwhile, whisk the egg whites until fairly stiff, and gradually add half the sugar. When stiff, satiny, and glossy, add the remaining sugar and cream of tartar, folding it in with a metal spoon.

When the tart has had its 20 minutes, dollop the meringue on top, sealing the edges well. Sprinkle with a teaspoon of sugar, and put back in the oven for a further 10 minutes, or until the meringue is golden and crisp.

This is good eaten half an hour after it's come out of the oven, but for me it's best of all eaten late at night at room temperature.

Serves 6–8.

DESSERTS

DESSERTS

When I was a restaurant critic, I was once teased for talking about "the pudding" and then proceeding to describe some elaborate, light, and most definitely unpuddingy French confection. But pudding is the word I stick to: can't help it and don't want to. Regardless of style or substance, if it's intended for the last, sweet course, it's pudding in my book—in America, it's given the name dessert.

On the whole, I take the line that you do not have to make dessert: the French have always bought their pâtisserie from those who really know how to do it. But in fact there is a good, lazy reason to cook dessert: unless you go out of your way to choose something complicated, the chances are that the process will not be difficult, and the reward gratifying. Quite apart from that essential sense of private satisfaction, people really do seem far more impressed by a homemade dessert, however simple, than they would be by the most lovingly produced main course. You know I'm not a cook-to-impress kind of a girl, so my point isn't so much that you can luxuriate in the astonished admiration of your friends by cooking dessert, but you can thereby lessen the culinary load all round.

Do you know how easy it is to make a steamed sponge? You just bung all the ingredients in a processor, blitz and scrape into a bowl, and then sit the bowl in boiling water for a couple of hours. In that time, you are required to do nothing, except maybe for the odd topping-up from the kettle so the pan doesn't boil dry. In other words, this is the easy option, the comforting one—for cook and cookee. What more do you want?

BLUEBERRY BOY-BAIT

When I saw this title, I had to make it. I came across it in a wonderful book by Christopher Kimball, the editor of *Cook's Illustrated* magazine, called *The Yellow Farmhouse Cookbook*. The recipe has just the provenance you want it to have: it was devised by a Chicago teenager for the Pillsbury $100,000 Recipe & Baking Contest 1954. (She came second in the junior division, incidentally.)

Now, the actual recipe didn't quite do it for me—though it's true I didn't test it out on its own terms. I wanted something different, something more luscious and perhaps something more English. My version, then, goes like this: aromatic custardy sponge, sweet gooey fruit and meringue, sugar-crisped—boy-bait Brit-style. And the proof of the pudding. . . .

for the crust:

¹/₂ cup plus 2 tablespoons fresh bread crumbs

3 tablespoons unsalted butter, plus more for greasing dish

2¹/₂ cups whole milk

2 teaspoons sugar

zest of 1 lemon

5 large egg yolks (and keep the whites for the topping)

1 5-cup oval or round dish, buttered

for the blueberry filling:

12 ounces blueberries

¹/₃ cup sugar

2 tablespoons all-purpose flour

2 tablespoons lemon juice

for the meringue topping:

5 egg whites

7 tablespoons sugar, plus extra for sprinkling

To make the bread crumbs, simply process some stale good white bread to rubble. Preheat the oven to 325°F and put in a baking sheet.

Heat the butter and milk in a saucepan until hot but not boiling. Stir in the bread crumbs, sugar, and lemon zest, take off the heat, and leave to steep for 10 minutes. Beat in the egg yolks very thoroughly and pour this bread-thickened custard into your greased dish. Bake for 20–30 minutes, until it's firm on top but still with a hint of wobble underneath. Let it stand for a few minutes to let the top form a skin while you get on with the blueberries.

Put the fruit, sugar, flour, and juice in a saucepan, and stir to coat. Heat to a robust simmer and cook until you've got a thick jammy sauce, stirring every now and again to prevent it catching. You should still have plenty of whole blueberries visible. Take this off the heat and set aside while you make the meringue topping.

Whisk the whites until stiff but not dry, then add half the sugar, a spoonful at a time, whisking as you do so. Fold in the remaining sugar with a metal spoon. Pour and scrape the cooked blueberries onto your set custard base, spreading evenly. Then dollop over the meringue topping, making sure you seal the edges well so that no dark syrup bubbles up and seeps out. Make peaks with the back of a spoon, sprinkle with a little sugar, and put back in the oven for a further 20 minutes or until the meringue is burnished and crisp. Underneath, however, it will still be desirably yielding.

Serves 6–8.

RHUBARB GRUNT

A grunt is like a cobbler or a slump: at its most basic, fruit stewed in the oven with a scone-like topping. Here it is made with cream in place of butter; I'd never come across it before and I doubt it's traditional, but it is gorgeously light and tender, and ridiculously easy to knock up. This version comes from *The San Francisco Chronicle Cookbook*, contributed by the illustrious Marion Cunningham.

for the filling:

about 1¹/2 pounds fresh rhubarb cut into 1 inch pieces

³/4 to 1 cup sugar depending on preference (and sourness of fruit)

scant 4 tablespoons unsalted butter cut into small pieces, plus more for greasing dish

8 x 12-inch shallow ovenproof dish, greased

for the topping:

1 cup cake flour

3 tablespoons sugar

¹/2 teaspoon salt

1 cup plus 2 tablespoons heavy cream, whipped

Preheat the oven to 375°F and, as with all desserts which could possibly bubble up and spill over the oven floor, put in a baking sheet.

Spread the chopped rhubarb over the bottom of the dish, sprinkle with the sugar, coating evenly, and dot with butter. For the topping, sift the flour, sugar, and salt into a mixing bowl. Gently stir in the cream, making a sticky dough. Spread this mixture over the fruit in handfuls, covering the top evenly. Bake for 45 minutes, or until the fruit is bubbling—it's easiest to judge this if you're using a Pyrex dish—and the top is golden.

Serve with cream, ice cream, or custard: there just isn't a bad way to eat this.

Serves 6–8.

PLUM AND PECAN CRUMBLE

There is absolutely nothing wrong with a plain crumble, and I reckoned it was better to offer you here the two crumbles I do most often when I've got people coming for dinner. This plum and pecan crumble (which can just as easily be made with walnuts) is comfortingly autumnal. If you want, use ordinary white sugar or turbinado sugar in place of the demerara; all I do urge is that you use self-rising flour, not the normally stipulated all-purpose.

for the filling:
approximately 2¹/4 pounds plums
8-inch round pie plate, buttered
2 tablespoons unsalted butter, plus
   more for greasing
2–4 tablespoons light brown sugar,
   depending on sourness of fruit
1 scant tablespoon cornstarch

for the crumble topping:
¹/2 cup plus 2 tablespoons cold
   unsalted butter, diced
1²/3 cups self-rising cake flour
¹/2 cup plus 2 tablespoons turbinado
   or demerara sugar
7 ounces pecans, some chopped finely,
   others left larger or whole

Preheat the oven to 375°F and put in a baking sheet.

Halve the plums and put them cut-side-up in the dish. You may find you don't need all of them, but squeeze in as many as will fit comfortably. Dot with the butter, sprinkle with the sugar and put, uncovered, in the oven for about 20 minutes. I know it's not normal to cook the base of a crumble first, but I find plums need a head start. You want the fruit's juices to have run a little and the fruit itself to be moving toward tender.

While the plums are cooking, make the crumble topping (or you can make this in advance if you prefer). Rub the butter into the flour, either with your fingers or in a free-standing mixer with the flat paddle. I find the food processor makes the crumb a little too fine and you want texture, not Caribbean sand, here. But what you can do to make this better is finish off by rubbing the mixture through your fingers for a while—soft pad of thumb fluttering against soft pad of index or first three fingers—to clump up some of the topping. Fork the sugar and nuts into the crumble mixture, and set aside for a moment.

When the plums have had their time in the oven, pour some of the liquid into a little bowl in which you have placed the cornstarch. Stir to a paste, then stir into the plum dish. Now add the crumble topping, pressing down lightly around the edges. Put the crumble back on the baking sheet in the oven and cook for 25 minutes or until the crumble is cooked and speckled golden brown.

Eat, for choice, with custard.

Serves 4–6.

GOOSEBERRY-CREAM CRUMBLE

If the above is essentially autumnal, this is an early summer delicacy. Gooseberries are around for such a short time that it's always good to make use of them when they are in season. Search them out in specialty markets or greengrocers. Do substitute the elderflower cordial I suggest with some elderflower heads if you have them. Put them in a pan with the fruit and sugar, heat till hot, and leave to steep for 20 minutes or so.

The first time I made this, I wanted to make a crumble that provided its own sauce. The first version, while it tasted wonderful, had too much of this eggy, elderflower-scented custard: on serving, the topping subsided into the fruit-studded sauce below. I'm not really a presentation queen, but I do see that a knobbly sludge isn't the most attractive sight, however good it might taste. So I fiddled and fiddled to come up with a recipe that would deliver on sauce but not fail on style. Be my guest. . . .

for the crumble:

³/4 cup cold unsalted butter, diced
1¹/3 cups self-rising cake flour
6 tablespoons light brown sugar
5 tablespoons vanilla sugar
pinch of salt

for the filling:

1¹/2 pounds gooseberries
7 tablespoons sugar
1 tablespoon plus 1 teaspoon
** elderflower cordial**
1 large egg plus one egg yolk
5 tablespoons heavy cream
1 pie plate, approximately 8 inches in
** diameter, buttered**

Preheat the oven to 375°F, and slip in a baking sheet to catch drips later.

Make the crumble topping by rubbing the butter into the flour and then forking in the sugars (see method above). Put the crumble mixture in the refrigerator while you get on with cooking the fruit.

If you can be bothered, trim the gooseberries. Put them into a pan with the sugar and the tablespoon of elderflower cordial and heat till just bubbling. All you really want to do is break down the skins slightly, so after a minute's gentle seething, remove from the heat.

In a measuring cup, beat together the egg, yolk, teaspoon of elderflower cordial, and cream, and pour into the pan of gooseberries, stirring to combine. Now pour this into the prepared dish and leave to sit for one minute before piling the crumble mixture on top. Put on the baking sheet in the oven and cook for 30–40 minutes, until cooked and golden brown.

You need nothing to accompany this, save perhaps a bottle of Frontignan.
Serves 4–6.

GIN AND TONIC GELATIN MOLD

I love gelatin molds and one of the wonderful things about them is that they are so simple to make. This has a definite kick and unarguable elegance: what better food to emanate from the modern woman's kitchen?

I remind you again of the necessity, in my book, of using sheets of leaf gelatin (also called sheet gelatin), since it is about a thousand times easier than the powdered sort. If you prefer powdered gelatin, one $^1/4$-ounce package is the equivalent of one 4-sheet package of leaf gelatin.

1$^1/3$ cups plus $^1/4$ cup water
1 cup sugar
zest and juice of 2 lemons
1$^2/3$ cups plus 1 tablespoon tonic
 water (not diet!)
1 cup plus 2 tablespoons gin
2 4-sheet packages of leaf gelatin

1 pint white currants or 1$^1/2$-2 pints
 raspberries, optional
1 teaspoon confectioners' sugar, if
 using raspberries
4-cup gelatin mold, lightly greased
 with almond or vegetable oil

Put the 1$^1/3$ cups water and sugar into a wide, thick-bottomed saucepan and bring to the boil. Let boil for 5 minutes, take off the heat, add the lemon zest, and leave to steep for 15 minutes. Strain into a measuring cup, then add the lemon juice, the tonic water, and the gin; you should have reached the 6-cup mark; if not, add more tonic water, gin, or lemon juice to taste.

Soak the gelatin leaves in a dish of cold water for 5 minutes to soften. Meanwhile, put the $^1/4$ cup of water into a small saucepan and bring to the boil. Remove from the heat, squeeze out the gelatin leaves, and whisk them in. Pour some of the gin and lemon syrup mixture into the saucepan and then pour everything back into the measuring cup. Pour into the mold and, when cold, put in the refrigerator to set. This should take about 6 hours.

When you are ready to unmold, half-fill a sink with warm water and stand the mold in it for 30 seconds or so. Clamp a big flat plate over the gelatin and invert to unmold, shaking it as you do so. If it doesn't work, stand it in the warm water for another half minute or so and try again. If you've used a dome mold, surround the gelatin with white currants, or fill the hole with them if you've used a ring mold. Raspberries are just as good, but dust these with confectioners' sugar—it sounds fancy, but it makes the pale-jade glimmer of the jelly and the otherwise-too-vibrant red of the fruit come together on the plate. The white currants should be left to glimmer, opal-like, without interference.

Serves 8.

VARIATION
To make a vodka and lime jelly, simply substitute 6 limes for the 2 lemons and use vodka in place of the gin.

STEAMED SYRUP SPONGE

Even though this dessert takes 2 hours to cook, that isn't as awkward as it sounds. You can assemble it all very quickly, and if you're serving it for a dinner party on a working day, just get started the minute you get in, before you've even taken your coat off, and then you should have no problems about timing.

Not being particularly good with my hands, I don't go in for all that foil-pleating farrago: I just use a plastic pudding basin that is manufactured for the purpose and comes with its own lid that fits. (Don't put either bowl or lid in the dishwasher, however, or the next time you use it it won't.)

I cannot tell you how glorious this is: light beyond words, feathery textured and comfortingly, not cloyingly, sweet. I know steamed sponges are so out of favor as to be, generally, beyond consideration now, but please do yourself a favor: cook it, eat it, and then tell me. . . .

for the sponge:

**3/4 cup very soft unsalted butter, plus
    more for greasing**

**1 cup plus 2 tablespoons self-rising
    cake flour**

1/2 cup plus 1 tablespoon sugar

3 large eggs

zest of 1 lemon and juice of 1/2 lemon

3 tablespoons milk

for the syrup base/topping:

**1 cup plus 2 tablespoons light
    corn syrup**

juice of other 1/2 lemon

7-cup pudding basin with lid

Put the kettle on, then put the butter, flour, sugar, eggs, lemon zest and juice, and milk in the food processor and whizz together, adding a little more milk if the mix is too thick (it should be a thick, pouring consistency).

Pour the boiling water into a large saucepan that has a lid (the water should come about half to two-thirds of the way up the side of the pudding basin when in) or into the base of a steamer. Put it on the heat. Meanwhile, butter the pudding basin, put the syrup in the bottom of it and stir in the lemon juice. Pour the sponge mixture on top of the syrup and put on the plastic lid, remembering to butter it first. Then put the pudding basin into the saucepan, put the lid on the saucepan, and that's it. The pan should keep just boiling, with the lid on. The important thing is that it shouldn't boil dry. Keep some water hot in the kettle to pour in when necessary.

I know one is supposed to put the basin on a saucer in the pan, but the rattling noise it makes drives me mad, and the pudding doesn't seem to suffer for being untriveted. Let it cook for a minimum of 2 hours, more won't matter. When it's ready, remove (I don't bother to make a handle out of string, but use two spatulas to lift it

out of the boiling water) and let rest for a couple of minutes, no longer. Turn out with great aplomb onto a large plate with a sauce-saving lip.

The usual trio of suggestions holds good here: cream, ice cream, custard. If custard, think of flavoring with lemon zest, not vanilla.

Serves 6–8.

VARIATIONS

The variation I do most—and chiefly because it is my father-in-law's favorite—is a marmalade sponge. Replace the corn syrup with 1¼ cups best marmalade and stir into it not lemon juice but 2 tablespoons of orange juice, replacing the lemon zest in the sponge above with the zest of ½ an orange.

And any other jam could go below, but in most cases I'd then flavor the sponge with a teaspoon of vanilla extract instead of zest.

CUSTARD

No chapter on desserts should leave out a recipe for custard. The only problem really is a fear of it splitting. Feel the fear, and cook it anyway. But first, half-fill the sink with cold water so that if you think the custard's about to split, you can plunge the pan into the sink and whisk like fury.

1 teaspoon vanilla extract or 1 vanilla bean
2¼ cups light cream

5 large egg yolks
1 tablespoon sugar

If you've got a vanilla bean, cut down its length so that the seeds will be released, and heat it in a pan with the cream till nearly boiling. Take off the heat, cover, and leave to steep for 20 minutes. If you're not using a pod, put the cream and vanilla on the heat, and beat the yolks and sugar together in a bowl. When the cream's warm, pour it over the sweet yolks, beating all the while. Pour the uncooked custard back into the rinsed-out and dried pan and cook over a medium heat, stirring constantly, until the custard's thickened. Ten minutes should do it, unless you're being very timid and leaving the flame too low. When the custard's thickened, plunge the pan into the cold water in the sink and whisk it for a minute or so. You can eat it straight away, or if you want to make it in advance, reheat later in a bowl over a pan of simmering water.

Serves 4.

APPLE-SYRUP UPSIDE-DOWN PIE

I include this here and not in the pie chapter mainly because you need to eat it hot and because I find it useful as a very easy way of turning a supper of leftovers into something a little more heartwarming. The pastry element is just a scone dough, which requires the minimum involvement on your part.

for the fruit:

2 tablespoons unsalted butter

4 Granny Smiths or other eating apples, peeled, quartered, and cored

4 ounces walnut (or pecan) halves

8 tablespoons light corn (or maple) syrup, plus extra for serving

8-inch shallow pie plate, buttered

for the scone dough:

1²/3 cups all-purpose flour

scant 1 tablespoon sugar

pinch of salt

1 scant teaspoon baking powder

3 tablespoons unsalted butter

1 large egg, beaten

¹/3 cup plus 1 tablespoon whole milk

Preheat the oven to 425°F, putting in a baking sheet.

Melt the butter in a pan, and gently fry the apples, curved side down, for about 10 minutes. Put the walnut halves in the pie dish flat side up. Pour over the syrup, and then arrange the fried apples curved side down. Leave it for a moment while you get on with the dough.

Put all the dry ingredients into a bowl. Cut the butter into cubes and rub into the flour mixture until it resembles coarse bread crumbs. Make a well in the center, pour in the milk and egg all at once, and mix to a soft dough. Using your hands, press the dough into a circle roughly the size of the pie dish and then place it over the fruit, taking care to seal the edges well against the edges of the dish. Bake in the oven for 15 minutes, then turn it down to 350°F for 10 minutes, by which time the top should be crusty and golden.

Let it sit out of the oven for a minute or so, and then place a large plate with an outer rim or lip over the top of the pie, and with one swift action (and wearing oven mitts; the dish will be very hot of course) turn it out onto the plate. It is best to do this over the sink as the syrup will be very hot and runny. Spoon about 3 tablespoons of syrup over the pie, and adjust any stray bits of apple or walnut that may have come off. If you want, and I resolutely do, put a pitcher of warmed syrup on the table for people to add when eating, as well as some light cream in another jug.

This sort of pastry becomes stodgy on cooling, so time it to be ready no more than 10 minutes before you'll be wanting to eat it.

Serves 6–8.

RED-GOOSEBERRY CLAFOUTI

A real clafouti, that vanilla-scented, dense batter pudding studded with fruit, is made with cherries. But that poses problems, the first being that the sour cherries that should punctuate the sweet billowy batter are not always available. The second is that, traditionally, even if you lay your hands on the correct cherries, you should not pit them. Most people, however, would find it difficult to eat a pudding studded with unpitted cherries; and if you do pit them, you lose some of that desirable, bitter-kernel taste (although a bit of Kirsch thrown over the pitted fruits might help). I have made it with the pitted sour cherries you can find bottled in tall glass jars from Poland, but by the time they have sat around in their syrup they tend to lose their edge, too. I wouldn't rule them out, though, particularly since the version here, made with red, or dessert, gooseberries is really only a possibility in midsummer. Red gooseberries, which I've only recently come across, are now easier to find than the tougher-skinned, bitter green ones and are still sour enough to provide the juicy contrast you're after here.

1 tablespoon butter	1 teaspoon vanilla extract
12 ounces red gooseberries	1 1/3 cups heavy cream
6 large eggs	1 1/3 cups whole milk
1/2 cup cake flour	confectioners' sugar for dusting
1/4 cup sugar	8-inch diameter pie plate (I use a
1/2 teaspoon orange-flower water	stainless-steel one for this)

Preheat the oven to 375°F, putting in a baking sheet at the same time. When it's reached temperature, grease the pie dish with the tablespoonful of butter and throw in the gooseberries. Put in the oven for 10 minutes.

Make the batter the easy way: put all the remaining ingredients into the food processor and blitz till smooth and combined. When the gooseberries have had their 10 minutes, pour the batter over them, put the dish back on the sheet in the oven, and cook for 35 minutes, by which time the pudding will be just set in the middle and golden brown and puffy at the edges. Indeed, all of it will be gloriously risen when you take it out, but it will have sunk—and that's just the way it goes—by the time it's at optimum eating temperature, about 20 minutes later. Dust with confectioners' sugar before bringing it to the table.

And boy, does it make a good breakfast tomorrow.

Serves 4–6.

MUSCAT RICE PUDDING

By providing this recipe for a slightly souped-up rice pudding, I am emphatically not suggesting that the basic, plain version is in any way deficient, but this muskily ambrosial pudding really is mellow heaven. And it's wonderful too with a dollop of the muscat jelly—coriander-seeded infusion and all—on page 352. Perfect dinner-party comfort food.

2¼ cups whole milk

2¼ cups heavy cream

scant ¼ cup sugar

pinch of salt

3 tablespoons unsalted butter

½ cup plus 2 tablespoons arborio rice

1 cup plus 2 tablespoons muscat

fresh nutmeg to grate over

6-cup flame-proof casserole

Preheat the oven to 300°F.

Combine the milk, cream, sugar, and salt in a measuring cup. In a casserole dish—and I use an age-old battered enamel oven casserole of my mother's—melt the butter over a medium to low flame, add the rice and stir well to coat, then throw in the muscat (much as you would wine in a risotto). Stir well and let the syrupy liquid bubble away for a couple of minutes. Then pour in the milk mixture, stirring while you do so. Let it all come back to a gentle bubble, stir well again, and grate over some fresh nutmeg.

Put in the oven and cook for 2 hours, though check after 1½ because the depth of your dish and the nature of your oven may make a significant difference. The rice should have absorbed the liquid, but still have a voluptuous creaminess about it. Remove and let cool for at least half an hour before eating.

Serves 6–8.

CALVADOS SYLLABUB

Syllabub is one of those ethereal, dreamy confections which seem at odds with the description "dessert." But this scented, whipped cream, piled up to swell cloudily out of its container, is a perfect way to end dinner and gloriously easy to boot.

8 tablespoons dry hard cider	**juice of 1 lemon**
2 tablespoons Calvados	**1 1/3 cups heavy cream**
1/4 teaspoon ground cinnamon	**4 cinnamon sticks (optional)**
4 tablespoons sugar	**4 6-ounce glasses**

Put the cider, Calvados, ground cinnamon, sugar, and lemon juice in a bowl and stir until the sugar's dissolved. Keep on stirring as you gradually pour in the cream. Now, using a wire whisk or an electric one at low speed, whip the syllabub until it is about to form soft peaks. It should occupy some notional territory between solid and liquid—you're aiming for what Jane Grigson calls "bulky whiteness"—so be careful not to let the cream become too thick or, indeed, to go further and curdle.

Spoon the syllabub into the glasses (and those you see here were bought by my maternal grandparents on their honeymoon in Venice) and puncture each semi-solid mound with a cinnamon stick. If that's just a little too frou-frou for you (and I quite understand), simply dust the uneven tops with the merest haze of ground cinnamon.

Serves 4.

OM ALI

I first ate this at Ali Baba, an Egyptian restaurant in London to which I was taken by Claudia Roden, about 10 years ago. How I remembered it, when I came to cook it myself, was as a kind of Egyptian bread-and-butter pudding; certainly, the idea is the same. Filo sheets are buttered and baked, then layered with nuts and dried fruit in a dish into which you pour cream-enriched sweetened milk before baking it again.

It looks beautiful—the white, the gold, the amber, the green—and it tastes just how you might imagine it would: light, comforting, fragrant. And, like most of the desserts here, it's extremely easy to make. I cook it in a dish made by Calphalon called an Everyday Pan, mainly because it's graceful, unfancy, and it looks the part, but any normal-sized (approximately 8-inch) pie plate should be fine.

7 ounces filo pastry	2 1/2 ounces pine nuts
scant 1/2 cup butter, melted, plus some for greasing	4 cups whole milk
	1 1/3 cups heavy cream
1/4 cup golden raisins	1/3 cup sugar
3 ounces dried apricots, diced small	fresh nutmeg
3 ounces slivered almonds	2 baking sheets
2 1/2 ounces pistachios, chopped	8-inch pie plate

Preheat the oven to 300°F.

Paint the filo sheets with melted butter and crumple loosely like wet rags, dividing them between the baking sheets. Cook for about 20 minutes until they turn crispy and golden.

Now turn your oven up to 500°F. Butter the dish you're using and crumble the filo sheets into it to cover the bottom, then sprinkle the raisins, apricot, and nuts on top, and continue layer by layer until all is used up. Heat the milk, cream, and sugar in a saucepan, and bring to the boil. As soon as it's come to the boil, pour over the filo and fruit layers, grate over some fresh nutmeg, and then put the dish back into the oven for 10–15 minutes. The top should be lightly browned, burnished, and billowed up with the heat. Leave for a few minutes before spooning into small bowls.

Serves 6–8.

PROFITEROLES, MY WAY

I couldn't write a book with this title without including a recipe for profiteroles. These, however, are not your usual profiteroles: they're stuffed with a burnt-sugar custard and have a toffee sauce poured over them. I haven't done this to be fancy, but simply because they're monumentally impressively better that way.

I am not going to pretend that making profiteroles is a completely effort-free exercise—there's an amount of fiddly preparation—but you can make it easier by cooking the little choux buns the day before you need them and keeping them, once cooled, in an airtight tin or Tupperware. And you can make the burnt-sugar custard earlier in the day, and keep it covered with wet baking parchment (but don't, unless it's the highest, hottest summer, put it in the fridge).

for the profiteroles:

1 1/3 cups all-purpose flour

1 1/2 cups water

1/2 cup plus 2 tablespoons unsalted butter, diced

pinch of salt

4 large eggs, beaten

2 baking sheets, oiled

Preheat the oven to 400°F.

Sift the flour. Put the water, butter, and salt in a decent-sized saucepan on the burner and heat until the butter's melted and the water's begun to boil. Take the pan immediately off the heat (you don't want the water to evaporate at all) and beat in the flour. Use a wooden spoon for this and don't worry about how lumpy or how unyielding it is, just keep beating until it comes smoothly together. Put the pan back on the heat for just long enough to finish this process off, about a minute or even less, until the dough begins to come away from the sides of the pan to form a smooth ball.

Now beat in the eggs: and you can do this either by hand (not difficult but you'll need muscle power) or by machine. So, either turn the dough into a mixing bowl and add spoonfuls of egg as you continue to beat with your wooden spoon, or turn it into the bowl of a food processor fitted with the metal blade and gradually pour the eggs through the funnel while blitzing until you have a smooth, gleaming dough, soft enough to pipe but still stiff enough to hold its shape. You may not need all of the eggs, so go carefully. Using a 1-inch plain tip, or just a spoon, pipe little rounds onto the oiled baking sheets and bake for about 15 minutes until golden and crisp. Remove to a cooling rack and pierce each profiterole with a pin, to let the steam out and prevent them going soggy.

for the custard filling:

1 cup plus 2 tablespoons milk

1 cup plus 2 tablespoons heavy cream

6 large egg yolks

1/3 cup sugar

2 tablespoons all-purpose flour

1 teaspoon vanilla extract

2 tablespoons sugar

2 teaspoons water

Warm the milk and cream in a saucepan. While you're waiting, beat the yolks and sugar until creamy, and then whisk in the flour. Stir the heated milk into the egg mixture and whisk until smooth. Pour back into the saucepan and stir or whisk gently over a low heat until the custard thickens. Add the vanilla and set aside. Then burn your sugar by putting the sugar and water in a little pan and turning the heat to high, letting the sugar and water turn to a dark brown caramel. Using an electric whisk for preference, though a fork would do, beat the custard as you pour in the molten liquid. When it's combined, pour into a bowl and let cool, placing a wet piece of wax paper on the top to prevent a skin forming.

for the toffee sauce:

6 tablespoons light brown sugar

4 tablespoons sugar

scant 1/2 cup unsalted butter

1 1/3 cups light corn syrup

4 tablespoons heavy cream

Put all the ingredients except for the cream into a saucepan, bring to the boil, and let bubble away for 5 minutes. Put to one side to cool a little while you assemble your profiteroles.

Get out a large shallow bowl. Fit an pastry bag with a small plain tip and fill with the cold burnt-sugar custard. Fill the profiteroles by splitting them with a small knife, inserting the tip into each one, and squeezing. As you fill them, arrange them in a loose pyramid in the bowl. Pour over some sauce to cover lightly about halfway through, and then again when your entire pyramid has been assembled. You should think of using half of your saucepan. The toffee will harden slightly, shining on top of the egg-yellow profiteroles. Just before you eat, add the cream to the remaining sauce and reheat, letting it bubble away for a few minutes. Decant to a warmed pitcher and stick a ladle into it so that people can pour their own. This sauce reheats easily, by the way.

Serves 8–10.

VARIATIONS

The easiest variation is the expected one: fill the profiteroles with some whipped cream and pour over them chocolate sauce, which you make by bringing 1 3/4 cups heavy cream and 12 ounces best bittersweet chocolate, chopped into little pieces, to the boil in a pan. Whisk till thick and smooth, let cool a bit, then pour over the cream-stuffed profiterole pyramid.

PISTACHIO SOUFFLÉS

Normally I hate the individually portioned, the mealymouthed ramekin of professional practice. But I make exceptions. I've made pistachio soufflé in one large dish and loved it, but you just don't get that perfect ratio of heat-singed exterior and tender interior unless you use dishes with a small diameter.

I have a particular love for pistachios, their scent, their fragrant, delicate taste, that clean eau-de-nil color, those romantic, *Arabian Nights* associations. The square of bitter chocolate, hidden dark and melting within, is the soufflés' killer secret. Don't ruin it by announcing it beforehand.

Lindt Excellence is a good chocolate to use here, because it comes in bars already scored with squares exactly the right size to be pressed into a ramekin (and it's generally stocked by supermarkets and shops). This picture was taken in a huge, cold studio in the dead of winter. I promise you that they rose higher, as yours will too.

2 tablespoons soft unsalted butter,
 plus extra for greasing soufflé cups
3 tablespoons sugar, plus extra for
 dusting soufflé cups, plus
 1 tablespoon for the egg whites
1 1/2 tablespoons all-purpose flour
1/2 cup plus 2 tablespoons whole milk
4 large eggs separated
4 ounces pistachios (shelled weight),
 ground

2 drops almond extract
1/2 teaspoon vanilla extract
1/2 teaspoon orange-flower water
5 large egg whites
pinch of salt
2 1-ounce squares, or similar, good
 bittersweet chocolate
confectioners' sugar for dusting over
6 8-ounce ramekins or soufflé dishes

Preheat the oven to 400°F and put in a baking sheet. Use a little butter to grease the insides of the ramekins and then tip in a little sugar, swirl about to cover, and tip out the excess.

Put the flour in a saucepan and add a little milk, just to blend. Then, stirring (I tend to use one of those little electric whisks here, but a wooden spoon would do fine as long as you're patient), add the rest of the milk and 1/4 cup sugar. Whisk over a medium heat until it comes to boiling point, then whisk for 30 seconds and take off the heat, by which time it should be very thick. Let it cool a little, then add the yolks, whisking in one at a time.

If you're making this in advance, beat in half of the butter and dot the rest on the top to stop a skin forming; otherwise just beat in all the butter now.

Add the ground pistachios, the almond and vanilla extracts and the orange-flower water, and mix in well. Then, whisk all 5 egg whites together with the salt until soft peaks form. Sprinkle over the tablespoon of sugar and then continue whisking until thick and glossy.

Lighten the pistachio mixture with some—up to a quarter—of the whites. Don't be afraid of this: just splodge them into the saucepan and stir briskly. Now fold in the rest of the whites, gently but purposefully.

Pour 1 scant inch of the mixture into each ramekin, then lie chocolate pieces on top and pour over the remaining mixture. Open the oven and as quickly but unhurriedly as possible, arrange the dishes on the heated baking sheet. Immediately, turn the oven down to 350°F and cook for 12–15 minutes, when the tops will be scorched gold and risen high above the ramekins' rims. Remove from the oven, dust with confectioners' sugar, and serve absolutely at once. But one note of reassurance: you can open the oven door to see that the soufflés are cooked and risen; they won't fall just because you've got the temerity to check on them. Serves 6.

CHESTNUT ICE-CREAM MERINGUE CAKE

Three layers of meringue, sandwiched with and topped by chestnut ice cream, covered with grated chocolate, then frozen: it sounds kind of fancy, doesn't it? Let me tell you that it's one of the easiest recipes in the book. The contrast of textures is wonderful because for some reason, which I can't quite fathom, meringue doesn't freeze. That's to say, even straight out of the freezer it tastes as if it's at room temperature, with its normal texture. This, then, is a useful template for any sort of ice cream cake you'd want to make. Chocolate meringues (see the gooey chocolate stack on page 185) layered with chocolate ice cream would indeed be fabulous: but making chocolate ice cream is a more long-winded process than this no-churn chestnut one culled from Shona Crawford-Poole's *Iced Delights*. You could always use a good bought one, I suppose.

But not but what—as my stepfather always used to say—this is just right as it is, so there's no onus on any of us to search anxiously for substitutions.

for the meringue layers:
6 egg whites
1 cup sugar
2 teaspoons cornstarch
1 teaspoon wine vinegar
1/2 teaspoon pure vanilla extract
3 baking sheets, covered with baking parchment

for the ice cream:
3 tablespoons rum
18 ounces canned sweetened chestnut purée
2 1/2 cups heavy cream
1/2 cup confectioners' sugar
1 ounce best bittersweet chocolate to grate over

Preheat the oven to 300°F.

Make the meringue layers first: whisk the egg whites until soft peaks form, then add the sugar a spoonful at a time as you carry on whisking. When you have a quarter of the sugar left, stop whisking and fold in the remaining sugar with a metal spoon. Finally, fold in the cornstarch, vinegar, and vanilla.

Draw three 8-inch circles (use a round cake pan and draw around it) on separate pieces of baking parchment and place on baking sheets. Divide the meringue equally between the 3, making flat discs. Don't get too nervous about handling: I've been brutally clumsy with this, to no detrimental effect. Cook for 1 hour, then turn the oven off, leaving the meringue discs to cool in the oven.

When the meringues are cold—and there's no reason why you can't make them days in advance—get started on the ice cream. You won't believe how pathetically low-effort this is. First, combine the rum and chestnut purée to make a smooth paste. Second, whip the cream and sugar to form soft peaks, and then fold into the chestnut and rum. This smooth mixture is your (unfrozen) ice cream.

To assemble the cake, put one meringue layer on a rimless plate and spread with one-third of the ice cream mixture. Repeat with the remaining layers of meringue and the remaining ice cream mixture. Then, on top of the final third of ice cream, grate over the chocolate. I suggest a Microplane grater for this, but use a grater you like.

Freeze the cake uncovered until it has set, then cover with plastic wrap and keep frozen until you need it. This is a fabulously rich dessert: even greedy people like me can't manage more than a modest slice.

Serves 12–14.

TRIFLES

I came to trifle relatively late in life, which is probably just as well. The three trifles that follow have very little in common with each other, but I feel they have equal claim on your attention.

The first, if not a traditional English trifle, is at least based on one and divinely so. The second is in some sense a tiramisù spin-off. Now, the third trifle I am excitedly pleased about. I came up with it a couple of summers ago: it was hot, I was hot, and I wanted to make something like trifle but lighter, sharper, less formal. The version I came up with is a modern, deconstructed trifle; the idea pared down to essentials. I have no favorites really, not when it comes to eating, but I can't help having a special maternal fondness for this, my own baby.

Trifles do need a certain amount of attention, but this can be spread over days if that makes life easier. Most satisfying, trifles are best when they're the fruitful result of leftover-inspired innovation. Use any stale cake lying around and create harmoniously, accordingly.

CHERRY TRIFLE

As with all trifles, it's hard to specify quantities: really you need to think of layers rather than amounts, but I can see that doesn't help much with the shopping list. The quantities below were enough to fill—just—a glass bowl such as you might expect to use for trifle: you can see from the picture. Otherwise, I tend to use a rather unsuitable terracotta dish with a capacity of about 2¹/₂ quarts.

for the trifle:
¹/₂ cup plus 2 tablespoons brandy
1 vanilla bean, cut into lengths
1¹/₃ cups whole milk
1¹/₃ cups heavy cream
8 large egg yolks
¹/₄ cup sugar
8 store-bought ladyfingers
approximately ¹/₂ cup best cherry jam

1¹/₂ pounds cherries

for the topping:
3 tablespoons slivered almonds
2¹/₄ cups heavy cream
1 tablespoon strained cherry jam
juice of ¹/₂ lemon
1 tablespoon water

First, make your vanilla-brandy infusion to flavor the custard later. So, in a small saucepan, bring about 4 tablespoons of brandy and the chopped vanilla bean to the boil, and then let it bubble away for 2 minutes. Remove from the heat and leave to cool.

Fill the sink with cold water, and get on with the custard: warm the milk and cream in a saucepan. In a bowl, whisk together the yolks and sugar, then beat the warm milk and cream into the yolks. Put everything back into the washed-out saucepan and, stirring or whisking constantly, keep on a low heat until it thickens. With this many yolks, it won't take long. But if you think there's any sign of imminent splitting, plunge the pan into the sink of cold water and beat like mad with an electric whisk or wire whisk till all danger is averted.

When the custard's thick, take it off the heat, stir in the brandy-vanilla infusion and set aside, covered with wet wax paper, till cold.

Split the ladyfingers and sandwich with the cherry jam and line a bowl (preferably glass) with them. Pour over the remaining 6 tablespoons brandy and now, holding them over the ladyfingers in the bowl for profitable juice-catching, pit the cherries. Boring work, time-consuming certainly, but not difficult. When all the cherries are pitted and in, pour over the cooled custard, cover with plastic wrap, and rest in the refrigerator for 24 hours, or at least 12.

When you're ready to eat, or almost, toast the almonds in a dry pan for a few minutes till golden and aromatic, then turn onto a cold plate to cool. Whip the heavy cream till thick but still soft, and pile it over the custard in the bowl. Put the strained cherry jam, lemon juice, and the tablespoonful of water into a little pan and bring it to the boil, letting it bubble away till you have a runny red syrup. Take the pan off the heat to let it cool down slightly, then scatter the almonds over the trifle and drizzle over the jam syrup.

Serves 10–12.

PASSIONFRUIT, MASCARPONE, AND MERINGUE TRIFLE

I have a weakness for anything with passionfruit, but this at least uses my weakness to good effect. You may as well let an obsession work for you. I don't for one instant expect you all to rush out to get a bottle of Passoa, though it is the most divinely camp liqueur you could ever come across. Cointreau is what I suggest if you have neither my sense of kitsch nor worrying extravagance. (Although, since my Passoa was a present, I actually have no idea how much it costs. Believe me when I say it doesn't taste expensive.) I'm not going to suggest an alternative fruit, but do substitute whatever you'd like.

for the soaking liquid:

15 passionfruit

2 limes, peeled and chopped

1 tablespoon confectioners' sugar

approximately 1²/3 cups Cointreau or Passoa

for the trifle:

juice of 1 lime, reserving skin

2 large egg whites

2 large egg yolks

7 tablespoons sugar

3¹/4 cups or 25 ounces mascarpone

12 meringue nests, bought or homemade

approximately 16 ladyfingers

12 passionfruit

glass dish measuring 13 x 10 x 2¹/2 inches

Put the passionfruit pulp, seeds and all, into a food processor or blender with the limes and confectioners' sugar, pulse a couple of times and then strain the liquid into a measuring cup. You should have about 14 tablespoons: make up the quantity to 2¹/₂ cups with Cointreau or Passoa.

Rub around a bowl with the skin of your juiced lime, then whisk the egg whites until stiff. Set aside for a moment. Beat together the egg yolks and sugar, preferably with an electric mixer. They will be a thick paste at first, but add the lime juice, keep beating, and the mixture will become like mayonnaise. Gently fold in the mascarpone and then the beaten egg whites. Take half of your meringue nests and crumble them into the mascarpone mixture, saving the rest to crumble on top afterward.

Dip the ladyfingers one at a time into the passionfruit liquid, then arrange them in a large, shallow dish. Pour in any remaining juice. Spread the mascarpone mixture over the top, covering the cakes evenly. Cover with plastic wrap and leave in the refrigerator for a day or so.

Just before you sit down to the meal at which you're going to eat this, crumble the remaining meringues on top and spoon the scooped-out pulp of the 12 passion fruit, including the seeds, over it.

Serves 14–16.

LEMON-RASPBERRY PLATE TRIFLE

This, as I've already buttonholed you about, is a deconstructed, pared-down version of the original: sliced lemon-syrup cake sprinkled with raspberries, topped with syllabub, and then scattered with almonds. It's simple, and it's perfect.

For the lemon-syrup loaf itself, see "Cakes," page 13, but double the amount of syrup stipulated: you want the cake drenched, not merely doused. In fact, you need only half the cake, but as you can't actually make half a cake, there will be some some left over—hardly a problem. If you want to make enough for 10 or 12, simply use the whole cake, and double the topping ingredients, below.

2 tablespoons sliced almonds
8 tablespoons dry sherry
4 tablespoons sugar
1/4 teaspoon rosewater (optional)
juice and zest of 1 lemon

1 1/3 cups heavy cream
1 lemon-syrup cake with double syrup
  (see page 13)
1 pint raspberries

Put the almonds into a dry frying pan over a medium to high heat to toast them. When they're golden and aromatic, remove to a plate and set aside to cool.

Mix the sherry, sugar, rosewater, and lemon juice and zest in a bowl large enough to take the cream when whipped. I find the best way to grate the lemon zest is by using a Microplane fine grater: this way the peel's tender and shredded enough not to need straining later. Leave for an hour if you've got it, or else give it a good stir and make sure the sugar's dissolved fully. Slowly, while whisking by hand, add the cream. Then—for ease—switch to an electric mixer and beat till airy and floppily bulky.

Slice half the cake onto a large oval plate, or one of whatever shape and size looks about right to you, and then empty out the raspberries on top. Flop over the syllabub and scatter the toasted almonds on top. Perfect for dessert outside on a summer's evening.

Serves 4–6.

VARIATION
Make the syrup cake with lime instead of lemon and replace the raspberries with a paw-paw, deseeded, peeled, sliced, and spritzed with lime. Make the syllabub with white rum instead of the sherry and 2 passionfruit in place of the lemon, and instead of topping with almonds, just scoop out the beady pulp of 2 or 3 passionfruit.

CHEESE BLINTZES

The cheese blintz is a wonderful thing: a pancake cooked on one side only, filled with a mixture of cottage cheese, lemon zest, vanilla, and egg yolk, folded into a parcel and then fried in butter before being splodged with some cold sour cream and perhaps some bitter fruit sauce. This is the traditional way, as eaten by generations of central Europeans; it comes originally, I think, from Hungary, but as with all dishes that are part of Jewish culinary culture, it's hard really to give an accurate provenance.

This version is changed only moderately. I've added some cream cheese to the cottage cheese, to make for a less grainy filling, and I've baked the pancakes rather than fried them. I could pretend this is to make the dessert more compatible with modern eating habits but it would scarcely be the truth. The reason is that it is a lot simpler.

I love these with the sour cream alone, but the blueberry sauce takes this to another realm. It's a doddle to make, and the fact that you can now get fresh blueberries practically all year round (or resort to frozen) makes things even easier. If using frozen blueberries, don't thaw them before cooking them. And this blueberry sauce has wider applications: it can be poured on top of ice cream, cooled and added to cream-topped meringues, eaten with a plain sponge, or spooned over a milky pudding.

for the blintzes:

2 large eggs

1/2 cup plus 2 tablespoons milk

6 tablespoons water

pinch of salt

**6–7 heaping tablespoons
    all-purpose flour**

scant 1/2 cup unsalted butter

zest of 1/2 lemon

few drops vanilla extract

for the blueberry sauce:

7 ounces blueberries

3 tablespoons sugar

juice of 1 lemon

1 teaspoon arrowroot

for the filling:

1 1/2 cups cottage cheese

7 ounces cream cheese

1 large egg

3 tablespoons sugar

to serve:

**2 heaping teaspoons confectioners'
    sugar**

1/2 teaspoon ground cinnamon

1 1/2 cups sour cream

First make the blintzes. Beat the eggs in a blender or by hand, and beat in the milk, water, and salt. Add the flour a tablespoon at a time, blending well after each addition. Stop when the batter's acquired the consistency of heavy cream, then pour into a pitcher through a sieve to get rid of any lumps. Let stand for half an hour.

Meanwhile, melt the butter and let cool a little. When the batter's resting time

is up, stir a tablespoon of the butter into it. Heat a crêpe pan or small frying pan about 8 inches in diameter and add a little of the melted butter, just to provide a light film. When hot, pour in enough batter to cover the bottom of the pan. Quickly swirl it around and drain the excess back into the pitcher. (This will form a slight lip on the side of the pan where the batter's been poured back. You want this, so don't worry.)

Cook on one side only until the sides curl up a little and the bottom is dry. Turn out onto a plate, cooked side up, and cover with a tea towel or cloth. Then cook the rest, stacking the pancakes up under the tea towel until you've finished. You should get 12 blintzes.

If you want you can now make the filling, stuff the blintzes and freeze them (wrapped in foil packages of 3), then cook from frozen as indicated below, only for another 10 minutes or so. Otherwise, preheat the oven to 400°F. Then, using some of the melted butter, brush the bottom of the dish you'll be cooking them in; something with the proportions of a lasagne dish should be about right. Mix the filling ingredients together until they're smoothly combined. Place a blintz, cooked side down, with the tab toward you. Dollop a generously heaped tablespoon of filling onto it, fold the tab over it, then fold the side edges in. Fold or roll over to make a rectangle and place in the prepared dish. Continue until all your pancakes are used up.

Brush generously with the melted butter that remains and cook for 20–30 minutes, when the blintzes will be turning golden and puffy. While they're cooking, get on with the sauce. Put the blueberries into a saucepan with the sugar and lemon juice, and bring to the boil over medium to high heat. Let bubble away for about 3 minutes until the berries have given out copious juice and have cooked down slightly. Stir in the arrowroot and cook for about 30 seconds or so, until the sauce is thick and glossy.

Remove the blintzes from the oven, and push the confectioners' sugar and ground cinnamon through a fine sieve or tea strainer over them, so that they are well dusted. Put on the table along with one bowl of cold sour cream, and another of warm blueberry sauce. Enjoy.

Makes 12, serves 6.

CHEESECAKES

From blintzes to cheesecakes: it's a natural progression. All it takes to make a beautiful dessert is a handful of berries scattered on a plate alongside.

NEW YORK CHEESECAKE

I ate a cheesecake just like this in New York once. I couldn't quite work out what gave it that airy lightness until I registered that, unlike the creamy, smooth, and dense cheesecakes I'd always known, the whites of the eggs must have been whisked.

I know the cooking instructions look odd (and if you want, you can go for the water-bath option and the more straightforward approach of the following two cheesecakes), but for me they're part of the Jewish cheesecake tradition.

for the crust:
1 cup plus 2 tablespoons or 9 ounces graham crackers crushed to fine crumbs
1/2 cup plus 2 tablespoons unsalted butter, melted
3/4 cup plus 3 tablespoons sugar
9-inch springform pan

for the topping:
2 tablespoons cornstarch

1 1/2 pounds cream cheese
6 large eggs, separated
2 teaspoons vanilla extract
1/2 cup plus 2 tablespoons heavy cream
1/2 cup plus 2 tablespoons sour cream
1/2 teaspoon salt
zest of 1 lemon
confectioners' sugar for dusting
raspberries or blackberries to serve

Mix together the crushed crackers, melted butter, and 3 tablespoons of sugar, and press into the base of the springform pan. Put into the refrigerator for about half an hour to set.

Preheat the oven to 325°F. In a large bowl, mix together the remaining sugar and the cornstarch. Beat in the cream cheese, egg yolks, and vanilla, either by hand or using an electric beater. Slowly pour in both creams, beating constantly. Add the salt and lemon zest. Whisk the egg whites to stiff peaks, then fold into the cheese mixture. Scoop onto the chilled base. Bake for 1–1½ hours without opening the oven door, until the cheesecake is golden-brown on top. Turn off the heat and let the cake stand in the oven for 2 more hours. Then open the oven door, take it out, and let it stand for a further hour. Serve chilled, dusted with confectioners' sugar and berries.

Serves 12–14.

LONDON CHEESECAKE

If I had a New York cheesecake, I had to have a London one, and this is surely it. My paternal grandmother instructed me in the art of adding the final layer of sour cream, sugar, and vanilla: and it's true, it does complete it.

I cannot tell you how much the velvety smoothness is enhanced by cooking the cheesecake in the water bath. It's not hard, though you really must wrap the pan twice in heavy-duty aluminum foil. Once you've tried it this way, you won't even consider cooking it any other.

for the crust:

1/2 cup plus 2 tablespoons or 5 ounces graham crackers

6 tablespoons unsalted butter, melted or very soft

20 ounces cream cheese

1/2 cup plus 2 tablespoons sugar

3 large eggs

3 large egg yolks

1 1/2 tablespoons vanilla extract

1 1/2 tablespoons lemon juice

8-inch springform pan

heavy-duty aluminum foil

for the topping:

3/4 cup sour cream

1 tablespoon sugar

1/2 teaspoon vanilla extract

Process the crackers until they are crumbs at this point, then add the butter and pulse again. Line the bottom of the springform pan, pressing the crumbs in with your hands or the back of a spoon. Put the pan in the refrigerator to set, and preheat the oven to 350°F.

Beat the cream cheese gently until it's smooth, then add the sugar. Beat in the eggs and egg yolks, then finally the vanilla and lemon juice. Put the kettle on.

Line the outside of the chilled pan with foil so that it covers the bottom and sides in one large piece, and then do the same again and put it into a roasting pan. This will protect the cheesecake from the water as it is cooked in its water bath.

Pour the cream-cheese filling into the chilled base, and then pour hot water from the recently boiled kettle into the roasting pan around the cheesecake. It should come about halfway up; don't overfill as it will be difficult to lift up the pan. Put it into the oven and cook for 50 minutes. It should feel set, but not rigidly so: you just need to feel confident that when you pour the sour cream over, it will sit on the surface and not sink in. Whisk together the sour cream, sugar, and vanilla for the topping and pour over the cheesecake. Put it back in the oven for a further 10 minutes.

Take the roasting pan out of the oven, then gingerly remove the springform, unwrap it, and stand it on a rack to cool. When it's cooled down completely, put it in the refrigerator, removing it 20 minutes before eating to take the chill off. Unmold and when you cut into it, plunge a knife in hot water first.

Serves 8.

PASSIONFRUIT CHEESECAKE

I am usually such a purist about cheesecake, loathing those that look as if they've got a pan of pie filling all over them, that I don't quite know what's come over me here. I was in a passionfruit phase when I first made it, and suddenly knew that a cheesecake flavored with the juice of this fragrant fruit, sharpened with lime maybe, would be wonderful. It was. It's up to you whether you put seeds or pulp over the finished cheesecake, but the shiny jet of the seeds (which you've got left over from the strained juice) looks wonderful against the thick off-white of the cheesecake; and it also makes this taste somehow more like dessert, and less like something you might be eating mid-morning with a cup of coffee.

for the crust:
¹/₂ cup plus 2 tablespoons or 5 ounces graham crackers
scant ¹/₄ cup melted or soft unsalted butter
8-inch springform pan
heavy-duty aluminum foil

for the topping:
20 ounces cream cheese
7 tablespoons sugar

3 large eggs
3 large egg yolks
³/₄ cup plus 2 tablespoons heavy cream
juice of ¹/₂ lime
¹/₃ cup plus 1 tablespoon passionfruit juice (from approximately 7 passionfruit pulped in the processor and strained)
4–5 passionfruit to decorate, optional

Preheat the oven to 325°F. Make the base and prepare the pan as before. Beat the cheese until smooth, add the sugar, then whisk in the eggs and yolks one at a time. Stir in the cream and lime and passionfruit juices, mixing everything together thoroughly. Remember, though, that beating cheesecakes too vigorously will introduce too much air, which in turn will make them rise and crack later. One of the benefits, in this respect, of a food processor is that you don't whip much air in.

Put the kettle on, then line the springform pan with foil as before. Place it in a roasting pan, then pour the cheesecake filling over the cracker base. Pour the hot water from the recently boiled kettle into the roasting tin so that it comes about halfway up the foil, but making sure you can still carry it safely to the oven. Cook for an hour, by which time it will have browned a little on the edges and the middle should be set, although retaining a hint of a wobble underneath.

Cool on a rack out of the foil, and then refrigerate before unmolding. If you can be patient, leave it overnight in the refrigerator: it will taste better.

Before eating, you can either spread with the reserved seeds or scoop out some more passionfruit to dollop all over the top. Your call.

Serves 8.

JOE DOLCE'S ITALIAN CHEESECAKE

I have become a bit of a bore. I can't hear anyone talk about a delicious something or other someone in their family cooks without asking for the recipe. This is the cheesecake my friend Joe Dolce told me his grandmother, Edith Guerino, always used to make. He e-mailed it to me with the message "Eat it and weep." You'll see.

12 large eggs
3¹/₄ pounds ricotta
³/₄ cup plus 2 tablespoons sugar, plus more for sprinkling

1 teaspoon vanilla extract or Amaretto
10-inch springform pan
paper towels

Preheat the oven to 350°F.

Beat the eggs until well mixed. In a separate bowl, beat the ricotta until creamy, then gradually add the sugar, eggs, and vanilla or Amaretto. Pour into the springform pan, and bake for 1¹/₄ hours. Do NOT open the oven before this time is up. It may be ready then, you may need to give it another 15 minutes. It's ready when the edges have risen into a crown of bronzed goldenness and the middle is parchment-pale and smooth but resistant, just, to the touch. At this stage, switch off the oven and leave the door open and the cheesecake inside for a further hour. Then take it out of the oven and let it sit on a rack at room temperature till cool.

Now for the difficult bit. Line two large rimless plates with paper towels. Gradually loosen the sides of the cheesecake with a spatula. Unclip the mold and turn the cheesecake, topside-down, onto one of the plates. Remove the metal base, now cover the cake with the other plate and turn right-side up. Remove the top plate, loosely cover the cake with the paper towels and put into the refrigerator. The towels should soak up any excess moisture—and there will be plenty. At least 12 hours in the refrigerator are necessary to let the cheesecake dry out adequately.

An hour before you want to eat it, remove the paper towels from the top and again turn the cake upside-down onto a paper-towel-lined plate, adding yet another layer of fresh towels on top. Finally, after an hour, turn the cake right-side up onto a large, flat serving plate and leave to get to room temperature.

All this turning this way and that is tricky, but if it's any consolation, I once broke it a bit, but when it had been wodged into place on the plate you didn't notice at all.

I think this is wonderful as it is, but for a dessert in the summer, halve about a pint of strawberries, sprinkle with sugar and a teaspoon or so of balsamic vinegar, cover with plastic wrap and leave to macerate for about an hour. When you eat, serve the cheesecake on one plate, the jewel-bright strawberries on another.

Serves 14.

CHOCOLATE

CHOCOLATE

If you asked me, I'd say that, unlike a lot of people I know, I am not particularly keen on chocolate. So why did this chapter grow more quickly than all the other chapters in the book? Well, it turns out there really are times when only chocolate will do. But for me, chocolate has to be good, not just brown and sweet. Actually, I'd go further: chocolate, in cooking, is better the less sweet, the more subtle it is.

While I don't want to get tiresomely prescriptive, it's obvious that the chocolate you choose is crucial to the brownies or cakes you make. I have a preference for Montgomery Moore buttons—dark, milk or white (the only white chocolate I'd ever want to eat); the chocolate is extraordinarily, seductively good, and melts beautifully and quickly, but these buttons can be hard to come by outside of England. Luckily, Nestlé does chocolate chips and chunks now too, which you may find more easily in the supermarket. Buying your chocolate already chopped saves time, but is hardly an imperative. Just stock up on the best bars of chocolate you can find, such as Valrhona, and proper, cooked-earth-colored cocoa. Look for brands containing a minimum of 70 percent cocoa solids.

One last thing: melting. The traditional method is to put broken-up pieces of chocolate in a bowl and that bowl on top of a pan of simmering water, making sure that the base of the bowl never comes into contact with the water (it is the steam that melts it). I am, however a complete convert to the microwave for this. I'm not quite enough of a microwave queen, though, to be confident of giving you precise instructions. What I do is give 4 ounces of broken-up chocolate about a minute on medium, then look to see if another minute's required. Not only is it easier to melt chocolate in the microwave than in a bowl over a pan of water, but it's much harder, even in my clumsy experience, to burn it so that it seizes up and becomes expensively unusable. Though if this does happen to you, you might be able to save it by whisking in, off the heat, a lump of butter or drop of vegetable oil. But it's safer to use the microwave and proceed slowly—a hard proviso for the impatient cook, I know, but if I can do it, so can you.

DENSE CHOCOLATE LOAF CAKE

I start with this because I think it is the essence of all that is desirable in chocolate: its dark intensity isn't toyed with, nor upstaged by any culinary elaboration. This is the plainest of plain loaf cakes—but that doesn't convey the damp, heady aromatic denseness of it. To understand that, you just have to cook it. And as you'll see, that isn't hard at all.

I also think this makes a wonderful dessert, either by itself with ice cream or, as when my in-laws were around for lunch one Sunday, with a bowl of strawberries and a pitcher of white chocolate–rum custard. The latter is a fussier option, but there are times when that's, perversely, what we want.

But simply sliced, with a cup of tea or coffee, it's pretty damn dreamy: as damp and sticky as gingerbread and quite as aromatic. And I will confess that I absolutely love it spread with cold cream cheese.

1 cup soft unsalted butter
1 2/3 cups dark brown sugar
2 large eggs, beaten
1 teaspoon vanilla extract
4 ounces best bittersweet chocolate, melted

1 1/3 cups all-purpose flour
1 teaspoon baking soda
1 cup plus 2 tablespoons boiling water
9 x 5-inch loaf pan

Preheat the oven to 375°F, put in a baking sheet in case of sticky drips later, and grease and line the loaf pan. The lining is important as this is a very damp cake: use parchment or one of those loaf-pan-shaped paper liners.

Cream the butter and sugar, either with a wooden spoon or with an electric hand-held mixer, then add the eggs and vanilla, beating in well. Next, fold in the melted and now slightly cooled chocolate, taking care to blend well but being careful not to overbeat. You want the ingredients combined: you don't want a light airy mass. Then gently add the flour, to which you've added the baking soda, alternately spoon by spoon, with the boiling water until you have a smooth and fairly liquid batter. Pour into the lined loaf pan, and bake for 30 minutes. Turn the oven down to 325°F and continue to cook for another 15 minutes. The cake will still be a bit squidgy inside, so an inserted cake tester or skewer won't come out completely clean.

Place the loaf pan on a rack, and leave to get completely cold before turning it out. (I often leave it for a day or so: like gingerbread, it improves.) Don't worry if it sinks in the middle: indeed, it will do so because it's such a dense and damp cake.

Makes 8–10 slices.

WHITE CHOCOLATE–RUM CUSTARD

And here's one way of transforming your cake into the perfect Sunday lunch dessert. Simply follow the instructions for the custard on page 134, omitting the vanilla, using only a scant tablespoonful of sugar, and adding 1–2 tablespoons of dark rum. Then, when the custard's thick, beat in 4 ounces of melted white chocolate off the heat. Leave to cool in a cup or bowl, but remember to cover the top with a piece of damp baking parchment to prevent it forming a skin. Throw some halved, lightly sugared strawberries into a bowl to serve alongside if the idea appeals.

VARIATION

I sometimes make these aromatic chocolate cupcakes to take as a present if we're going away for the weekend: they look so wonderful studded with gold Smarties or M&M's, though actually a plain, shiny brown M&M would have a certain chic allure.

for the cakes:

¹/₂ cup unsalted butter

³/₄ cup plus 2 tablespoons dark brown sugar

1 large egg, beaten

¹/₂ teaspoon vanilla extract

2 ounces bittersweet chocolate, melted and cooled a little

¹/₂ cup all-purpose flour

¹/₂ teaspoon baking soda

¹/₂ cup boiling water

12-cup muffin pan with paper baking cups

for the icing:

6 ounces bittersweet chocolate

3 ounces milk chocolate

³/₄ cup plus 2 tablespoons heavy cream

¹/₂ teaspoon vanilla extract

12 gold Smarties or M&M's, gold leaf, or other decorations of your choice

Preheat the oven to 350°F.

Using the method above, make the batter and fill the 12 muffin paper cups in the muffin pan. Bake for 30 minutes, remove from the pan and cool on a rack.

To make the icing, break all the chocolate into pieces (if no children are eating these you may prefer to use all bittersweet chocolate) and heat with the cream and vanilla in a saucepan until it has melted. Whisk until it's a good consistency for icing, and spoon some onto each thoroughly cooled cake. Spread with the back of the spoon and stud each one with a gold Smartie or M&M's or decorate as you wish. Leave to set somewhere cool, though preferably not in the refrigerator.

SOUR CREAM CHOCOLATE CAKE WITH SOUR CREAM ICING

For some reason, this is the only chocolate cake my daughter likes. Obviously, she has more sophisticated tastes than her mother.

It comes by way of, but not entirely from, the great American cake maker Rose Levy Beranbaum, and the sour cream provides a wonderful mouth-filling smoothness.

for the cake:

1 1/3 cups all-purpose flour

3/4 cup sugar

3/4 teaspoon baking powder

1/4 teaspoon baking soda

1/2 teaspoon salt

3/4 cup plus 2 tablespoons soft unsalted butter

3 tablespoons best cocoa

1/2 cup plus 2 tablespoons sour cream

2 large eggs

1 1/2 teaspoons vanilla extract

2 8-inch cake pans, buttered and lined with parchment or wax paper

for the icing:

3 ounces milk chocolate

3 ounces bittersweet chocolate

6 tablespoons unsalted butter

1/2 cup sour cream

1 teaspoon vanilla extract

1 tablespoon light corn syrup

2 cups confectioners' sugar, sifted (plus more if needed)

1/2 teaspoon hot water

Preheat the oven to 350°F.

Combine the flour, sugar, baking powder, baking soda, and salt in a large bowl. Then, using an electric mixer, add the butter. In a wide-mouthed measuring cup, whisk together the cocoa, sour cream, eggs, and vanilla, then slowly add this cocoa mixture to the ingredients in the bowl, beating until thoroughly mixed.

Pour the batter into the prepared pans and bake for 30 minutes; when they're ready the cakes should be starting to shrink back from the edges of the tins. Leave for 10 minutes in their pans on racks, then turn out to cool.

To make the icing, melt the chocolate and butter in a microwave, or in a bowl over hot water. Let cool a little, then stir in the sour cream, vanilla, and syrup. Add the sifted confectioners' sugar and a little hot water, blending until smooth. When you've got the texture right—thick enough to cover but supple enough to spread, adding more sugar or water as required—you can ice the cakes.

Cut four strips of baking parchment and make an outline of a square with them on a flat plate. Sit one layer on top of the paper pieces, spread with icing, sit the second layer on top and use the rest of the icing to cover the top and sides. Leave spatula-smooth or swirl with a knife as you wish.

Serves 6–8.

PANTRY-SHELF CHOCOLATE-ORANGE CAKE

This is a different sort of chocolate cake: the sort you can make in a few minutes once you get home from work. Hardly any trouble, and you've got a gorgeously aromatic cake either for dessert or just to eat, as supper in its entirety, in front of the television. I think of it as a pantry standby because I tend to have all the ingredients in the house at any given time and if I don't the local corner shop stocks them all.

Even if you don't like marmalade, you should try this: all you taste is orange. Lisa Grillo, who is one of my chief guinea pigs, Italian, and thinks marmalade is a peculiar British perversion, loves it.

1/2 cup unsalted butter

4 ounces bittersweet chocolate, broken into pieces

1 1/3 cups good, thin-cut marmalade

1/2 cup sugar

pinch of salt

2 large eggs, beaten

1 cup self-rising cake flour

8-inch springform pan, buttered and floured

Preheat the oven to 350°F.

Put the butter in a heavy-bottomed saucepan over a low heat to melt. When it's nearly completely melted, stir in the chocolate. Leave for a moment to begin softening, then take the pan off the heat and stir with a wooden spoon until the butter and chocolate are smooth and melted. Now add the marmalade, sugar, salt, and eggs. Stir with your wooden spoon and when all is pretty well amalgamated, beat in the flour bit by bit. Put into your prepared pan and bake for about 50 minutes or until a cake tester or skewer comes out clean. Cool in the pan on a rack for 10 minutes before turning out.

You can eat this still slightly warm (with crème fraîche, perhaps) or cold. For what it's worth, I haven't yet cooked it without someone asking for the recipe. It is, however, a plain-looking cake, and although I have no objection to that, if you want something slightly more elaborate, you could just dust it with confectioners' sugar pushed through a tea strainer (and obviously this goes for all cakes); and if you wanted to go one further, get a cake stencil (which you can you buy in packages containing a few designs, decorative or seasonal), stick on masking tape handles (imperative if you're to lift the stencil off the cake without blurring your design), place on the cake, and dust the confectioners' sugar on top. I am particularly partial to the star and leaf designs—and I don't care who knows it.

Serves 6.

VARIATIONS

As I've already said, you can substitute the jam of your choice, and I'd suggest, first off, raspberry or apricot; but you should also consider making this with the marmalade's weight in dark, aromatic, and velvety prune purée, which supermarkets tend to sell now, in their gourmet baking aisles. If you're going for this prune-thick chocolate cake, serve with crème fraîche to which you've added a few crucial drops of Armagnac; indeed, you could add a slug to the cake too, or just pour a little over as soon as you unmold it.

CHOCOLATE-CHESTNUT CAKE

This is a seriously compelling piece of cake bakery: definitely an after-dinner dessert—and an elegant one at that—rather than afternoon tea, though I think I might be able to force a slice down with a cup of coffee at unscheduled moments in the day. Really, you need serve nothing with it: apart from anything else, it's not so sweet as to need the masking properties of cream.

16 ounces canned unsweetened chestnut purée
1/2 cup soft unsalted butter
1 teaspoon vanilla extract
1 tablespoon dark rum
6 large eggs, separated

9 ounces melted bittersweet chocolate
pinch of salt
3 tablespoons sugar
2 tablespoons light brown sugar
8-inch springform pan, greased and lined with parchment or wax paper

Preheat the oven to 350°F.

Beat the chestnut purée with the butter, then add the vanilla, rum, egg yolks, and melted chocolate, blending well. I use my KitchenAid here, but an ordinary electric hand-held mixer would be fine—or even a bowl and wooden spoon. In another large bowl, whip the egg whites with the salt until they are foamy. Add the sugar gradually to form stiffer, glossy peaks, and then sprinkle the brown sugar over and either fold in or whisk in slowly. Fold the whites, gently but confidently, into the chestnut mixture, a third at a time.

Pour into the pan and cook for 45 minutes, until the cake has risen and is firm on top; it will look dry and cracked, but don't panic: it won't taste dry, and the cracks don't matter a damn.

Cool in the pan for 20 minutes, and then turn out on a rack.

When you want to eat it, dust with confectioners' sugar and serve with modest pride.

Serves 8–10.

TORTA ALLA GIANDUIA

Or, less fancily, Chocolate Hazelnut Cake. This is a fabulously easy cake, another that I draw into service for birthdays: the hazelnuts on top somehow give it a ceremonial look. Please don't feel obliged to rush out and buy a bottle of Frangelico, the most divinely déclassé hazelnut liqueur, its monkish derivation signaled by the rope that is hung from the holy-brother-shaped bottle.

I use hazelnuts bought ready-ground, but ones you grind yourself in the processor will provide more nutty moistness. Nutella, available in some U.S. supermarkets and specialty shops, is a rich, hazelnut-chocolate spread.

for the cake:

6 large eggs, separated

pinch of salt

½ cup soft unsalted butter

14 ounces Nutella, chocolate hazelnut spread
   (1 large jar)

1 tablespoon Frangelico, rum, or water

scant ½ cup ground hazelnuts

4 ounces bittersweet chocolate, melted

9-inch springform pan, greased and lined with parchment or wax paper

for the icing:

4 ounces hazelnuts (peeled weight)

½ cup heavy cream

1 tablespoon Frangelico, rum, or water

4 ounces bittersweet chocolate

Preheat the oven to 350°F.

In a large bowl, whisk the egg whites and salt until stiff but not dry. In a separate bowl, beat the butter and chocolate hazelnut spread together, and then add the Frangelico (or whatever you're using), egg yolks, and ground hazelnuts. Fold in the cooled, melted chocolate, then lighten the mixture with a large dollop of egg white, which you can beat in as roughly as you want, before gently folding the rest of them in a third at a time. Pour into the prepared pan and cook for 40 minutes or until the cake's beginning to come away at the sides, then let cool on a rack.

Toast the hazelnuts in a dry frying pan until the aroma wafts upward and the nuts are golden brown in parts: keep shaking the pan so that they don't burn on one side and stay too pallid on others. Transfer to a plate and let cool. This is imperative: if they go on the ganache while hot, it'll turn oily. (Believe me, I speak from experience.)

In a heavy-bottomed saucepan, add the cream, liqueur or water, and chopped chocolate, and heat gently. Once the chocolate's melted, take the pan off the heat and whisk until it reaches the right consistency to ice the top of the cake. Unmold the cooled cake carefully, leaving it on the base as it will be too difficult to get such a damp cake off in one piece. Ice the top with the chocolate icing, and dot thickly with the whole, toasted hazelnuts.

If you have used Frangelico, put shot glasses on the table and serve it with the cake. Serves 8.

CHOCOLATE-PISTACHIO CAKE

This is a straightforward cake to make, though an expensive one. While I know that pistachios cost more than other nuts, I can't help but prefer them, especially here. There's no need to ice it, but if you do, it looks spectacular in a rewardingly subtle way. It's a very useful cake to make for an elegant birthday dinner. I adore raspberries with it: the dark glow of the chocolate and the waxy jade of the nuts, perfect partners as they are, come newly alive with the matte ruby of those beaded berries.

for the cake:
5 ounces bittersweet chocolate
1/2 cup sugar
5 ounces pistachios
1/2 cup plus two tablespoons soft unsalted butter
6 large eggs, separated
1/2 lemon
pinch of salt
9-inch springform pan, lined with

parchment or wax paper and buttered

for the icing:
5 ounces bittersweet chocolate
1/2 cup plus 2 tablespoons heavy cream
drop of orange-flower water, optional
2–4 tablespoons coarsely chopped or slivered pistachios

Preheat oven to 375°F.

Melt the chocolate in the microwave or double boiler. Process ¼ cup of the sugar with the pistachios until they are like dust. Add the butter and another ¼ cup of the sugar and process until smooth. Add the egg yolks one at a time, pulsing after each, then, with the motor running, slowly pour in the cooled, melted chocolate.

Wipe the inside of a bowl with the lemon half, and in it whisk the egg whites with the salt. When peaks begin to form, slowly add the remaining ¼ cup sugar until gleaming, glossy and firm. Add a big dollop to the cake batter in the processor and pulse a couple of times to lighten the mixture. Now, a third at a time, dollop the cake batter over the whites and fold in gently but firmly.

Pour into the prepared pan, and bake for 20 minutes, then turn down to 350°F for a further 20–25 minutes, or until cooked. When the cake's ready it should be starting to come away from the sides of the pan. Leave to cool in its pan for 15 minutes on a wire rack before unmolding. Don't ice until it's completely cold.

The icing is once again a simple ganache; though the orange-flower water, if you've got it, does add a rather *Thousand and One Nights* note, which goes well with the exotic fragrance of the nuts themselves. Break the chocolate into pieces and put them in a heavy-bottomed saucepan with the cream and orange-flower water, if using. When the chocolate's melted, start whisking and when your mixture's thick enough to coat, but no more, pour it over the cake on its plate. I like a few drips, so just pour over and let it run down the sides of the cake; however, if you want a hatbox affair, let the icing get a little thicker by whisking some more and spread the sides with a spatula dipped in oil. And the less you touch this, the glossier it will dry. Sprinkle over the pistachios: as few or as many as you like, although here I feel less is more.

Serve with crème fraîche, plain, or with a drop of orange-flower water whisked in. Serves 10–12.

CHOCOLATE CHEESECAKE

If you'd ever told me that I'd write a recipe for chocolate cheesecake, I'd have denied it in horror. In theory, the cheesecake purist within me shudders at the idea of something so unorthodox, but for some reason I made one and I found that I shivered only with delight.

¹/₂ cup plus 1 tablespoon or 4 ounces graham crackers	**3 large egg yolks**
¹/₄ cup very, very soft or melted unsalted butter	**³/₄ cup sour cream**
	¹/₂–1 teaspoon lime juice (to taste)
18 ounces cream cheese	**5 ounces bittersweet chocolate, melted**
¹/₂ cup sugar	**8-inch springform pan**
3 large eggs	**heavy-duty aluminum foil**

Preheat the oven to 350°F and put the kettle on to boil.

Process the crackers and butter together and press into the bottom of the pan, then stick the pan in the refrigerator until the filling is ready.

Beat the cream cheese until smooth, then mix in the sugar. Add the eggs and yolks, one by one, beating in after each addition. Now pour in the sour cream and the lime juice and beat until smooth and creamy. Taste to see if you want a sourer base-note than this and, if so, add more lime juice. Gently fold in the melted chocolate; you want a cheesecake marbled with dark chocolate, so don't combine fully.

Line the springform with heavy-duty aluminum foil on the outside, and then tear off another square and repeat the exercise. Stand the pan in a roasting pan and fill it with the mixture. Pour hot water from the recently boiled kettle into the roasting pan to come ¾–1 inch up the side of the cake pan and place in the oven to cook for about 1 hour.

When the cheesecake's ready it should have browned a little on the edges and the center should be just set on top, with a hint of wobble underneath. Remove the cake tin and tear away the foil. Sit on a rack to cool, then refrigerate before unmolding and leaving it to get back to room temperature.

Serves 8.

CHOCOLATE MOUSSE CAKE

This is exactly what it says it is—as you can see from the picture. So if you feel like pure mousse, no cake, then chill it in a bowl rather than baking it in a pan.

For some reason people are put off by the words *water bath*, but if you think about it, it isn't so very hard to wrap a cake pan in foil, plonk it in a roasting pan, and then, when the cake mixture's in, pour hot water into that pan. And that little bit of extra effort makes a cake of such a dreamy, light texture.

11 ounces best bittersweet chocolate
2 ounces best milk chocolate
3/4 cup unsalted butter
8 large eggs, separated
scant 1/2 cup light brown sugar

1/3 cup sugar
1 tablespoon vanilla extract
pinch of salt
9-inch springform pan
heavy-duty aluminum foil

Preheat the oven to 350°F and put the kettle on to boil.

Line the inside of the springform with foil, making sure you press the foil well into the sides and bottom of the pan so that it forms a smooth surface. This will prevent water getting into the cake when it is cooked in its water bath.

Melt the chocolate and butter in a microwave or double boiler, and let it cool. In another bowl, beat the egg yolks and sugars until very thick and pale, as creamy as mayonnaise: the mixture should form and fall in ribbons when you lift up the whisk. Stir in the vanilla and salt, and then the cooled chocolate mixture. Whisk the egg whites in a large bowl until soft peaks form, then lighten the chocolate mixture with a briskly beaten-in dollop of whites before gently folding the rest of them into it.

Pour the cake batter into the foil-lined springform, which you have placed in a large roasting pan. Add hot water from the recently boiled kettle to come about 1 inch up the sides of the cake pan and carefully put the roasting pan with its cargo into the oven.

Cook for 50 minutes–1 hour. The inside of the cake will be damp and mousse-like, but the top should look cooked and dry. Let it cool completely on a cooling rack before releasing it from the pan. This calls for a little bit of patience, because you will need to peel the foil gently away from the sides. Just go slowly and remember that this is a very damp cake, and you won't be able to prise it away from its foil-lined base—though it's easy enough to tear off excess foil once you've set the cake on its plate. Dust with confectioners' sugar if you want, and serve with crème fraîche and maybe some raspberries.

Serves 6–8.

MOLTEN CHOCOLATE BABYCAKES

These are the acceptable face of culinary cute: their intensity guarantees the triumph of chic over prettiness. And, what's more, they're easy to make. You can make the mixture up a few hours in advance and put it ready and waiting in the prepared cups in the refrigerator until you want to cook them, which must be at the moment you're ready to eat them. You might think that preparing the cups sounds fiddly, but in fact the job is just demanding enough to make one feel uncharacteristically competent, but not so much that any actual dexterity is required.

This recipe comes by way of the great James McNair, America's gastro-compendium made flesh.

scant **1/4 cup soft unsalted butter,**
  plus more for greasing
12 ounces best bittersweet chocolate
1/2 cup sugar
4 large eggs, beaten with a pinch
  of salt

1 teaspoon vanilla extract
1/3 cup all-purpose flour
6 individual 6-ounce custard cups,
  buttered
baking parchment

Unless you are making these up in advance, preheat the oven to 400°F, putting in a baking sheet at the same time. Lay 3 of the custard cups on a sheet of doubled baking parchment. Draw round them, remove, and then cut out the discs as marked. Press them all into the base of the cups.

Melt the chocolate and let it cool slightly. Cream together the butter and sugar, and gradually beat in the eggs and salt, then the vanilla. Now add the flour, and when all is smoothly combined scrape in the cooled chocolate, blending it to a smooth batter.

Divide the batter between the 6 custard cups, quickly whip the baking sheet out of the oven, arrange the little cups on it and replace in the oven. Cook for 10–12 minutes (the extra 2 minutes will be needed if the puddings are refrigerator-cold when you start) and as soon as you take them out of the oven, tip out these luscious babycakes onto small plates or shallow bowls. Serve these with whipped cream, the same unwhipped in a pitcher, crème fraîche, custard, or ice cream.

Serves 6.

CHOCOLATE-COFFEE VOLCANO

Despite a move toward chic simplification, sometimes we need a touch of vulgarity in our lives. This dessert certainly provides that. The idea came from a dessert I had at Spago, the Los Angeles restaurant, comprising chocolate Bundt cake stuffed with raspberries and topped with crème brulée. This is my version: a light chocolate cake baked in a Bundt pan—that's to say, a turban-shaped one with a hole in the middle—its hole, once the cake's turned out and dampened with liqueur, filled with chopped walnuts with a creamy coffee custard poured over; finally, imagine sugar sprinkled over and that sugar set alight so that you've got a hard, crackle-glazed top (for which you'll need a small blowtorch). And funnily enough, although it is very much in composition and appearance a swaggering *pièce de résistance*, it's easy to make. Just isolate the three separate tasks: the making of the cake, which is infant-school easy; the making of the custard, which is so eggy it scarcely takes 5 minutes; and the final torching to turn the coffee custard into café crème brulée. Then—pa-dah!

for the cake:

1 cup sugar

scant 1 cup cake flour

1/3 cup plus 2 tablespoons cocoa powder

2 teaspoons baking powder

1 teaspoon baking soda

1/4 teaspoon salt

4 large eggs, separated, plus 2 more egg whites (from the yolks you need for the café crème)

1/2 cup vegetable oil

1/2 cup water

1 teaspoon vanilla extract

10-inch Bundt pan, oiled

for the café crème:

1 cup heavy cream

6 large egg yolks

3 tablespoons light brown sugar

1 tablespoon instant espresso powder

for the topping:

approximately 12 teaspoons (i.e., 4 tablespoons) Tia Maria or rum

1/2 cup plus 1 tablespoon chopped walnuts

4 tablespoons sugar

chef's kitchen blowtorch

It makes sense to get on with the custard first. So, warm the cream gently in a saucepan. Mix the yolks, sugar, and espresso powder together in a bowl, and pour the warm cream over this mixture, whisking to combine. Pour the mixture back into the rinsed-out saucepan and cook over a medium heat, stirring constantly, until it thickens; with this ratio of yolks to liquid, it won't take any time at all. Pour into a bowl, cover with wet baking parchment, and leave to cool.

Get on with the cake as soon as you've made the custard. It, too, must cool before assembly. (Indeed, you may well find it easier to make both cake and custard a day in advance.) Preheat the oven to 350°F, putting in a baking sheet as you do so. In a large bowl, mix together ¾ cup of the sugar, the flour, cocoa, baking powder, baking soda, and salt. In a measuring cup, whisk together the yolks, oil, water, and vanilla. Pour over the dry ingredients gradually, beating to combine.

In another bowl, whisk the 6 egg whites until they are foamy and forming soft peaks. Add the remaining ¼ cup of sugar, a spoonful at a time, still whisking, till the whites are thick and shiny and hold their shape. Briskly beat a large dollop of whites into the cake mixture to lighten it, then, a third at a time, fold in the remaining whites.

Pour the mixture into the oiled pan and place on the baking sheet in the preheated oven. Bake for 40 minutes, by which time the cake should be springy and coming away from the sides of the pan. Let the cake cool in its pan on a rack for 25 minutes before turning it out.

Pour or sprinkle the Tia Maria—or rum—onto the top of the cake, letting the liqueur soak in after each teaspoon. Of course, you could use tablespoons or just pour from the bottle, but you do want to make sure the cake's moistened rather than drenched.

When you are ready to serve, place the cake on a plate with a lip—or an almost-flat wide bowl—and fill the center with the walnuts. Pour the cold custard into the remaining space in the center, letting it overflow a little over the shoulders, so to speak, and the sides. Sprinkle the sugar, a little at a time, so that it doesn't soak in, on top of the cake, and use the blowtorch to caramelize the top.

Serves 8.

CHOCOLATE-MARSALA CAKE

The one true thing about ourselves is our palate, and so you will see Marsala included here and there to add resiny depth to whipped creams or a mascarpone filling, in the same way I often reach for the smoky intensity of a slug of muscat. This cake could, on reflection, use either—and if you were making it for a dessert, it might make sense to use muscat and serve the rest of the bottle to drink with it. If that's the case, reduce the sugar in the cake to ½ cup, though leave the icing as is.

for the cake:

scant ¹/2 cup unsalted butter

4 ounces bittersweet chocolate, broken up

4 large eggs

¹/2 cup plus 1 tablespoon sugar

¹/3 cup self-rising cake flour, sifted 3 times

3 tablespoons Marsala

8-inch springform pan, greased and lined with parchment or wax paper

for the icing:

4 ounces bittersweet chocolate

1 tablespoon Marsala

¹/3 cup plus 2 tablespoons heavy cream

Preheat the oven to 350ºF.

Melt the butter and chocolate together in the microwave or a double boiler, and then set aside to cool slightly. Beat the eggs and sugar together until thick, pale, and mousse-like and greatly increased in volume; they should double, triple even. Gently fold the sifted flour into the egg mixture, trying not to lose all of the air. Now fold the butter and chocolate very carefully into the cake mixture. (I should say at this point that of all the uncooked cake mixtures in this book this is without doubt my favorite: leave yourself a decent amount in the bowl for scraping-out purposes.) Pour into the pan and cook for 35 minutes, by which time the top should be firm and the cake underneath dense and desirably damp.

Cool on a rack for 5 minutes, and then pour over the Marsala. I find it easier to do this by the teaspoonful so that the liquid is evenly distributed. Leave the cake to cool completely before releasing it from its pan.

So, the icing: melt the chocolate, Marsala, and cream in a heavy-bottomed saucepan over a gentle heat. Take it off the heat, and whisk until it reaches a good icing consistency: smooth, thick, but not solid. I like to spread this just on the very top of the cake, which anyway sinks on cooling so that you should have a roughly circular sunken pond to fill, leaving an outline of cooked-cake rim. When set, you're left, beautifully, with a Sacher-shiny disc of ganache suspended on top of this dusty-brown, matte cake.

Serves 8–10.

GOOEY CHOCOLATE STACK

This is for those days or evenings when you want to usher a little something out of the kitchen that makes you thrill at the sheer pleasure you've conjured up. It isn't about showing off, it's about intensity: meringue that's marshmallow-gungy within and chewily crisp without, cocoa-flecked and feathery light; together with a slick, glossy crème patissière into which you've stirred the darkest of dark chocolates. I didn't think I believed in such things, but this is it: chocolate heaven.

Don't panic at the idea of crème patissière. It could hardly be easier: remember that the flour stabilizes it, so you don't have the knife-edge worry of its splitting; plus it's made in advance, as are the pavlova layers, so that it's just a simple stacking operation at the end.

You don't need to use the chopped pistachios I've suggested to scatter over the top: hazelnuts, almonds, indeed any nuts, would be fine; or you could go divinely retro with crystallized violets.

for the meringue discs:

6 large egg whites

1 cup sugar

3 tablespoons cocoa powder

1 teaspoon red wine vinegar

3 baking sheets

for the chocolate crème patissière:

6 large egg yolks

1/3 cup sugar

2 tablespoons cocoa powder

2 tablespoons all-purpose flour

1 1/3 cups whole milk

1 1/3 cups heavy cream

4 ounces the best bittersweet chocolate, melted

1 teaspoon vanilla extract

2 tablespoons pistachios, chopped

Preheat the oven to 250°F.

Line the baking sheets with parchment and draw an 8-inch circle on each one. The simplest way to do this is simply to find a bowl or cake pan with the desired dimensions, plonk it on, and draw around it.

Whisk the egg whites until stiff, then add the sugar a spoonful at a time, beating in well after each addition. Believe me—and I speak as someone often criminally impatient—it does make life easier to go slowly here. Sprinkle over the cocoa and vinegar and then fold in gently but firmly.

Divide the dusky meringue among the 3 circles, spreading evenly. You don't need to worry too much about beating the air out of them as you smooth; I find they withstand a modicum of brutality.

Cook for 1 hour, then turn off the oven, leaving the meringues in until cool. Often, I make them just before I go to bed and leave them in the switched-off oven overnight. It makes for less hanging about. And as long as you keep them airtight, with sheets of baking parchment in between, you can do these a good week or so in advance.

Now for the crème patissière: beat the egg yolks and sugar together, then add the cocoa and flour, whisking well. Warm the milk and cream in a saucepan, then, whisking, pour this onto the eggs and sugar before pouring everything back into the saucepan on the heat and, stirring constantly, bring it to the boil. When the mixture has thickened, take it off the heat and stir in the melted chocolate and vanilla.

Let it cool now, but avoid putting it into the refrigerator as it will become too solid. You can stop it forming a skin either by covering with buttered baking parchment or wax paper or by sifting a layer of confectioners' sugar over. What I often prefer to do, however, and which cuts out more waiting around, is to plunge the saucepan into a sink-ful of iced water and just keep stirring: it doesn't take long to get cold.

To assemble the cake, place one of the meringue discs on a flat plate (I rather like those tea shop cake stands, though preferably in glass), spread with a third of the chocolate cream, then carry on layering. Scatter over the chopped pistachios, which will gleam out, a tender grass-green against the dark chocolate. Then just cut in: and you'll find that it gives the illusion of a fine layering of multi-stacked, custard-bellied wafers; this is because each meringue, with its soft innards and crisp carapace, looks and tastes like three layers, not one.

This easily feeds 10 or 12 people, but I wouldn't let the fact that you've got fewer stop you from making it.

CHOCOLATE MACAROONS

Look at the picture of the pistachio macaroons on page 52, imagine them in chocolate and that's what we're talking about here. I suppose you could also describe them as fat little versions of the gooey chocolate stack above. Though description is irrelevant: the utter gorgeousness of just one mouthful of these chocolate macaroons—for which I have Kate Mellor's sister Lucy to thank—reveals the rank inadequacy of language. Eat them: that's enough.

for the macaroons:
1²/₃ cups confectioners' sugar
1/2 cup plus 1 tablespoon ground almonds
2 tablespoons cocoa powder
4 large egg whites
1 tablespoon sugar
2 baking sheets

1/2-inch plain pastry tip and pastry bag

for the ganache filling:
6 tablespoons heavy cream
5 ounces bittersweet chocolate, chopped
3 tablespoons unsalted butter

Preheat the oven to 350°F. and line the baking sheets with parchment.

Sift together the confectioners' sugar, ground almonds, and cocoa powder. Whisk the egg whites until half stiff, sprinkle over the granulated sugar and continue whisking until very stiff, but not dry. Gradually fold in the sifted ingredients.

Fit the piping tip into the bag, sit it in a tall glass, turn the bag back to form a cuff, and fill with the macaroon mixture. Pipe out 2-inch rounds on the lined baking sheets, then leave to stand for 15 minutes to form a skin.

Bake for 12–15 minutes: you want them dry on top, but still chewy underneath. Remove to cool on a wire rack, and when they are cool, sandwich with the ganache, which you make by heating all the ingredients in a saucepan until the chocolate's just melted. Off the heat, whisk until thick, and when cool spread with a knife on the underside of one macaroon, then stick another macaroon to it. Continue till you've used all of them up.

Makes 36 rounds, i.e., 18 macaroons.

CHOCOLATE-RASPBERRY TARTS

With their dark chocolate shells and their white-chocolate mascarpone filling, these look fancy enough, but when you eat them what strikes you is their cleanly balanced simplicity. The almost dry bitterness of the cocoa-darkened pastry balances the rich, fat creaminess of the filling, which in turn is perfectly offset by the tart, neatly-beaded berries.

I won't pretend that the chocolate pastry is that easy to work with. Yes, it does tear easily, but that doesn't matter, because it patches up perfectly too. Maybe the first time you make these you should try to get just 4 little tarts out of the dough; later on, when you're more confident, you should be able to make 6 without trouble.

Like anything that relies in great part on assembly, these are much easier to make than you might think.

for the tarts:
1 cup plus 2 tablespoons cake flour
2 tablespoons cocoa powder
2 tablespoons sugar
1/4 teaspoon salt
1/2 cup unsalted butter
1 large egg yolk
1 tablespoon ice water

for the filling:
2 ounces white chocolate
1 cup plus 2 tablespoons mascarpone
1/3 cup plus 1 tablespoon heavy cream
approximately 2 pints raspberries
6 2 1/2 x 5-inch tartlet pans with removeable bottoms

Your best bet is to make the pastry in a food processor, so put the flour, cocoa, sugar, and salt into the bowl and pulse to blend. Cut the butter into small pieces and pulse with the flour mixture until it looks crumbly. Beat the yolk and ice water together and add, down the funnel, to bind the pastry. When it starts to clump together, turn it out of the processor and work it together with your hands into two discs. Wrap them in plastic wrap and rest the pastry in the refrigerator for at least 30 minutes.

Roll out one of the dough discs; it will be quite a dry pastry because of the cocoa, so don't be too heavy-handed with the flour on your rolling surface. Then, using a tart pan as a guide, cut at least 3 rough squares or circles slightly bigger than each pan. Ease the pastry squares into the pans—don't worry if they break, just patch them as best you can—and cut off the excess pastry. Do this with all 6 pans, and then freeze them for about 30 minutes or until they feel frozen. While the pastry's in the freezer, turn on the oven to 350°F, and slip in a baking sheet to heat up at the same time.

Put the tartlets straight into the oven on the baking sheet, and cook for 10–15 minutes or until the pastry feels cooked and dry. The freezing plus the fact that the individual area is small means that they shouldn't puff up, which in turn means we're doing without the beans and all that blind-baking palaver. While the pastry's cooking, you might melt the chocolate for the filling, either in the microwave or in a double boiler.

When the pastry shells are cool, slip them out of their pans and finish the filling. This is simple: you just beat the mascarpone and cream together and fold in the melted, slightly cooled, white chocolate. Go gently with your whisking: you don't want this too thick; however, a little extra unwhipped cream stirred in at the end will thin it down if necessary. Fill the pastry shells with the cream, and then top with raspberries.

Makes 6.

PAIN-AU-CHOCOLAT PUDDING

Of course you can make a thoroughly chocolate bread-and-butter pudding, either by adding melted chocolate or cocoa to the eggy custard, or simply by using a sliced-up chocolate loaf. But if you ask me, you're better off with this gentler, subtler take on what a chocolate bread-and-butter pudding might be: all I've done is slice up some stale pains au chocolat. It looks beautiful and tastes divine.

If you want to, by all means replace the heavy cream and milk with 4½ cups of light cream.

3–4 stale pains au chocolat
2¼ cups milk
2¼ cups heavy cream
3 tablespoons sugar
1 large egg

4 large egg yolks
½ teaspoon vanilla extract
ovenproof dish with a capacity of
    approximately 6 cups

Preheat the oven to 325°F.

Butter your ovenproof dish (I always use one of those old-fashioned oval creamware dishes), cut up the pains au chocolat—I cut rough slices of about an inch—and arrange them in the dish. Put the milk and cream into a pan and bring near to boiling point. Whisk the egg, the yolks, and the sugar in a large wide-mouthed measuring cup. When the milk and cream are nearly boiling, pour over the eggs and sugar, whisking continuously. Add the vanilla and then pour over the slices of pain au chocolat and leave to soak for 10 minutes.

Transfer to the preheated oven and cook for about 45 minutes, or until the pudding is softly set. I can't tell you how comforting this is.

Serves 6.

BROWNIES

I don't understand why people don't make brownies all the time—they're so easy and so wonderful. My friend Justine Picardie gave me the idea for setting the brownies so gloriously alight when she asked me to make them for her husband's birthday. Ever since then, I've copied the idea: brownies are much quicker to make than a cake, and they look so wonderful piled up in a rough-and-tumble pyramid spiked with birthday candles. And I'd much rather eat a brownie than a piece of birthday cake any day; I think most people would.

1 2/3 cups soft unsalted butter
13 ounces best bittersweet chocolate
6 large eggs
1 tablespoon vanilla extract
1 2/3 cups sugar
1 1/2 cups all-purpose flour

1 teaspoon salt
1 1/3 cups chopped walnuts
pan measuring approximately
**   13 x 9 x 2 1/2 inches**
birthday candles and holders, if
**   appropriate**

Preheat the oven to 350°F. Line your brownie pan—I think it's worth lining the sides as well as the base—with foil or parchment.

Melt the butter and chocolate together in a large heavy-based pan. In a bowl or large wide-mouthed measuring cup, beat the eggs with the vanilla and sugar. Measure the flour into another bowl and add the salt.

When the chocolate mixture has melted, let it cool a bit before beating in the eggs and sugar, and then the nuts and flour. Beat to combine smoothly and then scrape out of the saucepan into the lined pan.

Bake for about 25 minutes. When it's ready, the top should be dried to a paler brown speckle, but the middle still dark and dense and gooey. And even with such a big batch you do need to keep alert, keep checking: the difference between gungy brownies and dry brownies is only a few minutes; remember that they will continue to cook as they cool.

Makes a maximum of 48.

VARIATIONS

You can really vary brownies as you wish: get rid of the walnuts, or halve them and make up their full weight with dried cherries; or replace them with other nuts—peanuts, brazil-nuts, hazelnuts—add shredded coconut or white chocolate chips; try stirring in some Jordan's Original Crunchy cereal. I had high hopes for chic, after-dinner pistachio-studded brownies, but found the nuts get too soft and waxy, when what you need is a little crunchy contrast.

CREAM-CHEESE BROWNIES

This version adds cream cheese, fridge-cold and sliced, to give an inner layer of almost salty sourness. Just think of cheesecake: rich, sweet, sharp, palate-cleaving. What's not to like?

4 ounces bittersweet chocolate
1/2 cup unsalted butter
2 large eggs
3/4 cup sugar
1 teaspoon vanilla extract

1/3 cup plus 2 tablespoons
  all-purpose flour
pinch of salt
7 ounces cold cream cheese
9-inch square pan, greased and lined
  with parchment or wax paper

Preheat the oven to 350°F.

Melt the chocolate and butter over medium-to-low heat in a heavy-based saucepan. While you're waiting for it to melt, idly beat the eggs in a bowl with the sugar and vanilla. Measure the flour into another bowl and add the salt. When the chocolate mixture has all but completely melted, take the pan off the heat. The bits of unmelted chocolate or butter will continue to dissolve if left. Leave for a bit longer to cool slightly before beating in the eggs and sugar. Finally, add the flour and beat until smooth. Pour half the mixture into the pan, slice the cream cheese as thinly as you can and top the brownie mixture in the pan with these thin slices. Pour over the remaining half of brownie-gunge, using a rubber spatula or whatever to make sure each bit of cheese is covered. Then put in the oven and bake for about 20 minutes: the top should be slightly paled and dry, but a cake tester poked within should reveal a still-sticky center. Cool for about 10 minutes before cutting into little squares, and eat warm or cold, though the cooler they are the easier they'll be to lift out. Reckon on a first, botched slice: cook's treat.

Makes 8–10.

WHITE CHOCOLATE AND MACADAMIA BROWNIES

Blonde brownies can never have the depth or intensity of their darker sisters (I'm not implying anything . . .) but that doesn't mean they haven't got anything going for them. The important thing is to maximize squodge, to try and create a buttery caramel flavor, but one that doesn't hit you about the head with migraine-provoking sugariness. This should fit the bill.

- 1/2 cup unsalted butter
- 9 ounces white chocolate, cut into chunks, or chips
- 4 large eggs
- 1 teaspoon salt
- 1 1/4 cups sugar
- 2 teaspoons vanilla extract
- 2 cups all-purpose flour
- 9 ounces macadamia nuts, roughly chopped
- 10 x 8 x 2 pan, buttered

Preheat the oven to 325ºF.

Melt the butter and chocolate either in a microwave or a double boiler. In a large bowl, beat the eggs with the salt until light and beginning to whoosh up in volume, then add the sugar and the vanilla, and continue beating until really thick and creamy.

Beat in the slightly cooled chocolate mixture and then add the flour and nuts, folding in gently. Pour into your prepared pan and cook for 35 minutes or until set on top and gooey in the middle. Leave for 3–5 minutes before cutting into small squares. Bear these in mind for giving to people to eat with coffee when dinner's ended with cheese. Not that you need to add anything sweet, but again it's that idea of supplementing shrewd and pleasurable shopping with the satisfactions of a little light home baking.

Makes 16.

ALL-PURPOSE CHOCOLATE ICING

The chocolate icing I use most, as you will have noticed, is a ganache (see page 22), which has the virtue of being as easy and quick to make as it is good to eat. But then, good chocolate mixed with good cream should taste like that. I think it's useful, though, to have another recipe, less elegant maybe, but helpful to turn a plain sponge into a chocolate-iced layer cake. It's also a good way of making a chocolate cake which otherwise may be too darkly adult into one fit for intergenerational eating.

It's only a blueprint, so fiddle about as you please: add orange oil or almond extract in place of the vanilla; use brandy instead of rum.

- 4 ounces bittersweet chocolate
- 6 tablespoons unsalted butter
- 2 large eggs, beaten
- 3 1/3 cups confectioners' sugar, sifted
- 1 teaspoon vanilla extract
- 1 tablespoon dark rum

Melt the chocolate and butter in the microwave. Beat in the eggs, then the sugar. Add the extract and rum, then leave to cool a little before using. This amount makes enough icing to cover the top, middle, and sides of an 8-inch layer cake.

CHOCOLATE-CHERRY CUPCAKES

These are very easy, very good—somehow light and dense at the same time—and I love their dark, glossy elegance. When I made them for the cake sale at my daughter's school fair, they sold, even at more than a dollar a piece, quicker than anything else. I'd have included them in the school party section (see page 235), except that they're perhaps too expensive to make a habit of. Still, if the cost considerations include time, then this probably counts as a cheap undertaking.

The jam I use for these is a morello cherry preserve; if you're using a less elegant, and probably sweeter confection, reduce the sugar in the cakes a little. And if you have any Kirsch about the place, then add a splash to the batter and icing.

for the cupcakes:
1/2 cup soft unsalted butter
4 ounces bittersweet chocolate, broken into pieces
1 1/3 cups morello cherry jam
1/2 cup sugar
pinch of salt
2 large eggs, beaten
1 cup self-rising cake flour

12-cup muffin pan and paper baking cups

for the icing:
4 ounces bittersweet chocolate
1/3 cup plus 1 tablespoon heavy cream
12 natural-colored glacé cherries

Preheat the oven to 350°F.

Put the butter in a heavy-bottomed pan on the heat to melt. When nearly completely melted, stir in the chocolate. Leave for a moment to begin softening, then take the pan off the heat and stir with a wooden spoon until the butter and chocolate are smooth and melted. Now add the cherry jam, sugar, salt, and eggs. Stir with a wooden spoon and when all is pretty well amalgamated stir in the flour.

Scrape and pour into the muffin baking cups in their pan and bake for 25 minutes. Cool in the pan on a rack for 10 minutes before turning out.

When the cupcakes are cool, break the chocolate for the icing into little pieces and add them to the cream in a saucepan. Bring to the boil, remove from the heat, and then whisk—by hand or electrically—till thick and smooth. Ice the cupcakes, smoothing the tops with the back of a spoon, and stand a cherry in the center of each.

Makes 12.

ESPRESSO CUPCAKES

You don't need to make the cappuccino cupcakes, opposite, to have with these, but they do look, and taste, wonderful together. They are on the edge of what my paternal grandfather, and my mother after him, used to condemn as landscape cookery, but I just couldn't help myself.

for the cupcakes:

¹/₂ cup soft unsalted butter

¹/₂ cup dark brown sugar

2 large eggs

³/₄ cup self-rising cake flour

1 tablespoon cocoa powder

1 tablespoon espresso coffee powder

2 ounces bittersweet chocolate, melted

1–2 tablespoons milk

for the icing:

11 ounces bittersweet chocolate

scant ¹/₄ cup unsalted butter

2 teaspoons instant espresso coffee powder

12-cup muffin pan with paper baking cups

Preheat the oven to 400°F.

Pulse the butter and sugar in a food processor, then add the eggs, pulsing again. Tip in the flour, cocoa, and coffee powder, and process until you have a smooth batter. Finally, add the chocolate, and thin the batter with the milk. Pour into the muffin baking cups in their pan and cook for 15–20 minutes. A quick poke with a cake tester (or uncooked stick of spaghetti) should let you know if they're sufficiently cooked. Let the cakes cool out of the oven in the pan for a few minutes, then take them out to cool completely on a rack.

While they're cooling, get on with the icing. Just put the chocolate, butter, and instant espresso powder in a large bowl and put it in the microwave till the chocolate's melted. (I find 2 minutes on medium does it, but I can't pretend to understand all manner of microwaves.) Whisk together to combine, then lop off a slice from the top of each cupcake so that you've got a perfectly flat surface. Spread the icing over this surface, until you've got 12 dark chocolate cupcakes doing their best to look like espressi. If you want, stud the center of each with a chocolate-covered coffee bean.

Makes 12.

CAPPUCCINO CUPCAKES

The only thing chocolatey about these is the white chocolate in the icing: underneath is just golden coffee sponge; I think of this combination as blonde mocha.

for the cupcakes:
3/4 cup self-rising cake flour
1/2 cup soft unsalted butter
7 tablespoons sugar
2 large eggs
1 teaspoon vanilla extract
1 teaspoon baking powder
1 heaped tablespoon instant espresso
2–3 tablespoons milk

for the icing:
5 1/2 ounces white chocolate
1/4 cup butter
1/2 cup plus 1 tablespoon sour cream
1 2/3 cups confectioners' sugar, sifted
scant teaspoon cocoa powder
12-cup muffin pan with paper
  baking cups

Preheat the oven to 400°F.

Put all the cupcake ingredients except for the milk into the food processor and blitz to combine. Pulse again, adding milk down the funnel to form a batter with a soft, dropping consistency. Spoon into the baking cups in their pan and put in the oven to cook for about 20 minutes. When ready, remove from the oven and leave in the pan to cool for 5 minutes before turning out onto a wire rack.

When they're completely cold, get on with the icing. Melt the chocolate and butter in the microwave or in a double boiler, and after it's cooled a little, stir in the sour cream. Gradually beat in the sifted confectioners' sugar. And if the consistency isn't right for icing, add either hot water to thin or more sifted sugar to thicken. Spread roughly and generously over the top of each cupcake, and then dust sparingly with cocoa, by pressing a little through a tea strainer, so that they look like little cups of chocolate-dusted cappuccino.

Makes 12.

BANANA, CHERRY, AND WHITE CHOCOLATE CUPCAKES

Isn't the name enough? If not, then note that these are risibly easy to make. The recipe comes from a much-loved American book of mine, *One-Pot Cakes* by Andrew Schloss—who's also the inspiration behind the chocolate-cherry cupcakes and the chocolate-orange cake above—and it's true, you do need just one pot, and the least energetic stirring with any old fork, to make this. Perfect for lunch box or picnic basket. What am I saying? Perfect for anything.

1/2 cup unsalted butter
3/4 cup sugar
1 teaspoon vanilla extract
3 ripe bananas
4 tablespoons sour cream
2 large eggs
1 teaspoon baking soda

1/2 teaspoon baking powder
2 cups all-purpose flour
3 tablespoons dried cherries, chopped
2 ounces white chocolate, chopped, or chips
12–cup muffin pan with paper baking cups

Preheat the oven to 350°F.

Melt the butter in a saucepan, then, off the heat, add the sugar, vanilla, and soft bananas, mashing them with a fork in the pan. Stir in the sour cream and the eggs and—still using your fork or a wooden spoon if you prefer—beat to mix. Add the baking soda and the baking powder, and stir in as well, then finally stir in the flour, cherries, and chocolate.

When the mixture's just blended, divide among the 12 muffin cups and cook for 20 minutes or until golden and springy on top. Remove the cupcakes in their paper cups to a wire rack and leave till cool.

Makes 12.

NIGHT-AND-DAY CUPCAKES

This, like the cream-cheese brownies, uses my favorite combination of densely sweet and smoothly sharp. I love the way chocolate-coated coffee beans look like buttons or studs on top of the creamy whiteness of the icing, but use dark chocolate coarsely shaved through a grater if you prefer.

for the cupcakes:
2 scant tablespoons cocoa powder
2 tablespoons boiling water
1/4 cup sugar
scant 1/4 cup dark brown sugar
3/4 cup self-rising cake flour
2 large eggs
1/2 cup very soft unsalted butter
1 teaspoon vanilla extract
1 tablespoon milk

**12-cup muffin pan with paper
  baking cups**

for the frosting:
1 1/3 cups confectioners' sugar, sifted
4 ounces cream cheese
**juice of 1/2 lime (or 1 tablespoon
  lemon juice)**
**12 chocolate-coated coffee beans or
  bittersweet chocolate**

Preheat the oven to 400°F. Mix the cocoa to a paste with the boiling water and set aside while you make the cupcake mixture.

This couldn't be easier: just put the sugars, flour, eggs, and butter in the processor and blitz to combine smoothly. Scrape the mixture from the sides, and then pulse while you add the cocoa paste and milk down the funnel. You should have a batter with a soft dropping consistency: if not, add a little more milk. Dollop into the paper baking cups in the pan and bake for about 20 minutes, until an inserted cake tester comes out clean.

Leave in the pan for 5 minutes, then remove, in the paper baking cups, to a wire rack. When cool, make the frosting by beating together the sifted confectioners' sugar and cream cheese till soft; add lime or lemon juice to taste and then spread roughly over the waiting cupcakes. Stud each one with a chocolate-coated coffee bean or shave over some bittersweet chocolate.

Makes 12.

FLORENTINES

This is the one recipe using glacé cherries in which I won't beseech you to use the dark natural-colored ones; we want that garish red here. I won't claim this isn't a fiddly recipe, but you need patience rather than dexterity or expertise, and they are so good it would be a pity if you never found the calmness from which to produce them. Hettie, who's worked with me on this book, customarily calls me Frank, as in Spencer, and if I can make these, so can you. These taste so much better than any florentines you've ever bought.

4 ounces whole, blanched almonds

7 tablespoons mixed candied peel, in whole chunks, not ready chopped

1 1/2 ounces glacé cherries

2 tablespoons unsalted butter

1/3 cup sugar

1 tablespoon all-purpose flour

1/2 cup plus 2 tablespoons heavy cream

4 ounces bittersweet chocolate

4 ounces white chocolate

2 baking sheets, greased

Preheat the oven to 375°F.

Chop the almonds so that you have some fine pieces and some chunks of nut. Chop the candied peel and cherries into fairly small, even pieces. In a heavy-bottomed saucepan, melt the butter and sugar without letting it scorch. Add the flour rather as if you were making a roux for a white sauce; it should form a ball of paste. Take off the heat and whisk in the cream. The mixture should be smooth, so put it back on the heat briefly to beat out any lumps. Stir in the fruit and almonds.

Drop heaping teaspoonfuls of this florentine mixture onto the greased or nonstick baking sheets. It will look quite liquid and will spread, so leave generous space between the blobs. Place the sheets in the oven and cook for 10–12 minutes. They're ready when they've spread into larger circles and the edges are golden brown. Take them out of the oven and leave for 2–3 minutes to firm up; at this point you can ease them back into shape if you need to, as they will be very malleable. When you feel they can be lifted, slip a metal spatula or palette knife underneath them and transfer to a wire rack to cool, ensuring you leave them flat.

Melt the dark and white chocolate in separate bowls in the microwave, and paint the flat side of each florentine; I use a pastry brush for this. Be prepared to paint over and over to get a good thick coating, although it's more of an issue with the white chocolate.

Using a fork, make wavy lines on the chocolate on each florentine, and leave to dry.

Makes approximately 30.

GRANNY BOYD'S COOKIES

The recipe for these cookies was given to me, at my insistent request, by my editor, Eugenie Boyd. I don't think there is a more chic accompaniment to a tub of good vanilla ice cream: they're sturdy, dark, smoky, and melting.

2 cups self-rising cake flour

2 tablespoons cocoa powder

**1 cup plus 2 tablespoons soft
    unsalted butter**

7 tablespoons sugar

2 baking sheets, greased

Preheat the oven to 325°F.

Sift together the flour and cocoa, and set aside for a moment. Cream the butter and sugar until pale and soft, then work in the flour and cocoa. It might look like it needs liquid, but keep working the ingredients in and it will form a dough. Roll into walnut-sized balls and arrange these with a decent space between them (as they'll spread) on the baking sheets, then press down on them with the back of a fork: you can see the marks the tines make on them in the picture opposite page 61.

Put the sheets in the oven and cook for 5 minutes, then turn the oven down to 300°F and bake for a further 10–15 minutes. It's hard to tell by looking when the cookies are ready since the dough starts off so dark, but they should feel firm on top, although not hard; they will continue to cook and harden as they cool. Remove from the oven and transfer immediately to a wire rack to cool.

Makes about 35.

WHITE CHOCOLATE AND PISTACHIO COOKIES

The pale gold of these buttery cookies together with the waxy green of the nuts and rich whiteness of the chocolate is the perfect combination: elegance and comfort.

scant ¹/2 cup soft unsalted butter
7 tablespoons sugar
scant ¹/2 cup soft brown sugar
1 teaspoon vanilla extract
1 large egg
1 cup all-purpose flour

1 teaspoon baking soda
scant ¹/2 cup ground pistachios
4 ounces whole pistachios
4 ounces white chocolate, chopped
2 baking sheets, lined

Preheat the oven to 350°F.

Cream together the butter and sugars until soft and almost mousse-like. Add the vanilla and the egg, then the flour and baking soda. Don't worry if the mixture looks almost curdled after you've beaten in the egg. When you've got a smooth, thick dough, add the nuts and chocolate and mix to combine.

Pinch off pieces of dough and roll them into walnut-sized balls in your hands. Place these, generously spaced, onto the baking sheets, and put in the oven for 10–12 minutes, by which time the cookies should be a pale gold, with a darker gold around the edges.

Leave to set for a couple of minutes on the baking sheets before transferring to a wire rack to cool.

Makes about 36.

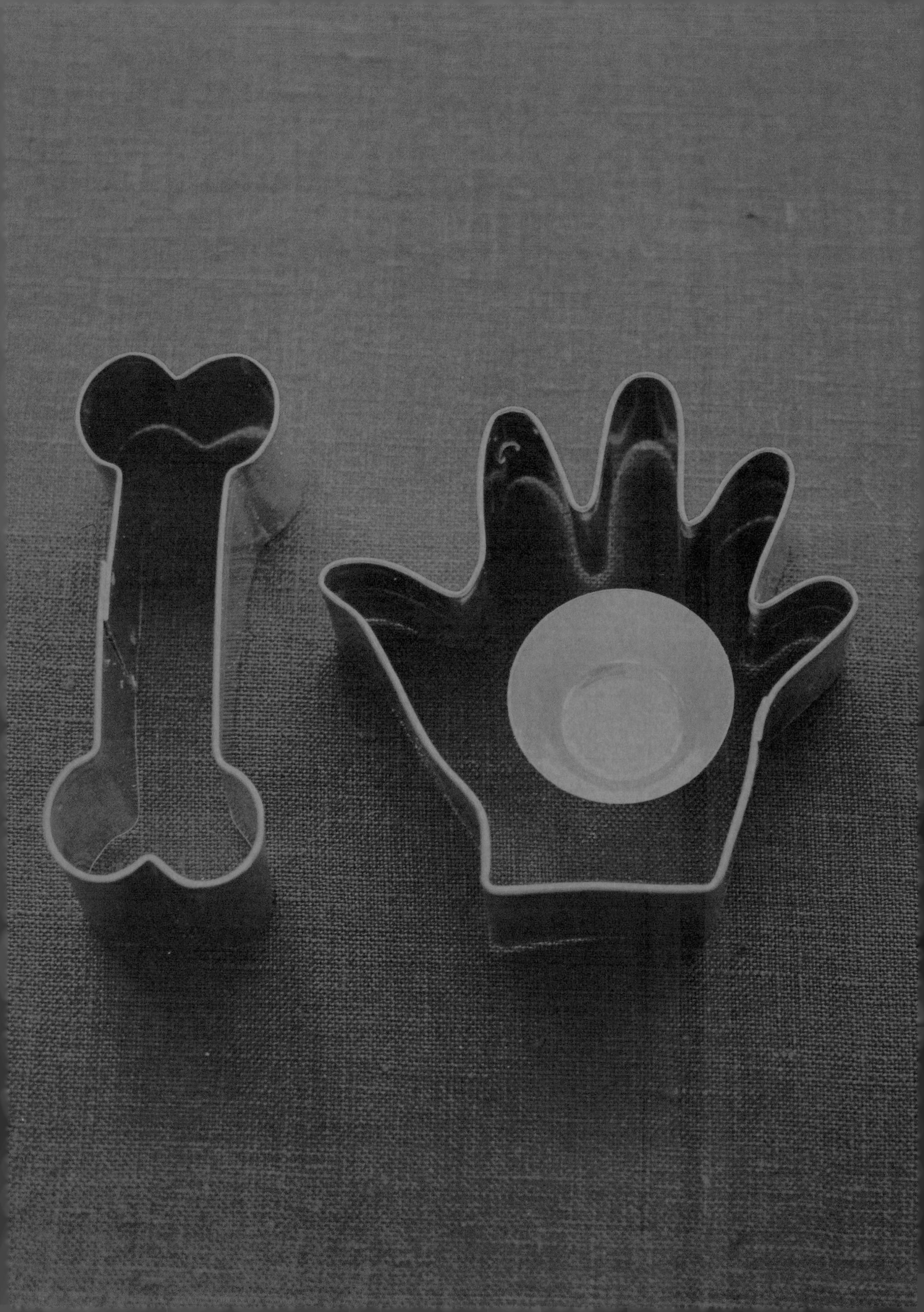

CHILDREN

CHILDREN

Although in cooking I resist strongly the idea that there is such a thing as children's food, as distinct from "real" food, in baking I have, I suppose, to lighten up. Not that I think that peanut-butter squares are therefore unfit for adult consumption—sadly, that doesn't appear to be the case— or that candy-covered cupcakes cannot lie happily with a child-free life, but they are both the sort of thing I have in mind when I talk about baking for children. Indeed, many of the recipes here can be made by children, too, although it would be hard to make a useful distinction throughout the chapter between cooking for and cooking with children— that would inevitably depend on their age. And actually, so much of children's baking isn't about what they can be left alone to get on with, but about what you do together. I love hanging around the kitchen with the children, stirring mixtures, licking out bowls, baking fairy cakes, or cutting out and icing cookies. But it's also incredibly important to me that that doesn't usurp everyday cooking; I like them with me in the kitchen helping—or not, as the case may be—with ordinary lunch or supper, not just on-the-side kiddie cuisine. In fact, even though I'm lucky enough to work at home, I'm hopelessly negligent and never actually do much with my children other than cook.

BUTTERMILK BIRTHDAY CAKE

Of course, you can make birthday cake simply enough by following the Victoria sponge recipe on page 14, and I often do just that. But this is one of my most ecstatic discoveries: a cake that holds its shape whatever mold you want to cook it in, that can bear the weight of as much frosting as you want to drape it with, and is, after all that, the best-tasting birthday cake you will ever come across. Not, of course, that is has to be a birthday cake. My children like it on nonceremonial occasions baked in two cake pans and then filled and iced with the chocolate frosting on page 195.

The following quantities are enough to make a cake in one 9-inch square pan, 2 inches deep. So, for a birthday I would make two of these and sandwich them together with the butter icing. The quantities below will make a lot of icing, but if you're going to use various shades of food coloring—and is there a birthday cake that doesn't require it in some quantity?—then you'll need more than if you were using just one color.

It would be impossible for me to give exact quantities for all the sorts of molds you might want to fill (and you can buy or even rent molds at most specialty cake-decoration shops), but let me succumb to guilt-free stereotyping and give guidelines for one boy-cake and one girl-cake. If you're using a train-shaped mold or one of those conical affairs that when unmolded reveal themselves to be Barbie's lower half (all you have to do is plunge a bare-naked Barbie doll into the cake and cover her, pert plastic torso and all, in icing), double the quantities. You may end up with a bit left over, but not enough to make it worth cutting down on quantities. I should reckon on 45 minutes at 350°F for the train and probably 1 hour for Barbie.

for the cake:
1²/3 cups all-purpose flour
1¹/2 teaspoons baking powder
¹/2 teaspoon baking soda
¹/4 teaspoon salt
³/4 cup plus 2 tablespoons buttermilk
   (or ¹/3 cup plain yogurt mixed with
   ¹/2 cup low-fat milk)
1¹/2 teaspoons vanilla extract
¹/2 cup soft unsalted butter
³/4 cup sugar

3 large eggs
1 9-inch square cake pan or 2 8- or
   9-inch round cake pans, lined with
   parchment or wax paper and
   greased

for the icing:
1¹/3 cups butter
4¹/2 cups confectioners' sugar, sifted
1 teaspoon vanilla extract
2 tablespoons milk

Preheat oven to 350°F.

Sift flour, baking powder, baking soda, and salt together into a bowl and set aside. Pour the buttermilk (or yogurt and milk) into a measuring cup and stir in the vanilla. Cream the butter and sugar in a large bowl with an electric mixer at medium speed (or by hand, of course) until light and fluffy. Reduce the speed if using the mixer and add the eggs one at a time, beating for 30 seconds between additions. Add alternating increments of the flour mixture and the vanilla-buttermilk, blending well after each addition; this should take 3–5 minutes.

Pour into the prepared pan or pans, and bake for about 40 minutes (30 if using the layer cake pans) until the cake is beginning to shrink away from the sides and a cake tester comes out clean. Cool in the pan on a wire rack for 10 minutes before unmolding to let cool completely. If I'm using a mold with a lot of patterning—the train, for example—I leave it for 20 minutes in the pan before unmolding.

NOTES ON ICING

I find butter icing easiest to use to conjure up the train in all its Thomas-the-Tank-Engine glory. Black is difficult to get right, but as with all food-coloring activities, I urge you toward the pastes rather than the liquid colorings. The black paste, called "Liquorice," is still not emphatic enough for train black. Either go with fashionable charcoal, or add some melted chocolate to add intensity.

For these complicated shapes, squeezing a pastry bag and tip is easier than laying out fondant, but for Barbie I tend to change tack. I buy great wodges of made-up ready-to-roll icing in pink, pink, pink. There is something faintly disturbing about plunging a naked doll into a cone of sponge and then painting her pointy plastic bosoms with apricot glaze so that the sugar-icing bustier you're about to cut out for her will adhere. I mean, there are grown men who'd pay to do this. Tie up her hair with twisty wire, then just brush the Barbie-skirt cake and the doll herself with warmed-up apricot jam before wrapping and sticking the cut-out pieces onto her.

Buy all manner of sparkles and sweets, dip them briefly in cold water and stick on to create a sumptuously jeweled gown. You can buy jelly beans by weight in their separate colors; there are about 6 different pinks that come into their own here—and at girls' birthday parties generally.

BUTTER CUT-OUT COOKIES

It's not hard to make cookies that hold their shape well while cooking; it's not hard to make cookies that taste good and have a melting, buttery texture: what's hard is to find a cookie that does all of these things together. This one, by way of a wonderful American book, *The Family Baker*, does: so any time you want to play supermummy in the kitchen, here is where you start.

Like all doughs, it freezes well, so it makes sense—in a smug, domestic kind of a way—to wrap half of this in plastic wrap and stash it in the deep freeze until next needed. It's hard to specify exactly how much icing you'll need, but you might end up using more than specified below if you're using a lot of different colors. I always cut out the newly acquired age of the child on his or her birthday. My children couldn't contemplate a birthday party without them.

³/₄ cup soft unsalted butter

³/₄ cup sugar

2 large eggs

1 teaspoon vanilla extract

2²/₃ cups cake flour, plus more
    if needed

1 teaspoon baking powder

1 teaspoon salt

2 cups confectioners' sugar, sifted,
    and food coloring

cookie cutters

2 baking sheets, greased or lined with
    parchment or wax paper

Preheat the oven to 350°F.

Cream the butter and sugar together until pale and moving toward moussiness, then beat in the eggs and vanilla. In another bowl, combine the flour, baking powder, and salt. Add the dry ingredients to the butter and eggs, and mix gently but surely. If you think the finished mixture is too sticky to be rolled out, add more flour, but do so sparingly as too much will make the dough tough. Halve the dough, form into fat discs, wrap each half in plastic wrap, and rest in the refrigerator for at least 1 hour. Sprinkle a suitable surface with flour, place a disc of dough on it (not taking out the other half until you've finished with the first), and sprinkle a little more flour on top of that. Then roll it out to a thickness of about ¹/₄ inch. Cut into shapes, dipping the cutter into flour as you go, and place the cookies a little apart on the baking sheets.

Bake for 8–12 minutes, by which time they will be lightly golden around the edges. Cool on a rack and continue with the rest of the dough. When they're all fully cooled, you can get on with the icing. Put a couple of tablespoons of just-not-boiling water into a large bowl, add the sifted confectioners' sugar, and mix together, adding more water as you need to form a thick paste. Color as desired: let the artistic spirit within you speak, remembering with gratitude that children have very bad taste.

Makes 50–60.

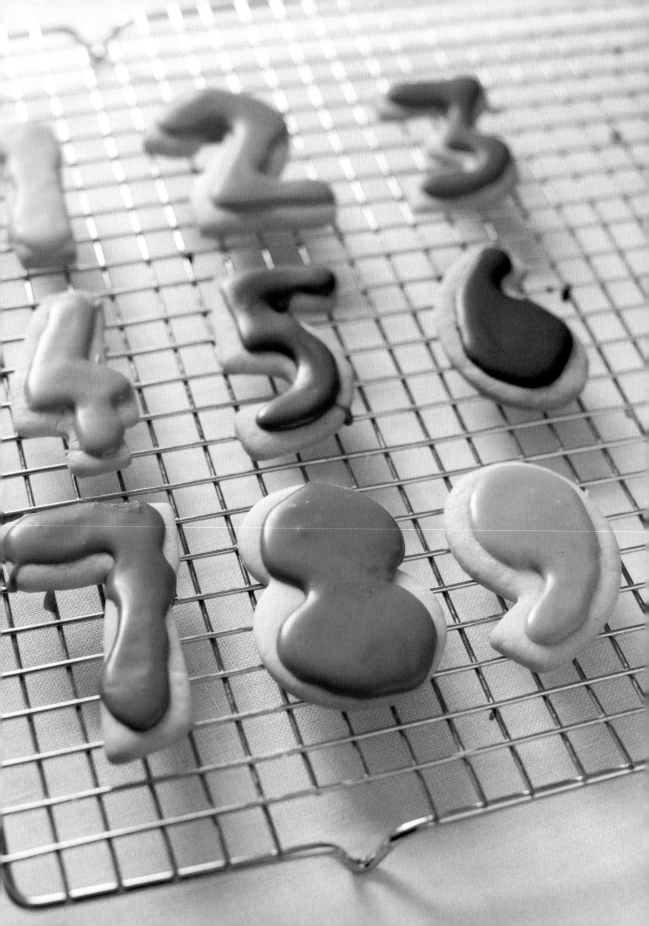

BIRTHDAY-PARTY AND CHILD-FRIENDLY FAIRY CAKES

Fairy cakes that you make for a child are no different from the cupcakes with which you adorn your dinner-party table (pages 39–42); that's partly the point. I would say one thing, though: you should always keep some margarine, or similar, in the fridge so that you can make up a quick batch whenever necessary. (OK, I'm not mad about margarine, either, but I promise you this is an accommodation that makes sense.) Butter just won't soften quickly; the margarine you can bung straight from fridge to processor, and thus you are never more than about 20 minutes away from a tray of fairy cakes.

TRADITIONAL FAIRY CAKES

To make 12 fairy cakes, use the recipe on page 40 and ice with pink icing, using 1⅓ cups confectioners' sugar (or instant royal icing), a tablespoonful or so of water, pink food coloring, and 12 natural-colored or shriekingly artificial glacé cherries.

CANDY FAIRY CAKES

All children love these and I find them curiously therapeutic to make. Choosing the patterns and sticking down the sugary cubes is entirely absorbing without being in any way demanding. Two packages of candies make for leftovers but artistic freedom. So important.

for the cakes:
as on page 40

for the icing:
1 cup plus 2 tablespoons or 9 ounces instant royal icing (and you may

need more if you're using lots of colors)
coloring of your choice
4 ounces assorted small candies

Use the regular recipe for cakes, cutting any risen bit of cake off so you've got a flat surface to adorn. Make up the icing, following package instructions. Dollop a tablespoonful or so into a bowl, add the coloring of your choice (I enjoy a bit of mix-and-match artistry here) and blend. Ice the cake in question, smooth with the back of an ordinary dessert spoon, and leave a few minutes before studding with various colored candy. If you decorate before the icing is beginning to dry, the candies will slide off.
    Makes 12.

HALLOWEEN CUPCAKES

for the cakes:

as on page 40

for the icing:

³/4 cup plus 2 tablespoons or
7 ounces instant royal icing
4 ounces bittersweet chocolate
black and red food coloring

This is more a guide to the icing than anything else, since the cake beneath is, again, the ordinary fairy cake.

For the cobwebs, you need to make up a batch of white icing using the instant royal icing, and another of black, which you make by melting the chocolate in the microwave (on a medium heat for a minute or two) or in a bain-marie (i.e., a bowl sitting over a pan of hot water, with the sides of the bowl not touching the water), and, when it's liquid, stirring in the black food coloring.

Cut any peaks off the cupcakes so you've got a flat surface to work on, and ice them in white. Now, just drizzling with a teaspoon, make a dark spiral on top. Then, using either a knife or (this is what I prefer) a bamboo skewer, draw lines from the center to the edge as though you were doing the rays of the sun or the spokes of a wheel. Don't worry too much about perfection. In the first place, you can always get your children to do them, and in the second, they look just as good when they're not perfect.

Another easy, spooky cupcake can be made by topping with white icing, then adding splodges of red icing to make a cartoon blood-stained effect.

Makes 12.

VARIATION

Obviously, too, you can use the technique to make Halloween cookies; just follow the recipe for butter cut-outs and use a spider's web cutter. You may want to make up some other thematically linked ones too—the cutters tend to come in packs of ghost, spider's web, witch, cat, and pumpkin. The last just need orange icing, but if you get some angelica and cut out stalks for them, it will greatly enhance the finished effect. For the cats, make up some glacé icing, say ½ cup, of sifted confectioners' sugar and a few drops of boiling water, then stir in melted dark chocolate, as above, adding some black food-coloring paste once the chocolate and icing are combined. Place two silver balls on each cat's face for eyes.

BUTTERFLY CAKES

for the cakes:

**as on page 40, plus 1 heaped
teaspoon baking powder added
to the flour**

for the icing:

scant ¹/₂ cup very soft unsalted butter
¹/₂ cup confectioners' sugar, sifted
food coloring if wanted

Follow the instructions and quantities for normal fairy cakes, only add a heaped teaspoon of baking powder on top of the self-rising flour so that you end up with appropriately peaked cakelets.

Cut the tops off with a small sharp knife and set aside, leaving the fairy cakes perfectly level. While they're cooling on a wire rack, make up the butter icing. Beat the butter in a bowl and add the confectioners' sugar gradually, until you have incorporated all of it into the butter. This is not an exact science; your icing might be the right consistency before you have added all the sugar or you might want more butter at the end. Put a splodge of butter icing onto the middle of each cake, and then cut the top in half vertically before placing it back on top of the cake upside-down. With a little adjustment they should now resemble a butterfly's wings.

Makes 12.

CORNFLAKE CRISPIES

Do you really want to have a child's birthday party without these?

4 ounces milk chocolate
2 tablespoons unsalted butter
1 teaspoon light corn syrup

¹/₄ cup cornflakes
28 petit-four paper cups

Melt the chocolate and butter—and see my introduction to the chocolate chapter for various methods—and add the syrup. Coat the cornflakes well with the chocolate mixture—the easiest way is just to fold them into the semi-liquid mix—and fill the petit-four paper cups. Put the paper cups on baking sheets and leave them to set in the refrigerator.

Makes 28.

SNICKERS AND PEANUT BUTTER MUFFINS

These muffins have a special charm: I think the ingredients speak for themselves. But what I should perhaps add is that they taste seriously good to adults too.

1²/3 cups all-purpose flour

6 tablespoons sugar

1¹/2 tablespoons baking powder

pinch of salt

6 tablespoons chunky peanut butter

¹/4 cup unsalted butter, melted

1 large egg, beaten

3/4 cup milk

3¹/2 full-size (2.07 ounces) Snickers
   bars, chopped

12-cup muffin pan with paper
   baking cups

Preheat the oven to 400°F.

Stir together the flour, sugar, baking powder, and salt. Add the peanut butter and mix until you have a bowl of coarse crumbs. Add the melted butter and egg to the milk, and then stir this gently into the bowl. Mix in the Snickers pieces and dollop into the muffin cups.

Cook for 20–25 minutes, when the tops should be risen, golden, and firm to the (light) touch. Sit the pan on a wire rack for 5–10 minutes before taking out each muffin in its paper cup and leaving them on the wire rack to cool. If you can.

Makes 12.

BANANA MUFFINS

Any sort of muffin is easy and quick for a child to make: the whole point is that the mixture must not be too vehemently or smoothly combined. The bonus here is that small children seem to have an inordinate passion for mashing bananas. In other words, a fairly calm two-year-old can feel he or she is making these almost unaided. You will have to melt the butter and so on yourself, but—although I am perhaps irresponsibly insouciant about infantile involvement here—on the whole, you can take a serenely noninterventionist approach to the whole exercise.

All the ingredients can be bought at any unglamorously stocked corner shop, as can the ingredients for the recipe below. It doesn't matter whether you use mini-muffin pans or full-size ones: you will get about 24 of the former, 10 of the latter. For what it's worth, the tiny ones taste better when eaten still warm; the larger ones when cold. Just remember to buy the right-sized paper baking cups for whichever pans you've got.

snickers and peanut-butter muffins

2 tablespoons unsalted butter

¹/₄ (two oozingly, bulgingly heaping
   tablespoons) clear honey

¹/₂ teaspoon vanilla extract

2 large, very ripe bananas

1 cup all-purpose flour

1 heaping teaspoon baking powder

¹/₂ teaspoon baking soda

¹/₂ teaspoon cinnamon

pinch of salt

mini-muffin pans and paper baking
   cups, or 12-cup muffin pan lined
   with 10 paper baking cups

Preheat the oven to 375°F.

Put the butter, honey, and vanilla extract in a pan on a low heat to melt, then remove and set aside for a few minutes.

Mash the bananas and, in another bowl, measure out the flour, baking powder, baking soda, cinnamon, and salt. Mix the melted-butter mixture with the bananas and then mix that into the dry ingredients. Don't overmix: just stir a couple of times; you will have a not terribly attractive lumpy sludge, but don't worry about it.

Put the paper cups in the muffin trays and fill them about two-thirds full of mixture. Put in the oven and cook for about 25 minutes. Leave in the pans for 5 minutes, then remove the muffins in their cups to a wire rack for another 5–10 or till cool.

Makes 24 mini-muffins, 10 full-size muffins.

JAM-DOUGHNUT MUFFINS

I have to try and steer myself away from making these, as I know that every time I suggest them, simperingly pretending that I have only the pleasure of my kids at heart, it's because I am dying to eat them, and then do. There is something about the melted butter and sugar that they're turned in while still warm that makes them irresistible. Of course, these are much easier than actual doughnuts, and the children can do most of the work themselves. All you need to do is help to eat them.

¹/₂ cup milk

scant 7 tablespoons corn or other
   vegetable oil, plus more for
   greasing

1 large egg

¹/₂ teaspoon vanilla extract

1¹/₃ cups self-rising cake flour

¹/₃ cup superfine sugar

12 teaspoons strawberry jam

scant ¹/₂ cup unsalted butter

¹/₂ cup granulated sugar

1 incredibly well-greased or nonstick
   12-cup mini-muffin pan

Preheat the oven to 375°F.

With a fork, beat together the milk, oil, egg, and vanilla extract. Stir this into the flour and ⅓ cup sugar to combine (just): the lumps don't matter and if you overbeat the muffins will be tough. Spoon the mixture into each muffin cup so that it's just under a third full. Then with a teaspoon add a dollop of strawberry jam—about the size of a fat lima bean—then top with more muffin mix so that the cases are just about full.

Put them in the preheated oven and cook for about 20 minutes or until the tops feel springy and resistant and the muffins have puffed up into little toadstools.

Meanwhile, melt the butter slowly in a thick-bottomed pan, and lay the remaining sugar out in a wide, shallow bowl. As soon as the muffins are ready, remove them from their cups, dip them in the butter, and roll them in the sugar. Eat warm.

Makes 12.

PEANUT BUTTER AND JAM JEWELS

This is really just a cookie evocation of the American child's favorite combination, peanut butter and jelly. I am not convinced about this in a sandwich, but here, in a soft, buttery cookie, the taste is wonderful. And they look beautiful, like the sort of jewels worn by fairy-tale princesses.

½ cup soft unsalted butter

½ cup sugar

½ cup plus 1 tablespoon soft light brown sugar

¾ cup plus 2 tablespoons creamy peanut butter

2 large eggs

1 teaspoon vanilla extract

2 cups all-purpose flour

½ teaspoon baking powder

¼ teaspoon salt

enough strawberry jam for 50 large spoonfuls

2–3 baking sheets

Preheat the oven to 350°F.

Cream together the butter and sugars, and add the peanut butter, beating to combine, then the eggs and vanilla. Mix in the flour, baking powder, and salt to make a damp, sticky dough, and put it in the refrigerator to firm up for at least 1 hour, the bowl covered with plastic wrap.

Pinch off small amounts of dough, about as much as would make a scant table-spoonful, and roll between the palms of your hands into small balls, 1 to 1½ inches in diameter and place on a baking sheet, flattening slightly with your hand. Make a thumbprint in each cookie, being quite firm or the indent will disappear during baking.

When the baking sheets are full, put into the oven and bake for 10–15 minutes, by which time the cookies should be just cooked. It doesn't matter if they're a bit soft, as they'll firm up on cooling, but just check the underside of one to make sure they're no longer actually doughy.

As soon as you've taken the cookies out of the oven, spoon a small amount of jam (about a teaspoonful) into each indent to make a jewel. Transfer them to a wire rack to cool, by which time the jam will have melted slightly, and will be sitting, bulging shinily, a red gem in the middle of its peanut-butter setting. The jam seems to harden slightly, not enough to make it unpleasant but enough to make it stay put, so you can pack these up, on top of each other, in pans or Tupperwares, without their coming to any harm.

Makes about 50.

PEANUT BUTTER SQUARES

If you've ever eaten Reese's Peanut Butter Cups, you'll recognize these homespun versions of them. And if you discount melting the chocolate (which in any case the microwave can do) there is no cooking involved. You may think that seeing how the dough is made—just peanut butter, butter, and sugar—might put you off eating them. Sadly not.

for the base:
scant ¼ cup dark brown sugar
1⅓ cups confectioners' sugar
scant ¼ cup unsalted butter
¾ cup plus 2 tablespoons creamy
  peanut butter

for the topping:
7 ounces milk chocolate
4 ounces bittersweet chocolate
1 tablespoon unsalted butter
1 9-inch square pan, greased

Stir all the ingredients for the base together until smooth. I use the paddle attachment to my mixer which my children love operating, but a bowl and a wooden spoon will do the job just as well. You will find, either way, that some of the dark brown sugar stays in rubbly, though very small, lumps, but don't worry about that. Press the sandy mixture into the brownie pan and make the surface as even as possible.

To make the topping, melt the chocolates and butter together (in a microwave for ease, for a minute or two on medium) and spread on the base. Put the pan in the refrigerator to set. When the chocolate has hardened, cut into small squares—because, more-ish as it undeniably is, it is also very rich.

Makes approximately 48.

ROCKY ROAD

Ever since I read that brazil nuts are inordinately good for you, containing essential selenium, and that you should probably have three a day, I have chosen to regard these as health food. What they really are are clumps of brazil nuts and mini-marshmallows bound together by a mantle of melted chocolate. You can alter the ratio of dark to milk chocolate as you wish, but, as ever, I really do think it's worth using the best chocolate that you can.

7 ounces milk chocolate

1 ounce bittersweet chocolate

3 ounces brazil nuts

⅓ cup mini-marshmallows

1 baking sheet, lined with wax paper or oiled foil

Melt the chocolates either in the microwave or using a bowl over a pan of barely simmering water. Roughly chop the brazil nuts, and mix into the chocolate with the mini-marshmallows.

Drop heaping teaspoons onto a lined baking sheet, and leave to cool in a cold place, though not the refrigerator if at all possible; it will take some of the gleam from the chocolate.

Makes 24.

VARIATION
You could chop these up and stir into slightly softened vanilla or chocolate ice cream.

TOFFEE APPLES

However much this recipe is geared toward children it's not one you can do with them. I burned myself twice doing this: not badly, but I wouldn't have wanted a child anywhere near.

Of course, you can use toffee-apple sticks, specifically made and sold for the purpose, but twigs straight from the tree look so wonderful. If you haven't got a garden, just take a strong pair of scissors out with you one day.

You could use this amount of toffee for several more apples, if you need them.

10 apples, preferably organic
10 strong but slender twigs or sticks
4¹/₂ cups sugar
1¹/₃ cups water
1 tablespoon vinegar

3/4 cup unsalted butter
2 tablespoons light corn syrup
1 baking sheet, lined with oiled foil

If you're not using organic apples, which are unwaxed, wash your apples: the wax stops the toffee from adhering properly. Dry them, then remove the stalks and impale them, where the stalks have been, with the twigs or sticks.

Put the sugar and water into a large, heavy-bottomed pan and heat. When the sugar's dissolved, add the vinegar, butter, and syrup. Boil rapidly for approximately 45 minutes, though start testing after 30. To do this, fill a large bowl with ice water and drop a small amount of the toffee into the bowl: if it is ready it should harden on contact. Keep the water close because you'll need it for the apples later.

Dip each apple in the toffee, rotating on its stick. Then hold it over the pot of toffee (keeping the heat on but now turned down to low) and twirl it about 10 times so that the toffee forms a good shell around the apple. Now plunge the toffee apple into the iced water, and twirl, submerged, another 10 times. Remove to the lined baking sheet and continue with remaining apples.

Makes 10.

DREAM BARS

These are one of those chewy, fudgy, nutty, crisp bar cookies that the Americans are so good at. The base is a buttery, crumbly shortbread you press into the pan and on top is a sticky mixture of nuts and coconut bound by a tender, toffeelike chewy gunge. The name suits them well.

You can use whatever chopped nuts you prefer; I just like the brazils and cashews for their rainforest-crunch qualities.

for the base:

3/4 cup plus 2 tablespoons unsalted butter, very soft

4 tablespoons light brown sugar

4 tablespoons sugar

1 1/2 teaspoons vanilla extract

1 2/3 cups all-purpose flour

pinch of salt

for the topping:

3 large eggs

1 1/2 teaspoons vanilla extract

1/2 cup plus 1 tablespoon brown sugar

3 tablespoons self-rising cake flour

pinch of salt

1/2 teaspoon baking powder

scant 1/2 cup shredded coconut

1/3 cup or 3 ounces brazil nuts, roughly chopped

3 ounces raw, unsalted cashews

1 9-inch square pan, greased and lined with parchment or wax paper

Preheat the oven to 350°F.

Cream the butter and sugars together and, when light and soft, add the vanilla, flour, and salt, mixing well to combine. Tip this into the prepared pan and press down and in with your fingers. Put in the oven and bake for 10 minutes, then remove and let cool a little before spreading the topping on it.

To make this, beat the eggs together with the vanilla and then, still beating, add the sugar. Stir the flour, salt, and baking powder together, and fold into the sugar-egg mixture. Now fold in the coconut and nuts and spread this on top of the part-baked shortbread base.

Put the pan back in the oven for 30 minutes, then remove and let cool, still in the pan, on a wire rack. Cut into squares or bars as you like.

Makes 10–12.

FUDGE

I think fudge was one of the first sweet things I made as a child (we never went in for cakes much as a family) and I still love it. I like chocolate fudge, too, but real fudge for me is this sort—buttery, vanilla-flavored, and teeth-achingly sweet.

Don't get alarmed by mention of sugar thermometers and specific temperatures. Just keep a bowl of ice water next to the stove, periodically drop a little bit of fudge into it, and if it keeps its shape it's ready. That simple. I do occasionally faff around with a sugar thermometer, since I happen to own one, but I can't say I get a tremendous amount of joy out of it. Still, there are those who prefer to tackle these things scientifically, so I give precise desirable temperatures too.

1²/3 cups sugar
scant ¹/4 cup unsalted butter
¹/3 cup plus 1 tablespoon evaporated milk

1 teaspoon vanilla extract
8 x 6 inch or similar pan or 6 x 5-inch or similar foil pan buttered

Put the sugar, butter, and evaporated milk into a heavy-bottomed saucepan and bring to the boil. Boil this mixture gently, stirring occasionally to prevent it sticking. Carry on until a thermometer reaches 225°F, or the mixture's holding its shape in the water. This will take between 5 and 10 minutes.

Take the pan off the heat, beat in the vanilla, and continue beating until the fudge becomes thick and creamy—grainy almost—and then pour the mixture into your buttered pan and allow to cool.

Cut the fudge into little squares, or however you like.

Makes 25–30 squares.

CINDER TOFFEE

This is just a more poetic and old-fashioned name for honeycomb—"cinder" presumably referring to the splintered texture made by the whoosh of air introduced by the baking soda.

3/4 cup sugar
4 tablespoons light corn syrup

1 tablespoon baking soda
8-inch square pan, well-greased

Grease the 8-inch square pan generously with butter.

Off the heat, mix the sugar and syrup in a heavy-bottomed saucepan, then put over a medium to low heat and simmer for 3–4 minutes (this is based on using an 8-inch diameter saucepan). The mixture is ready to come off the heat when it's a thick bubbling mass, the color of rusty caramel—no darker.

Take off the heat and quickly whisk in the baking soda and watch the caramel foam up in a sudsy and opaque golden cloud like something out of a sci-fi film. Pour into the waiting pan and leave to set. This takes a few hours. Then you can try and cut it, but the best way of treating this is to bash it into splintered pieces.

VARIATION

You can slice this the best way you can, not worrying too much about uniformity and neatness, and dip into melted chocolate before letting dry on oiled foil to make your own Crunchies.

Or, to make your own hokey-pokey ice cream, fold splinters of this, unchocolated, into homemade or good store-bought vanilla ice cream.

EASTER NESTS

Yes, these are cute; yes, they are kitsch, but I love them all the same. Can't say I'm absolutely mad about eating them, but luckily my children are.

7 ounces milk chocolate

1 ounce bittersweet chocolate

2 tablespoons unsalted butter

4 ounces (about ½ cup) shredded wheat

about 25 multicolored sugar-coated little chocolate eggs

1 baking sheet, lined with oiled foil

Break up the chocolate into small pieces and put it in a glass bowl with the butter. Melt on a medium heat in the microwave for about 2 minutes—I give it a minute, then look to see how much more it might need—or over water. When it's melted, give it a stir, then leave it to one side for a moment or two. You need it to be a bit cooler or it might burn the children's hands. Crumble the shredded wheat into another bowl.

Now mix the contents of the two bowls and remove a small handful of messy mixture to the lined baking tray and form into a round nest shape, about 3 inches in diameter. Don't worry if you feel it won't stick together: it will as it cools. Leave in a cool place (though not the refrigerator) until set, then remove to a plate or a wooden board and fill the center with the eggs (about 5 per nest).

Makes 5.

MERINGUES (AND MERINGUE NESTS)

I've never met a child who didn't like meringues, and they're child's play to make, too. The best way of getting meringue-making fixed into your (or your child's) head is to remember that for each egg white you need 3 tablespoons sugar, and that this in turn will make you around 10 2-inch-diameter meringues. For this reason, I give method only:

Preheat the oven to 250°F.

Whisk the egg white(s) till stiff, but not dry; peaks should be firm and hold their shape. Resume whisking, adding the sugar tablespoon by sprinkled tablespoon till all's incorporated and you have a gleaming, satiny mass. You can pipe meringues onto lined (but not greased) baking trays, but I mound dessertspoonfuls onto the trays and then use the back of the spoon, wiggling it around so that I have neat-nippled, small-bosomed shapes. To make nests, simply use the back of the spoon to make a nest shape. Bake for 60–70 minutes, then leave in the switched-off oven for 20 minutes before removing to cool.

SOOT'S FLAPJACKS

Flapjacks as made in England are such old-fashioned, comforting things, the sort of food you should make from a mother's recipe—and nothing like American-style griddle cakes. My mother, however, didn't go in for this sort of cooking. Hettie, who has been a reassuring and calming spirit throughout our work on this book, luckily had a mother, Soot, who did. This is the recipe we took out of the handwritten book Hettie inherited from her.

It's not orthodox, but following the advice of a friend who's eaten them like that in Alderney, one of the Channel Islands off England's coast, I add a scant tablespoonful of sesame seeds, sprinkled on them before baking.

2 cups rolled oats
1/3 cup soft brown sugar
1 1/3 cups unsalted butter

1/4 cup light corn syrup
sesame seeds, optional
9-inch square pan, buttered

Preheat the oven to 375°F. Mix the oats with the sugar, then melt the butter with the syrup very gently over a low heat, and stir in the oats and sugar. Press the mixture into the pan, sprinkle over sesame seeds if using, and cook for 25 minutes. While they're still warm, about 10 minutes out of the oven, cut the flapjacks into 9 squares, and then cut each of the squares into triangles.

Makes 18.

COCA-COLA CAKE

I really don't plan to become the Coca-Cola cooking queen of Europe, but I came across several versions of this cake in various American books and naturally had to try it. It's really just a divinely tender-crumbed chocolate cake—and there's nothing wrong with that. And however odd you might think it, everyone loves it when I make it.

for the cake:
1 1/3 cups all-purpose flour
3/4 cup plus 1 tablespoon sugar
1/2 teaspoon baking soda
1/4 teaspoon salt
1 large egg

1/2 cup buttermilk (or 2 tablespoons
  plain yogurt mixed with 1/3 cup
  plus 1 tablespoon low-fat milk)
1 teaspoon vanilla extract
1/2 cup unsalted butter
2 tablespoons cocoa powder

³/₄ cup Coca-Cola

8- or 9-inch springform pan lined with foil to prevent the batter leaking, then greased

for the icing:

1¹/₂ cups confectioner's sugar

2 tablespoons butter

3 tablespoons Coca-Cola

1 tablespoon cocoa powder

¹/₂ teaspoon vanilla extract

Preheat the oven to 350°F and put in a baking sheet at the same time.

In a large bowl, combine the flour, sugar, baking soda, and salt. Beat the egg, buttermilk (or yogurt and milk), and vanilla in a measuring cup. In a heavy-bottomed saucepan, melt the butter, cocoa, and Coca-Cola, heating gently. Pour into the dry ingredients, stir well with a wooden spoon, and then add the liquid ingredients, beating until everything is well blended.

Pour into the prepared pan and bake on the warm sheet for 40 minutes or until a cake tester comes out clean.

Leave to stand for 15 minutes in the pan before unmolding. Then unclip, unwrap, and turn out on a wire rack, making sure you've got a sheet of newspaper or something underneath the rack to catch any icing that drips through.

Sift the confectioners' sugar and set aside for the moment. In a heavy-bottomed saucepan, combine the butter, Coca-Cola, and cocoa and stir over a low heat until the butter has melted. Remove from the heat, add the vanilla, and spoon in the sifted sugar, beating as you do so, until you've got a good, spreadable, but still runny, icing.

Pour this icing over the cake, while the cake is still warm, and leave till cool before transferring to the plate on which you're serving it.

Serves 8–10.

VARIATIONS

Fold 2 ounces chopped walnuts into the cake batter just before pouring it into the pan, and then press a few, or as many as you want, walnut halves on top of the iced cake.

Or make Coca-Cola cupcakes by pouring this batter into a 12-cup muffin pan lined with paper baking cups. Pour the icing over just after you've taken them out of the oven. Instead of studding each with a walnut half, you could buy those wine-gummy candies which look like miniature bottles of Coke and press one in on top of each cupcake once the icing's cooled a little but before it has set hard.

Makes 12.

MINT DOMINOES

These are simply small, flat bricks of peppermint cream dipped in dark chocolate to resemble dominoes. I'm not sure I'd want to bring these out with the coffee after dinner—though you never know—but for a childish culinary conceit, they're perfect. Besides, the contrast between bitter chocolate and sinus-clearing mint is a good one. Even though these are for children, I still use the darkest, blackest, meanest chocolate I can find.

3 1/3 cups confectioners' sugar
2 egg whites, beaten till frothy

1/2 teaspoon peppermint extract
4 ounces bittersweet chocolate, melted

Sift the confectioners' sugar into a bowl and add enough beaten egg white to form a stiff dough. Add a few drops of peppermint extract to taste. Knead the paste lightly, and then roll out to about ¼ inch thickness on a work surface lightly dusted with confectioner's sugar. Cut into domino-sized rectangles, and then leave them to dry for a day.

Paint half of each domino with the melted chocolate, drop little dots of chocolate on the white halves, using a wooden skewer, and arrange the dominoes on a piece of oiled foil to dry.

Makes about 22.

VARIATION

To make traditional peppermint creams, after rolling out the kneaded paste cut into 1-inch rounds using a plain cutter. Leave them to dry as before, and dip them entirely in the chocolate.

Makes about 25.

COOKING FOR THE SCHOOL FAIR

There comes a certain time in your life when you are suddenly required to be a provider of cakes, cookies, and assorted sweetmeats for whatever fund-raising event or fair your children's school goes in for; and there will be many. Of course, you don't need to make anything—many parents bring along bought stuff—but it's strange how one batch of homemade cupcakes can assuage a term's guilt at being late for parents' night.

MINI-CHEESECAKES

These are very easy to make, but I do have to say that lining the mini-muffin pans with the graham cracker crust can get a little tedious. This is where your darling children come in—their little fingers are made for the job.

scant 1/2 cup unsalted butter	1 large egg
1 cup plus 2 tablespoons or 9 ounces graham crackers	2 tablespoons sour cream
	1/2 teaspoon vanilla extract
7 ounces cream cheese	2 teaspoons lemon juice
2 tablespoons sugar	2 12-cup mini-muffin pans

Preheat the oven to 375°F.

Melt the butter in a pan. Put the graham crackers, broken up roughly, in the processor, and blitz. Still processing, add the melted butter down the funnel and turn this wet sand onto a plate or into a bowl. Put a heaped teaspoonful of the biscuit base into each mini-muffin cup, press it around the edges and up the sides of the cup with your fingers, and let it harden in the refrigerator.

Beat the cream cheese until it's smooth, and then add the sugar. (You can do all this in the washed-out processor bowl.) Add the egg, beating well, and then the sour cream, vanilla, and lemon juice, combining everything until it's smooth and creamy.

Put the cream-cheese mixture into a measuring cup and pour some into each mini-muffin cup, leaving the top of the crust still visible. Put in the oven and cook for about 10 minutes, by which time the cheese mixture should have set.

Let them cool and then put them in the refrigerator for at least 3 hours before gently easing them out of the pans. Or, if you're like me and lose patience, after some cautious prising with a rubber spatula turn the pans upside-down and rap firmly, and the little cheesecakes fall out unharmed.

Makes 24.

FRESH GINGERBREAD WITH LEMON ICING

Having run the cake table at my daughter's school last year, I can say that there are two types of optimum bake sale fare: small, individual pieces that look cute and fetch high unit-prices and sheet cakes that can be made without effort or dexterity and sliced up easily. This recipe fits the latter category and has the added virtue of appealing to parents and grandparents who feel that something from the sale should be gratifyingly old-fashioned. The fresh ginger is a modern touch, admittedly, but I always keep some in the fridge and wanted to try it in a less contemporary, pan-Asian way one day (it worked). The lemon icing may not be conventional either, but there is another starkly practical reason for it: brown things—if they're not gooily chocolate—don't sell so well; and the lemon spruceness of the topping is perfect with the musky sweetness beneath it.

for the gingerbread:

½ cup plus 2 tablespoons unsalted butter

½ cup plus 2 tablespoons brown sugar

¾ cup plus 1 tablespoon light corn syrup

¾ cup plus 1 tablespoon molasses

2 teaspoons fresh ginger, finely grated

1 teaspoon ground cinnamon

1 cup plus 2 tablespoons milk

2 large eggs, beaten to mix

1 teaspoon baking soda, dissolved in 2 tablespoons warm water

2 cups all-purpose flour

roasting pan, approximately 12 x 8 x 2 inches, greased and lined with foil or parchment paper

for the icing:

1 tablespoon lemon juice

½ cup plus 2 tablespoons confectioners' sugar, sifted

1 tablespoon warm water

Preheat the oven to 325°F.

In a saucepan, melt the butter along with the sugar, syrup, molasses, ginger, and cinnamon. Off the heat, add the milk, eggs, and baking soda in its water.

Measure the flour out into a bowl and pour in the liquid ingredients, beating until well mixed (it will be a very liquid batter). Pour it into the pan and bake for ¾–1 hour until risen and firm. Be careful not to overcook it, as it is nicer a little stickier, and anyway will carry on cooking as it cools.

And when it is cool, get on with the icing. Whisk the lemon juice into the confectioners' sugar first, then gradually add the water. You want a good, thick icing, so go cautiously and be prepared not to add all the water. Spread over the cooled gingerbread with a palette knife, and leave to set before cutting.

Makes 20 squares.

MINI-PAVLOVAS

Because of the fruit—and the cream, for that matter—these are not cheap to make, but I always have a stash of egg whites in my freezer so I reckon I'm halfway there before I start. And actually, you can probably sell them for quite a lot at a bake sale. You need to make sure that you've got a supply of paper plates and napkins, though, as they're not small enough to eat in one neat mouthful.

What I do is take with me a large Tupperware container of meringues, another air-tight bowl of the whipped cream, and in another, or still in their baskets, the berries. I also bring with me my tea strainer, a teaspoon, a package of confectioners' sugar, paper plates, and little plastic forks. When I arrive at the sale, I set out the meringue bases, dollop the cream on top, arrange the fruit, and dust with sugar, being ready to top up from time to time as the sugar dissolves into the berries. It's a job, but worth it: they look so pretty people can't stop themselves spending whatever extortionate price you've put on them.

8 large egg whites	**3 cups plus 2 tablespoons heavy**
pinch of salt	**cream, duly whipped**
1¹/2 cups sugar	**1¹/2 pints blackberries**
4 teaspoons cornstarch	**1¹/2 pints raspberries**
1 scant teaspoon vanilla extract	**confectioners' sugar for dusting**
2 teaspoons white wine vinegar	**3 baking sheets, lined with parchment**
	tea strainer or fine-mesh sieve

Preheat the oven to 350°F.

Whisk the egg whites with the salt until they're holding firm peaks but are not stiff. Gently add in the sugar, spoonful after spoonful, still beating, until you've got a bowl full of gleaming, satiny, snowy meringue. Sprinkle the cornstarch, a few drops of vanilla, and the vinegar on top and fold in to combine.

Draw 6 circles of approximately 4 inches on each of the parchment-lined baking sheets. Spoon the meringue onto the baking parchment into the delineated circles, and spread and smooth to fill. You want to make the meringue slightly higher at the rims, or just use the back of the spoon to make an indentation in the center to hold the cream and fruit later. Put into the oven, turn it down to 300°F, and bake for 30 minutes. Turn the oven off and leave them in for another 30 minutes, then take out of the oven to cool. I just transfer them, on their baking parchment, to wire racks. When you want to assemble the pavlovas, dollop cream into the indentation, and smooth it with the back of a spoon, leaving the odd peak. Place, one by one, a few blackberries and a few raspberries so that they look well filled but not crammed. Dust with confectioners' sugar.

Makes 18.

ROXANNE'S MILLIONAIRE'S SHORTBREAD

This is the recipe, given to me by a fellow mother at my daughter's school, that introduced me to the notion of melting chocolate in the microwave. I am now a complete convert: it is truly the best way to do it. And you make the caramel in the microwave, too, so what would normally take a good couple of hours takes only a few minutes. Another revelation. It's not that I had never used a microwave before, but I hadn't ever realized it could do things better as opposed to just faster.

You can make this a good week in advance if you like. Keep the shortbread in a cold place or in an airtight pan, and it'll be fine. Or you can even freeze it for up to 6 months. If frozen, the squares should be allowed to defrost for 3–4 hours at room temperature.

1 1/2 cups all-purpose flour

1/4 cup sugar

1 2/3 cups unsalted butter

14-ounce can sweetened condensed milk

4 tablespoons light corn syrup

12 ounces bittersweet chocolate

1 9-inch square pan or similar, greased and the bottom lined with parchment or wax paper

Preheat the oven to 325°F.

Put the flour and sugar into a bowl and rub in 12 tablespoons of the butter, clumping the dough together to form a ball. Press this sandy shortbread mixture into the pan and smooth it with either your hands or a spatula. Prick it with a fork and cook for 5 minutes, then lower the oven to 300°F, and cook for a further 30–40 minutes until it is pale golden and no longer doughy. Let it cool in the pan.

Melt the remaining butter in the microwave (in a large microwavable bowl) for 2–3 minutes, then add the condensed milk and syrup. Whisk the mixture well until the butter is thoroughly incorporated. Heat for 6–7 minutes until it is boiling, stirring thoroughly every minute. As a microwave novice, I found this bit difficult and had to watch that I didn't burn the toffee mixture (I did once), which is why I caution you to check and stir every minute. It's ready when it's thickened and turned a light golden brown. Pour this molten toffee evenly over the cooled shortbread and leave it to set.

Break the chocolate into pieces and melt it in a bowl in the microwave. Pour and spread it over the fudge mixture (the less you touch it, the shinier it will be) and leave it to cool. Once set, cut the caramel shortbread into pieces. The squares can be stored in the fridge to keep them firm, though if it's winter that shouldn't be necessary.

Makes about 24.

MINI KEY LIME PIES

The base for these is the same as for the cheesecakes, and the filling is taken from one of the lime pies from pages 103–104. I have sometimes dyed these green with just a little food coloring, otherwise you can't quite tell the difference between these and the mini-cheesecakes. But, for a chic alternative (if you'd rather not use the food coloring) just grate some lime zest over the top once they're cooked and cooled.

scant ¹/₂ cup unsalted butter
1 cup plus 2 tablespoons or 9 ounces graham crackers
2 large eggs, separated
7-ounce can sweetened condensed milk

zest and juice of 2 limes
pinch of salt
2 12-cup mini-muffin pans

Preheat the oven to 325°F.

Make the cracker base as for the cheesecakes, leaving the pans in the refrigerator as above.

Beat the egg yolks until thick—I use an electric mixer for this—then add, still beating, the condensed milk and lime juice. If you're making these the day before they're needed, keep the lime zest in an airtight bag, or just bag up the lime-halves and zest them the next day.

In a separate bowl, whisk the egg whites with the salt until soft peaks form and gently fold into the yolk mixture. Using a dessert spoon (and a teaspoon for scraping), fill the cracker-crusted mini-muffin pans. Transfer to the oven and cook for 10 minutes. Remove, let cool in the pans, then refrigerate for a day.

Turn out the mini key lime pies following the advice for the cheesecakes. Using very fine grater, dust with the zest of the limes.

Makes 24.

MINI LIME-SYRUP SPONGES

This is really just the miniaturization of the lemon-syrup sponge on page 13. You could do them in lemon here, too, or use a mixture of ordinary orange juice and lime juice to evoke the wonderful acerbity of Seville oranges. (Or indeed use those when in season.) It doesn't matter what the citrus is: there is just something about these small-scale, perfectly formed loaves that makes them particularly appealing.

1/2 cup unsalted butter, softened

1/2 cup plus 1 tablespoon sugar

2 large eggs

zest of 1 lime

1 cup plus 2 tablespoons self-rising cake flour

pinch of salt

4 tablespoons milk

8-cup mini-loaf pan, buttered very well

for the syrup:

4 tablespoons lime juice (of 1–2 limes), plus zest for decoration

1/2 cup confectioners' sugar

Preheat the oven to 350°F.

Cream together the butter and sugar, and add the eggs and lime zest, beating them in well. Add the flour and salt, folding in gently, and then the milk. Spoon into the mini-loaf pan, and cook for 25 minutes.

While the cakes are cooking, prepare the syrup by putting the lime juice and sugar into a small saucepan and heating gently so that the sugar dissolves.

As soon as the mini-sponges are ready, take them out of the oven and prick them with a cake-tester all over. Pour over the syrup evenly. Try to let the middle absorb the liquid as well as the sides, then leave it to soak up the rest. Don't try to take the cakes out of the pan until they have cooled slightly and the syrup looks like it has been absorbed, but be aware that if you leave these to cool completely they might be very difficult to get out of the pan.

So, after an hour or two, turn them out onto a rack and grate some lime zest over them before serving (or selling).

Makes 8.

CHRISTMAS

CHRISTMAS

I think it is probably the case that even people who never, ever bake might consider doing so at Christmas. This doesn't mean I'm going to load you down with homework, presenting this chapter as a kind of holiday-season project; the real point is that at Christmas you might feel you've got more time to play around with some of these recipes (or indeed any of the recipes in this book).

I must emphasize that, having never been someone to bake her own Christmas cake or make her own Christmas pudding, it is deeply satisfying when you do. This doesn't mean it has to become a yearly obligation, a source of pressure rather than pleasure. One of the best things about being adult is that you can decide which rituals and ceremonies you want to adopt to give shape to your life and which you want to lose because they just constrain you. True, I think it takes more determination to shuck off the habits that you've inherited but don't actually want at Christmastime; it's hard not to feel that the way you always did it when you were a child is the way it should be done. So, I've consciously enjoyed setting my own pattern here, choosing what I want to be part of my family's Christmas.

You surely know by now that, as ever, what follows is suggestion, not instruction.

CHRISTMAS CAKE

I think you do need to have a blueprint for a basic fruitcake that you can make up in whatever size you need. I've already given you recipes from Hettie Potter, who's worked with me on this book; she gave me this, too, from her brother-in-law's mother, Hazel, in New Zealand. The only change I make is to ignore the suggestion of brandy or sherry in favor of Marsala. You do entirely as you wish.

As with all rich fruitcakes, this one should be made at least 3–4 weeks before you plan to eat it. And the actual preparation does have its *Blue Peter* moments—you'll need brown paper, as well as baking parchment, to line the pan and stop the cake from scorching.

Place all of the fruit in a large bowl, and add the brandy or sherry. Cover and let the fruit soak overnight.

Preheat your oven to 300°F. Line your pan with a double thickness of brown paper, then line again with baking parchment, both to come up a good 4 inches above the rim of the pan.

Cream the butter and sugar, then beat in the orange and lemon zest. Add the eggs one at a time, beating well after each addition, and then the marmalade. Sift the dry ingredients together, then mix the fruit alternately with the dry ingredients into the creamed mixture. Add the almond essence and combine thoroughly.

Put the cake mixture into the prepared pan and bake following the table below, or until a cake tester comes out clean.

When the cake is cooked, brush with a couple of tablespoons of extra liqueur. Wrap immediately in its pan—using a double thickness of aluminum foil—as this will trap the heat and form steam, which in turn will keep the cake soft on top. When it's completely cold, remove the cake from the pan and rewrap in foil, storing, preferably in an airtight tin or Tupperware, for at least 3 weeks.

For icing, see my comments in the recipe for black cake (page 250).

AMOUNTS OF INGREDIENTS FOR FRUITCAKES
OF VARIOUS WEIGHTS

	4 ounces (^{1}/4lb)	8 ounces (^{1}/2lb)	12 ounces (^{3}/4lb)
golden raisins	1^1/2 cups	3 cups	4^1/3 cups
raisins	^{1}/2 cup	1 cup	1^1/2 cups
currants	^{1}/4 cup	^{1}/2 cup	^{3}/4 cup
glacé cherries	^{1}/4 cup	^{1}/2 cup	^{3}/4 cup
mixed peel	^{1}/4 cup	^{1}/2 cup	^{3}/4 cup
brandy or			
sherry	^{1}/4 cup	^{1}/2 cup	^{3}/4 cup
butter	^{1}/2 cup	1 cup	1^1/2 cups
brown sugar	7 tablespoons	^{3}/4 cup plus 2 tablespoons	1^1/3 cups
orange zest,			
grated	^{1}/3 teaspoon	1 teaspoon	1^1/2 teaspoons
lemon zest,			
grated	^{1}/2 teaspoon	1 teaspoon	1^1/2 teaspoons
large eggs	2	4	6
marmalade	1 tablespoon	2 tablespoons	3 tablespoons
all-purpose flour	1^2/3 cups	2^1/4 cups	3^1/2 cups plus 2 tablespoons
mixed spice	^{1}/2 teaspoon	1 teaspoon	1^1/2 teaspoons
cinnamon	pinch	^{1}/4 teaspoon	^{1}/4 teaspoon
nutmeg	pinch	^{1}/4 teaspoon	^{1}/4 teaspoon
almond extract	^{1}/2 teaspoon	1 teaspoon	1 teaspoon
salt	pinch	pinch	^{1}/4 teaspoon
pan: round	7–8 inches	9 inch	10 inch
or square	6 inches	8 inch	9 inch
temperature	300°F	300°F	300°F, reduce to 250°F after 1 hour
cooking time	2–2^1/2 hours	3–3^1/2 hours	4–4^1/2 hours

BLACK CAKE

This recipe comes from one of my favorite books, Laurie Colwin's *Home Cooking*. There are few food books that have such genuineness of tone, such love of food and of life. Laurie Colwin died young, and I often think of her family, her daughter, whom she writes about with such passion and interest. It's an extraordinarily powerful legacy that she's left her.

This cake was introduced to Laurie Colwin by her daughter's West Indian babysitter: "Its closest relatives are plum pudding and black bun, but it leaves both in the dust. Black cake, like truffles and vintage Burgundy, is deep, complicated and intense. It has taste and aftertaste. It demands to be eaten in a slow, meditative way. The texture is complicated, too—dense and light at the same time," she writes. Here is the recipe, altered only slightly by me.

for the fruit:

- 1 cup plus 2 tablespoons or 9 ounces raisins
- 1 cup plus 2 tablespoons or 9 ounces prunes
- 1 cup plus 2 tablespoons or 9 ounces currants
- 1 cup plus 2 tablespoons or 9 ounces natural-colored glacé cherries
- 1/2 cup plus 3 tablespoons mixed citrus (orange, lemon, lime, grapefruit) peel (the real thing, not the chopped stuff in containers)
- 1/2 750-ml bottle Madeira (about 1 1/2 cups)
- 1/2 750-ml bottle darkest rum you can find (about 1 1/2 cups)

Chop all the fruit very finely in the food processor. I advise you to go slowly, one fruit at a time, or else you'll find you've got purée.

Put the chopped fruit into a huge Tupperware container and mix pleasurably and stickily with your hands to combine and then pour over the Madeira and rum. I should perhaps say that Laurie Colwin suggested Passover wine, but unless you're doing this around Easter/Passover you'll never find it; and Madeira is, I'm told, the best substitute for it.

Cover the fruits and leave to steep for at least two weeks, but up to six months. I say up to six months—which is what Colwin writes in *Home Cooking*—but I must tell you that I steeped all the fruits one year in November only to find in December that I was just too exhausted to make the cake. So I used it up the following year, after 13 months' marinating. It was strong, but it was good.

To make one cake, you need only half of this fruit mixture. Save the other half for a second cake—there's no point mixing up less than this. It's so good and keeps so well.

for the cake:

**1 cup plus 2 tablespoons soft
   unsalted butter**

**1 cup plus 2 tablespoons dark
   brown sugar**

1/2 the marinated fruit mixture

1/2 tablespoon vanilla extract

1/4 teaspoon freshly ground nutmeg

1/4 teaspoon ground cinnamon

6 large eggs

2 cups all-purpose flour

1 1/2 teaspoons baking powder

9 tablespoons molasses

deep, 9-inch cake pan, lined as for
   Christmas cake, above

Preheat the oven to 350°F.

Cream the butter and sugar, and beat in the fruit, rum, and wine mixture. I use my KitchenAid free-standing mixer for this: it wouldn't be impossible to do by hand, but it takes a lot of muscle. Add the vanilla, nutmeg, and cinnamon, and then beat in the eggs. Stir in the flour and baking powder, and finally the molasses. The batter should be dark brown.

Pour this dark batter into the prepared pan and cook for 1 hour, then turn the oven down to 325°F and cook for a further 2½–3 hours. Remove to a wire rack but do not unmold till the cake's completely cold, at which stage, wrap it in a double-thickness of foil and put it back in a Tupperware container until you want to ice it.

for the icing:

1/2 jar marmalade (about 3/4 cup)

confectioners' sugar for sprinkling

18 ounces marzipan

**2 pounds 3 ounces ready-to-roll
   fondant icing**

1 pair of holly-leaf cutters

I was teased mercilessly last year for proposing my white-on-white holly-decorated Christmas cake, but as precious as it sounds, it is simply beautiful. And I promise you those who at first mocked, ate their words and my cake.

I don't think there is anything better than an all-white cake—especially with an interior as dense and dark as this one's—but you could easily cut holly leaves out of dark green icing if you wanted. Holly-leaf cutters tend to come in pairs—a smaller and a larger leaf—complete with vein-stamping *truc*. The berries you have to roll yourself, but for this I suggest in any case you buy the icing ready to roll. Of course you can whisk sifted confectioners' sugar with egg whites until it's the right consistency to roll out and ice, but the bought stuff, especially if it comes from a cake-decoration shop, is fine.

Heat the marmalade in a saucepan and when hot and runny strain into a bowl to remove rind. With a pastry brush, paint all over the cake to make a tacky surface. Dust a work surface with confectioners' sugar, roll out the marzipan and drape over the cake. Then press against the cake and cut off the excess with a sharp knife. If you need to do this twice (with half the marzipan), that's fine, but make sure to smooth over any joins, so that the icing on top lies smoothly. Dust the work surface again with confectioners' sugar and plonk down your block of icing. Beat it a few times with the rolling pin, then dust the top with confectioners' sugar and roll out. Cover the cake with it, again cutting off the excess and sticking bits together to patch up as you need, sprinkling with cold water first. Transfer the cake to a cake stand or board: once you've added the leaves you really don't want to move it again.

Re-roll the remaining icing and start stamping out the larger holly leaves (dipping the cutter into confectioners' sugar first) and pressing down on them with the vein-stamper. Wet the underneath of each with a little cold water and stick onto the cake to form a circle about 1 inch in from the cake's edge. Don't make all the holly leaves face the same way: you want this to look a bit like a holly wreath, which means that although most leaves should be placed aslant, they shouldn't be in a uniform ring. Now do the same with the smaller leaves, sticking them to make a circle around the base of the cake, in other words, blurring the line between cake board and cake. Make tiny balls, to resemble the berries, out of some of the icing that remains. Again, don't be uniform about the way you stick them on: put one berry between some leaves, a bunch of three between others, and so on.

SNOW-TOPPED SPICE CAKE

This cake—fruitless, light but aromatic—is the perfect replacement for the standard Christmas cake for those who hate it or just haven't got time to make it. The dripping blanket of royal icing certainly lends a seasonal touch, but the dark gingerbread spiciness is enough on its own if you'd prefer to keep it very simple.

I know the list of ingredients is long, but check out the method before deciding this is too labor-intensive: as you'll see, it's about the easiest cake you could make. And if you want to see what it looks like, give or take, turn to the picture of the chocolate-coffee volcano (page 180); I use the same cake mold for both.

for the cake:

4 large eggs, separated, plus 2 extra-large egg whites

1/2 cup vegetable oil

1/2 cup water

2 tablespoons honey

3/4 cup plus 2 tablespoons dark brown sugar

1/3 cup ground almonds

1 cup all-purpose flour

2 teaspoons baking powder

1 teaspoon baking soda

pinch of salt

1 teaspoon ground ginger

1 teaspoon cinnamon

1/2 teaspoon allspice

1/4 teaspoon ground cloves

zest of 1/2 an orange

1/3 cup sugar

10-inch Bundt pan, well buttered

for the icing:

9 ounces instant royal icing

Preheat the oven to 350°F.

Whisk together the yolks and oil, then add the water, honey, and dark brown sugar. Add the almonds, flour, baking powder, baking soda, salt, spices, and zest, folding in gently. In another bowl, beat the egg whites until soft peaks form and then gradually add the granulated sugar. Fold the whites into the cake mixture, and pour into the Bundt pan. Cook for 45 minutes, or until the cake is springy on top and beginning to shrink away from the edges. Let the cake cool in its pan on a rack for 25 minutes before turning it out.

When it's completely cold, you can make up the icing. Put the icing mix in a bowl with as much water as specified on the package and whisk till thick. And you do need this to be thick, or else it will just melt into the damp stickiness of the cake. Use more icing if you want a thicker coating, but leave to dry before slicing.

CERTOSINO

This is the most fabulous Italian spicy fruitcake, decorated glossily with candied fruits and nuts, and best eaten in the tiniest slices with a glass of vin santo or, crossing continents for a moment, Australian black or orange muscat. I'm afraid I've taken terrible liberties with the recipe given to me by Anna del Conte; this is an anglicized version insofar as I've greatly augmented the apples to give a much wetter cake. I do think Italians appreciate a dry cake in the way that we don't. I've also, for purely personal reasons, got rid of the candied peel. As for the decorative topping: I've been vague about quantities because it depends completely on what you want to use and how.

¹/₃ cup seedless raisins

2 tablespoons Marsala

2¹/₄ cups all-purpose flour

2 teaspoons baking soda

¹/₂ cup plus 2 tablespoons honey

¹/₂ cup sugar

3 tablespoons unsalted butter

3 tablespoons water

1 tablespoon anise or fennel seeds

1 teaspoon ground cinnamon

2 medium tart apples, roughly grated

³/₄ cup plus 2 tablespoons or
   7 ounces blanched almonds,
   coarsely chopped

scant ¹/₄ cup pine nuts

3 ounces bittersweet chocolate,
   chopped

¹/₃ cup walnuts, chopped

10-inch springform pan, buttered and
   lined with parchment or wax paper

suggestions for decorating:

4 tablespoons apricot jam to glaze

pecan halves

natural-colored glacé cherries

blanched whole almonds

marrons glacés

glacé fruits

Soak the raisins in the Marsala for 20 minutes, and while they're steeping, preheat the oven to 350°F. Measure the flour and baking soda out into a large bowl. Heat the honey, sugar, butter, and water in a saucepan until the sugar dissolves. Add the anise or fennel seeds and cinnamon, pour this mixture over the bowl of flour and stir to combine.

Mix in all the other ingredients, not forgetting the soaked raisins and their liquid, then spoon into the pan and cook for ³/₄–1 hour; and should you find the cake needs that final 15 minutes, you may need to cover it with foil to stop it from scorching. When the cake has cooled, heat the apricot jam in a small pan and, using a pastry brush, paint most but not all of it over the top of the cake to glaze and give a sticky surface to which the fruits and so forth will adhere. Decorate with glacé fruits and nuts of your choice, leaving no gaps of cake visible on top. Brush with scant remaining glaze so all looks burnished and shiny.

CHRISTMAS PUDDING

"Stir-up Sunday," the day on which we're all supposed to make our puddings before they're left to mature for Christmas Day itself, falls toward the end of November, on the Sunday after Trinity. Of course, the real stirring-up—as in, "Stir up, we beseech thee, O Lord, the wills of thy faithful people"—was a religious injunction rather than a culinary one, but it's still a good time, faith or no, to mix up the pudding. Traditionally, as well, everyone in the house is meant to give one stir, wishing for luck as they do so; thus superstitious paganism gets a look-in too, and everyone's happy.

Don't worry too much over every detail in the list of ingredients. Use it rather as a guide toward general bulk rather than specific, must-have items.

If you can't buy candied peel in whole strips, which you then cut up yourself, don't bother with it at all. Just augment quantities of other fruits.

scant 1/2 cup currants
scant 1/2 cup black raisins and
    golden raisins
1/4 cup natural-colored glacé cherries,
    chopped into quarters
1/4 cup dried blueberries
1/4 cup prunes, roughly chopped
1/4 cup marron glacé pieces, chopped
1/4 cup candied peel, finely chopped
1/2 cup plus 2 tablespoons rum
silver dollars, cleaned (see below)
1/2 cup self-rising cake flour
generous 1/2 cup white bread crumbs

1/2 cup plus 2 tablespoons or 5 ounces
    vegetable shortening
1 quince or 1 medium cooking apple,
    to provide 1/2 cup, roughly grated
1/2 cup plus 2 tablespoons dark
    brown sugar
1/2 teaspoon mixed spice
pinch of salt
3 large eggs
zest of 1 orange
1/2 cup vodka for flambéing
sprig of holly for decoration
1 6-cup plastic pudding basin with
    fitted lid

Soak the fruit in the rum overnight.

Mix all the ingredients together in a large bowl and then add the soaked fruit. At the same time, add the cleaned silver dollars. I know a dollar a serving sounds extravagant but the heaviness of these coins, and their glinting shininess, makes them most appropriate; soak in Coca-Cola overnight to clean. Butter the pudding basin and put the mixture into it. Cover with a piece of wax paper in which you have folded a pleat, and put on the lid. Boil or steam the pudding for 3½ hours. Rewrap the pudding and store somewhere cool until Christmas. Reheat in the same way, that's to say, steam or boil for another 3½ hours. Now, the flambéing. I know brandy's traditional, but ever since I read that Fanny Cradock advised vodka (because it burns for longer), I have, of course, followed suit. Put the vodka in a small pan and heat on the burner. Light it, pour it over the pudding, add a spring of holly, and bring ceremoniously to the table.

THREE SAUCES

I hate to recycle recipes, but Christmas puts me into something of a quandary because it's not about innovation but tradition, and you can't have Christmas pudding or mince pies without brandy butter. And so evangelical have I become about the Sauternes custard and iced rum sauce, I really couldn't bear to leave them out.

BRANDY BUTTER

This is what was always traditionally called hard sauce, but somehow it looks affected and twee to call it that now. We all know it as brandy butter these days. I add ground almonds because my mother did, and so it's the taste I know, and because they give it a glorious marzipanny depth and velvetiness.

You need the butter to be as soft as possible before you start but not at all oily. Obviously it makes life a lot easier if you can do this in a machine, either a mixer or food processor; I prefer the former. There is one new modification to this: I now use golden unrefined confectioners' sugar, which gives a gorgeous fudginess to it all. This may be hard to find, so use regular confectioners' sugar instead.

1/2 cup plus 2 tablespoons softened unsalted butter
1 1/2 cups confectioners' sugar
1/4 cup ground almonds
3 tablespoons brandy, or to taste

Cream the butter until soft and then add the confectioners' sugar and beat them together till pale and creamy. Mix in the ground almonds and when all is smooth add the brandy. Add a tablespoon at first, then taste, then another and see if you want more. You may find that the suggested 3 is far from enough: it is a question of taste and what is lethally strong for one person seems insipid to another; you must please yourself since you can't please everyone.

ICED RUM SAUCE

This is a rum-sodden and syrupy eggnog with cream that's put in the fridge for a few hours before eating. You put it on the searing hot pudding and it melts on impact. A taste sensation.

1 1/3 cups heavy cream
2 large egg yolks

2 tablespoons light corn syrup
2 tablespoons dark rum

Beat the cream until stiff. In another bowl beat the yolks until extremely frothy. Add the syrup and the rum to the frothy eggs, still beating. Then fold this mixture into the thick cream, transfer to an airtight container and stash in the freezer (though it's pretty good as it is, unfrozen).

Leave in the freezer to set hard, and then remove to the refrigerator to ripen for about 40 minutes before eating, so that it isn't absolutely rock hard.

SAUTERNES CUSTARD

You don't actually need to use Sauternes for this; any desirably ambrosial and honeyed dessert wine will do. To tell the truth, I hadn't thought of making this to go with the Christmas pudding until a magazine did. Now I always do.

2 1/4 cups light cream
3/4 cup plus 2 tablespoons Sauternes

7 large egg yolks
3 tablespoons sugar

Half fill the sink with cold water. Put the cream and wine into separate saucepans and heat both to just under boiling point. Whisk together the egg yolks and sugar and, still whisking, add first the hot wine and then the warm cream. Pour into one of the saucepans and cook over a low to medium heat, stirring constantly, until the custard thickens. If at any time it looks as if it's about to curdle, plunge the saucepan into the cold water in the sink and beat like mad—preferably with an electric whisk.

MINCE PIES

I always think I don't like mince pies: in my memory, they're too sweet, too dense, too cloying. And then I eat one. I think the trick is, if you're using store-bought mincemeat, to grate over a little sharp apple and squeeze in some lemon juice. But you'll see from the recipes below that making your own mincemeat is not a strenuous activity.

I've given three recipes here, and I should say that I've copied the small, star-topped ones, in idea if not actual recipe, from the mince pies I used to buy from a supermarket in London called Waitrose. They are the perfect size: one small mouthful.

MANGER MINCE PIES

Originally, I learned fairly recently, mince pies were cooked in barquette (little boat) molds because they were meant to represent the manger. Since this tin is routinely used by French pâtissiers to make small fruit tarts, it's not hard to find the wherewithal to make them now. I've added a shredded filo topping, in part to make them different from the usual, but also in a clumsy attempt to carry on the symbolism: think of it as the straw bedding. If you can get hold of konafa (a sort of shredded-wheat version of filo) so much the better.

And, even if you're using homemade mincemeat, add the extra seasonings here; this version should be even more aromatic than usual.

for the pastry:
2 cups all-purpose flour
1/3 cup vegetable shortening
6 tablespoons cold unsalted butter
juice of 1 orange
1 teaspoon orange-flower water
pinch of salt

for the filling:
approximately 1 3/4 cups or 14 ounces mincemeat
1/4 teaspoon ground cloves
finely grated zest of the orange
1/2 teaspoon orange-flower water
6 sheets filo or 3 1/2 ounces konafa
scant 1/4 cup unsalted butter, melted
confectioners' sugar for dusting
12-mold barquette tray

Measure the flour out into a shallow bowl or dish and, using a teaspoon, dollop in little mounds of shortening, add the butter, diced small, combine with your hands and put in the freezer for 20 minutes. Mix the orange juice, the orange-flower water, and the salt in a small pitcher and put this in the refrigerator.

Empty out the flour and fat into the bowl of the food processor and blitz until you've got a pale pile of oatmeal-like crumbs. Add the salted juice down the funnel, pulsing till it looks as if the dough is about to cohere; you want to stop just before it does (even if some orange juice is left). If all your juice is used up and you need more liquid, add some ice water. Turn out of the processor and, in your hands, combine to a dough. Then form into two discs. Roll out one of the discs to make a rectangle approximately 16 by 14 inches. Lay this on top of the tray, gently pushing the pastry down into the molds with your fingertips. Give yourself a lot of slack. When you feel all the molds are lined with pastry, take your rolling pin and roll over the top of the pastry to cut off the excess. When you take that away you should be left with 12 lined barquette molds. Put the tray in the refrigerator for 20 minutes, preheating the oven to 400°F as you do so.

Empty the mincemeat into a bowl and stir in the ground cloves, orange zest, and orange-flower water, then drop 2 scant teaspoons into each barquette mould, spreading it gently to fill. Add more if you want, but remember that the pastry sides will slip down as they bake. Either snip the filo into shreds with scissors or pinch off bits of the konafa and crumble over the mincemeat in the molds. Drizzle the filo or konafa with the melted butter, transfer to the oven, and bake for about 15 minutes, or until the pastry cases and filo topping are cooked and golden.

Remove from the oven and, using a palette knife, help the pies out of the tray and onto a wire rack to cool. When the barquette molds are cold, start again with the second disc of pastry.

Dust with confectioners' sugar sifted through a tea strainer or fine-mesh sieve before serving. Makes 24.

STAR-TOPPED MINCE PIES

Please don't think these will be better if you make the pastry out of butter rather than the butter and vegetable shortening mixed; it's the vegetable shortening which makes the pies so celestially light (though by all means use lard if you object to "fake" fats). And it's the acid in the orange juice that makes the pastry especially tender.

1²/₃ cups cake flour
¹/₄ cup vegetable shortening
¹/₄ cup cold unsalted butter
juice of 1 orange
pinch of salt
approximately ³/₄ cup plus 2 tablespoons or 7 ounces mincemeat

1 large egg, mixed with a tablespoon water, to glaze, optional
confectioners' sugar for dusting
tray of miniature tart pans, each indent about 2 inches in diameter
2¹/₂-inch fluted round biscuit cutter
1¹/₂-inch star cutter

Make the pastry following the method for manger mince pies, but form it into three discs (since you're going to have to make these in three batches, unless you've got enough tart tins to make all 36 pies at once). Wrap each in plastic wrap and put in the refrigerator to rest for 20 minutes. Preheat the oven to 425°F.

Roll out the discs one at a time as thinly as you can without exaggerating; in other words, you want a light pastry shell, but one sturdy enough to support the dense mincemeat. Out of each rolled-out disc cut out circles a little wider than the indentations in the trays. Press these circles gently into the molds and dollop in a scant teaspoon of mincemeat. Then cut out your stars—re-rolling the pastry as necessary—and place them lightly on top of the mincemeat.

If you want to glaze the mince pies, then brush the stars with a pastry brush dipped into the egg and water mix (actually, the pies in the picture on page 261 haven't been glazed). Sometimes I do, sometimes I don't: the difference really is one of appearance and only you can decide whether you want them pale and matte or gold and shiny.

Put in the oven and bake for 10–15 minutes: keep an eye on them, they really don't take long. Remove from the oven, prising out the little pies right away and letting the empty tin cool down before you start putting in the pastry for the next batch. Carry on until they're all done. Dust over some confectioners' sugar by sifting it through a tea strainer before serving them.

Makes 36.

FRANGIPANE MINCE PIES

If you try making these in little molds, you'll drive yourself mad. But if you've already got a batch of tiny pies and another of manger-shaped ones, it's a good idea to make a third that are the size of real, grown-up mince pies. These are no light, airy mouthfuls, but dense, almondy, buttery mounds—rather like a Christmas version of Bakewell tart, now I come to think of it. And indeed there's nothing stopping you from making this in a 10-inch quiche pan to make one sliceable Bakewellian pudding.

for the pastry:
- **1 cup plus 2 tablespoons cake flour**
- **2 tablespoons ground almonds**
- **6 tablespoons confectioners' sugar**
- **pinch of salt**
- **1/2 cup cold unsalted butter, diced**
- **2 large egg yolks, beaten with a tablespoon of ice water**

for the topping:
- **approximately 3/4 cup plus 2 tablespoons or 7 ounces mincemeat**
- **2 large eggs**
- **1/3 cup sugar**
- **7 tablespoons unsalted butter, melted**
- **1/3 cup ground almonds**
- **4 tablespoons flaked almonds**
- **2 12-cup tartlet trays**
- **3-inch fluted biscuit cutter**

Make the pastry by putting the flour, ground almonds, sugar, and salt into the bowl of the food processor and pulse to combine. Add the diced butter and process till you've got a flaky, crumbly mix. Now start adding, tablespoon by tablespoon, the egg and water mixture down the funnel, pulsing as you do so, until the pastry looks like it's about to form a ball around the blade. Turn it out onto a surface, press to form a cohesive dough, shape into 2 discs, cover with plastic wrap, and put into the refrigerator to rest for 30 minutes. Roll out one of the discs and stamp out 12 circles slightly larger than the tart indentations. Press these in gently, patting base and sides, and put back in the refrigerator for 15 minutes. Preheat the oven to 400°F.

Put a scant teaspoon of mincemeat into each pastry-lined cavity. In a bowl, beat together the eggs and sugar, then pour in, still beating, the melted butter. Stir in the ground almonds and then dollop a tablespoon of this mixture on top. Sprinkle with flaked almonds and then put in the oven to cook for 15 minutes, or until the pastry is cooked through and the frangipane gold and brown flecked.

Take out of the oven and leave to cool in the tins for 5 minutes before transferring to a wire rack to cool. When the pan's cool, repeat with the second disc, remaining mincemeat, and frangipane.

Makes 24.

HETTIE POTTER'S SUET-FREE MINCEMEAT

I know it looks illogical to give the recipe for mincemeat after the mince pies, but I thought I'd make you *want* to have it. And once you've decided to make your own mince pies, why compromise, undermining your satisfaction, by missing out what is the easiest part of the exercise?

So many people object to suet that it seemed sensible to begin with Hettie's recipe for a suetless mincemeat. The extra apples make up for the fat by keeping everything tender and moist.

1 cup plus 2 tablespoons dark
   brown sugar
1 cup plus 2 tablespoons medium-dry
   hard cider
2¹⁄₄ pounds tart cooking apples,
   peeled, halved, and quartered
¹⁄₂ teaspoon mixed spice
¹⁄₂ teaspoon ground cinnamon
1 cup plus 2 tablespoons currants

1 cup plus 2 tablespoons raisins
¹⁄₃ cup natural-colored glacé cherries,
   roughly chopped
¹⁄₃ cup blanched almonds, fairly finely
   chopped
rind and juice of ¹⁄₂ lemon
6 tablespoons brandy or rum
4 1-pint or 2 1-quart canning jars

In a large saucepan, dissolve the sugar in the cider over a gentle heat. Roughly chop the apples, and add them to the saucepan. Then add all the other ingredients except the brandy or rum, and simmer for 30 minutes or until everything looks pulpy. Take off the heat and when it has cooled a little, stir in the brandy or rum. Spoon into sterilized jars.

This should make around 4 pounds.

QUINCEMEAT

I came across this recipe of Frances Bissell's in *The (London) Times* when I was in the first flush of my love affair with the quince, and of course I had to make it straight away. This "quincemeat," as we call it at home, is a model of seasonal exploitation.

You don't need to go out and buy a bottle of eau de vie de coings—you can use brandy instead—but I did, and have since found it strangely useful in prinking up all manner of other things. (Or, really making the most of the short season, follow the recipe for homemade quince brandy on page 340.)

Since I've already given a recipe for a suet-free mincemeat, I should clarify my own position on suet: I love it. Ideally, you want fresh suet from the butcher, which you then grate yourself. Failing that—since it's virtually disappeared from sale now—buy boxed, shredded vegetable shortening.

2¹/₄ pounds quinces

2 tablespoons unsalted butter, melted

1 cup plus 2 tablespoons or 9 ounces golden raisins, chopped

1 cup plus 2 tablespoons or 9 ounces raisins, chopped

1 cup plus 2 tablespoons or 9 ounces dried apricots, chopped

1 cup plus 2 tablespoons or 9 ounces light brown sugar

1 cup plus 2 tablespoons or 9 ounces shredded vegetable shortening

1 teaspoon ground cardamom

1 teaspoon ground cloves

1 teaspoon ground cinnamon

¹/₂ teaspoon ground mace

scant ¹/₂ cup real crystallized peel, chopped

¹/₃ cup eau de vie de coings, Poire William, or my quince brandy, see page 340

shallow roasting pan

4 1-pint or 2 1-quart jars or equivalent

Preheat the oven to 300°F.

Peel and quarter the quinces and cut into wedges (this is the hardest part of the whole operation). Toss them in the melted butter and put them in the pan and into the oven to roast gently, for 40 minutes or so, until tender.

Remove and leave to cool, then chop or grate or process the fruit (but do not pulp it) and put in a large bowl along with any cooking juices. When completely cold, stir in all the remaining ingredients and put in your clean jars. Now, was that so hard?

Makes 4 pounds.

CHRISTMAS CUPCAKES

These beauties also make a very good alternative to mince pies. I buy the icing ready-made and dyed (which is why it isn't a very convincing color for holly, let's be frank) and use cranberries as the holly berries. The cake underneath is somewhere between chocolate and gingerbread. If you're thinking of taking anything to friends' houses, may I suggest these?

1 cup all-purpose flour
1 teaspoon baking powder
1/2 teaspoon baking soda
1 teaspoon ground mixed spice
pinch of salt
scant 1/2 cup soft unsalted butter
1/2 cup plus 3 tablespoons dark brown sugar
2 large eggs
3 tablespoons sour cream
1/2 cup boiling water

3 ounces bittersweet chocolate, broken into pieces
1 teaspoon instant coffee
1 cup plus 2 tablespoons or 9 ounces instant royal icing
1 12-ounce package green ready-to-roll fondant icing
about 30 cranberries for decoration
small holly-leaf cutter with veining stamp
12-cup muffin pan and paper baking cups

Preheat the oven to 400°F.

In a large bowl, mix together the flour, baking powder, baking soda, mixed spice, and salt. In another bowl, cream the butter and sugar with an electric mixer. Add the eggs one at a time, mixing well after each addition, and then beat in a third of the flour mixture followed by a tablespoon of the sour cream, repeating till all is used up.

Put the water, chocolate, and instant coffee in a pan and heat gently, just until the chocolate's melted. Fold this into the cake batter, but don't overbeat. The mixture will be very thin, but don't worry about that: just pour carefully into the waiting muffin cups and put in the oven for about 20 minutes, until each little cake is cooked through but still dense and damp. Let cool in the pan for 5 minutes, then slip out the cakes in their papers and sit on a wire rack until completely cold.

To ice them, make up the royal icing according to the package instructions and cover the tops of the cupcakes thickly. Cut out holly leaves and sit two on each cake, and then press on your berries, perhaps putting two on some, three on others.

Makes 12.

Some people really cannot stomach mincemeat, so it's useful to have some little pie to serve as a substitute for mince pies. The recipe from the Maids of Honour tea rooms in Richmond, Surrey, England, is what is commonly called a "closely guarded secret," but unofficial recipes abound for these tarts, with their filling somewhere between cheesecake and custard. This one is the result of a collaboration between me and one of my oldest friends, Tracey Scoffield.

I like a shortcrust pastry shell, but if you prefer puff pastry—which many, including my collaborator, do—you should find 9 ounces of packaged puff pastry enough for the job.

for the pastry:
2 cups cake flour
6 tablespoons cold unsalted butter, diced
1/3 cup vegetable shortening in scant teaspooned lumps
2 large eggs
2 teaspoons lemon juice
pinch of salt
1 12-cup tartlet pan
3-inch plain round cutter

for the filling:
1 vanilla bean
generous 1/2 cup plus 2 tablespoons heavy cream
scant 1/4 cup unsalted butter
2 tablespoons sugar
scant 1/4 cup ground almonds
1 large egg, beaten
zest of 1 small lemon and juice of 1/2 lemon
fresh nutmeg

Preheat the oven to 425°F, and prepare the pastry following the method on page 83. Cut lengthways down the vanilla bean with the tip of sharp knife, put it in a saucepan over medium heat with the cream, and heat till just below boiling point. Take out the bean, scraping some of the seeds into the milk, then add the butter, sugar, ground almonds, egg, and lemon zest and juice. Stir, take off the heat, and leave to stand for about 5 minutes.

Roll out half the pastry, cut out 12 rounds and place these into the tart molds, pressing down with your fingers so they're well lined. Spoon in the filling (remembering you'll have a second batch to do). Leave a good inch below the rim, as the custard will rise up as it bakes. Grate over some fresh nutmeg and transfer carefully to the oven and bake for 15–20 minutes until the custard's golden and puffy.

Let the tarts sit in the pan for a few minutes before standing, unmolded, on a wire rack to cool. When the pan is cool, repeat with the remaining ingredients. Leave the tarts to cool a little before serving, but they are best eaten still slightly warm. And unlike mince pies, they don't keep at all.

Makes 24.

MULLED WINE

With mince pies, goes mulled wine. Don't fight it.

1 750-ml bottle red wine	**2 cinnamon sticks**
4 tablespoons dark rum	**1 star anise**
½ cup brewed Earl Grey tea	**1 tablespoon dark brown sugar**
1 orange, quartered, each quarter	**1 tablespoon honey**
stuck with 1 clove	

Put all the ingredients in a saucepan, bring almost to the boil, but before the aromatic wine actually boils, turn down to the lowest possible heat and keep it warm as you ladle it into any nearby glass.

VARIATION

If you need to make mulled wine that isn't really mulled wine because you have to provide drink that's nonalcoholic (as I had to do for the Christmas fair at my daughter's school last year) then you can substitute a bottle of red grape juice for the wine, half a bottle of rum flavoring (I'm sorry) for the rum.

SWEDISH GLÖGG

I was sent this recipe during a culinary crusade on the part of some Swedish trade mission, and I'm sure the interested party will be only too pleased that I've now passed it on to you.

1 750-ml bottle red wine	**12 cardamom seeds**
½ cup plus 2 tablespoons Swedish	**1 tablespoon sugar**
(or other) vodka	**2 tablespoons blanched almonds**
2 cinnamon sticks	**2 tablespoons raisins**
8 cloves	

Combine all ingredients except for the raisins and almonds in a large pan and let steep, preferably overnight.

To serve, put a sprinkling of raisins and almonds in the bottom of everyone's mug, put the pan on the heat and slowly bring almost to the boil. Strain into a pitcher and pour over the raisins and almonds in the waiting mugs.

CHRISTMAS DECORATIONS

I like these as spiced and peppery as German *Lebkuchen* and decorated only in white and silver or gold. I tend, also, to limit myself to bells, angels, and stars, but if you want to go bolder and brighter, you should. And if you want these to be milder and therefore more likely to please young children, use the smaller amount of pepper. But keeping them peppery is also a good way of keeping them hanging on the tree. . . .

Of all Christmas rituals up for adoption, making these is probably the most satisfying one.

for the cookies:

2 cups all-purpose flour

pinch of salt

1 teaspoon baking powder

1 teaspoon mixed ground spice

1–2 teaspoons freshly ground pepper

scant 1/2 cup unsalted butter

scant 1/2 cup dark brown sugar

2 large eggs beaten with
  4 tablespoons honey

set of Christmas cutters

2 baking sheets, lined with parchment
  or wax paper or nonstick

for the icing and trimmings:

2 cups confectioners' sugar, sifted

3 tablespoons boiling water

gold or silver balls or sprinkles

florists' ribbon for hanging

Combine the flour, salt, baking powder, mixed spice, and pepper in the processor. With the motor on, add the butter and sugar, then, slowly, the eggs and honey, though don't use all of this liquid if the pastry has come together before it's used up. Form two discs and put one, covered in plastic wrap or in a freezer bag, into the refrigerator while you get started on the other. Preheat oven to 325°F.

Dust a surface with flour, roll out the disc, also floured, to about 15 inches and cut out your Christmas decorations. Re-roll and cut out some more, setting aside the residue from this first disc, well covered, while you get on with rolling out the second. When you've got both sets of leftover clumps of dough, roll out and cut out again and keep doing so till all the dough's used up. Now take a small piping tip and use the pointy end to cut out a hole just below the top of each cookie (through which ribbon can later be threaded to hang them).

Arrange on the baking sheets and cook for about 20 minutes: it's hard to see when they're cooked, but you can feel; if the underside is no longer doughy, they're ready.

Transfer them to cool on a wire rack. Make up ordinary glacé icing by mixing approximately 3 tablespoons of boiling water with the sifted confectioners' sugar and stir till you've got a thin, glossy glaze. Ice the cold decorations using a teaspoon (the tip for dripping, the back for smoothing) and scatter sparkles or sprinkles as you like.

BAKLAVA

Of course, I don't really think this is a part of the traditional Yuletide feast, but there is something about the intense sweetness and aromatic succulence that makes it appropriate. It is so temple-achingly sweet that one small marked-out diamond, or maybe two, is enough. But even so, I love its perfumed sugariness—as much as I love the tender, rose-shot green of its equally fragrant nubbly interior. It's also a very good present to take to people over Christmas, which is why I've indicated one of those foil baking pans below.

for the syrup:
1 ¹/3 cups water
1 ¹/2 cups sugar
juice of ¹/2 lemon
1 tablespoon rosewater
1 tablespoon orange-flower water

for the pastry:
1 ¹/3 cups pistachios, chopped in a
    processor until medium–fine
¹/2 cup unsalted butter, melted
1 16-ounce package filo pastry
square foil pan, 9 x 9 x 1 ¹/2 inches
    from a supermarket or kitchen shop

To make the syrup: bring the water, sugar, and lemon juice to the boil, and keep it at boiling point for 5 minutes. Add the rosewater and orange-flower water, and then remove it from the heat. Pour it into a pitcher, let it cool, and then chill it in the refrigerator.

Preheat the oven to 350°F.

Brush the pan with butter, and then each of the filo pastry sheets as you line the pan with them. Use one package for the bottom layer, placing them in the pan evenly so that the pastry goes up the sides with a little overhang. As the pan is square and the filo pastry is often a rectangular shape, you should try to arrange the sheets so that each side is covered in turn. When you have used one package, spread the pistachios evenly over the filo sheets. Then carry on with the rest of the pastry in the same way. The last sheet on top should also be buttered well, and then with a sharp knife trim around the top edge of the pan to give a neat finish. Cut parallel lines 1¹/2 to 2 inches apart to form diamond shapes, making sure you cut the baklava right through to the bottom of the pan.

Put in the oven and cook for 30 minutes, by which time the filo will have puffed up and become golden brown. As soon as it comes out of the oven, pour over half the cold syrup. Leave it a few minutes to soak in and then pour over the rest.

Makes approximately 16 pieces.

I came across loukamades in a wonderful book called *The Food of the Jews of Greece* (and yes, I do know this is the Christmas chapter) when I was writing a piece about food and Hanukkah, the Jewish Festival of Lights, about which until that time I knew absolutely nothing. For the record, Hanukkah is an eight-day affair that tends to fall in December and has thus been appropriated as a kind of Yiddisher Christmas by Jewish-Americans who want their own party to go to as well. It is, in fact, a significant but small commemoration of the victory of the Maccabees in 165 BC, and is called the Festival of Lights because—the story goes—when the Jews returned to Jerusalem after the Maccabean victory, they found that the pagans had desecrated the temple, polluting the oil and stopping all but one lamp from burning. There was only enough oil to let it burn for one more day, but when the Jews poured it into the lamp it burned for eight, allowing them to clean the temple and replenish their supplies of holy oil. The miracle of the oil is celebrated culinarily by using it in great vats into which are dunked, splutteringly, latkes, doughnuts, batter-wrapped pieces of chicken, fritters—the Jewish genius is that this festival provides divine ordinance to eat fried food.

Eating latkes—desirably stodgy little potato cakes—is the commonest British way of marking Hanukkah. I like them with cold meats but they are perhaps at their best palate-skinningly hot with cold, cinnamon-infused apple purée dolloped on top.

about 1 1/2 pounds potatoes, peeled

1/2 medium onion, peeled and coarsely chopped

1 large egg

good pinch of salt

good grind of fresh pepper

1–2 tablespoons self-rising flour or matzo meal

vegetable oil for frying

heavy-bottomed frying pan

Push the potatoes through the grater disc of the food processor. Remove and drain in a sieve, pushing well to remove all excess liquid. Then fit the metal blade and put the onion, eggs, salt, pepper, and the self-rising flour (or the matzo meal, which is better according to my mother-in-law) in the bowl and process briefly. Then add the grated potatoes and give a quick pulse till the mixture is pulpy but not totally puréed. This should be a thick sticky mess; if it is at all runny add more flour.

Fry the latkes in lumps of about a tablespoonful in the frying pan with hot oil bubbling away in it to a depth of about 1/2 inch About 5 minutes a side should do it, maybe even less.

Makes 20.

*

Edda Servi Machlin, in her resonant, elegiac book, *The Classic Cuisine of the Italian Jews*, writes of her aunt's *frittelle di chanukà*, yeasty, diamond-shaped doughnuts fried till golden and then drenched in a lemon and honey syrup. It's the Greek version, loukamades (eaten all over Greece all the year round, in fact, regardless of ethnicity), that I have adopted as part of our family ritual. They have the virtue, too, of not being yeast-leavened and therefore requiring less time to make. They're not really doughnuts, but spoonfuls of choux pastry, deep-fried and then rolled, straight out of the fiercely hot oil, in a chilled aromatic syrup. Make them and hand out to waiting children (and inevitably their parents), to be eaten straight away with fingers.

for the syrup:

1¹/3 cups sugar

2¹/4 cups water

1 stick cinnamon

1 teaspoon orange-flower water

for the loukamades:

¹/2 cup all-purpose flour

³/4 cup water

6 tablespoons unsalted butter, diced

pinch of salt

2 large eggs, beaten

approximately 4 cups olive (or vegetable) oil for frying

heavy-bottomed frying pan

You can make the syrup in advance if you like. Put the sugar, water, and cinnamon stick in a saucepan, slowly bring to the boil (you want the sugar to dissolve before it boils), then turn up the heat and let bubble ferociously for about 7 minutes. Add the orange-flower water and give it another minute or 3. What you want is a syrup that isn't exactly runny, but isn't honey-thick either, for it will thicken as it cools. Pour the syrup into a pitcher or bowl to cool and remove the cinnamon stick. Now, you will have a lot of syrup, but that's because I like lots: I want these doughnuts swimming in it. If your tastes are more austere, make less.

Now for the loukamades. Pour the oil for frying into a wide pan to come up to about 1¹/₂ inches. I specify, first, olive oil, because it is, in this context, the holy oil. Of course, substitute vegetable oil if you want, but it isn't *echt*. If you're using olive oil it shouldn't be extra virgin: just the ordinary, pale golden, faster flowing (and cheaper) stuff. In my pan (which is 8 inches in diameter and 3 inches deep), the oil takes a good 20 minutes to get hot enough for deep-frying, so there's no rush. Just make sure you've got everything for the choux weighed out and at hand before you start.

Sift the flour. Put the water, butter, and salt in a medium-sized saucepan on the burner and heat until the butter's melted and the water's begun to boil. Take the pan immediately off the heat (you don't want the water to evaporate at all) and beat in the flour. Use a wooden spoon for this and don't worry about how lumpy it is or how unyielding, just keep beating until it comes smoothly together—a minute or so should do it. Put the pan back on the heat and keep beating until the dough begins to come away from the sides of the pan to form a smooth ball.

Now beat in the eggs, either by hand (but you'll need muscle power) or by machine. So, either turn the dough into a mixing bowl and add spoonfuls of egg as you continue to beat with your wooden spoon, or turn it into the bowl of the food processor fitted with the metal blade and pour, gradually, the egg through the funnel while blitzing. You may not need all of the egg, so go carefully, until you have a smooth, gleaming dough, soft but still stiff enough to hold its shape.

When the oil for frying is haze-waftingly hot, dip a teaspoon into it (so the dough doesn't stick) and then into the mixture. Push the dough off the spoon, spoonful by spoonful, into the hot oil and watch the lumps of choux paste swell up and grow golden as they cook. I find 4 minutes does them (and I cook 4–5 at a time). But just taste as you go along (make that sacrifice) to check the insides are soft but cooked, rather than still doughy. As you remove the spiky little doughnut balls from the pan—with one of those fine-meshed stock de-scummers for preference—put them immediately on a waiting plate, spoon the syrup over and continue to roll them in it. In fact, this is best done by a pair of you: the one to cook the loukamades; the other to ladle over the syrup and then roll them assiduously in it.

Makes about 30. Enjoy.

CHRISTMAS-MORNING MUFFINS

I do think that part of creating a family life is establishing those shared rituals, as important as getting out the same old familiar box of decorations for the tree each year. Now, it's true that children are too excited about their presents to take a lively interest in breakfast on Christmas Day, but consider making these all the same: there's something so warmly reassuring in knowing that soon this cinnamon-sweet smell of baking and oranges will come to signify Christmas morning to them.

You may find it easier to measure out the cranberries, flour, baking powder, baking soda, and sugar the night before, so that all you've got to do is mix together the orange juice, milk and eggs, melt the butter, and combine all the ingredients on Christmas morning itself.

for the muffins:

1 1/3 cups all-purpose flour

3 teaspoons baking powder

1/2 teaspoon baking soda

1/3 cup sugar

good grating fresh nutmeg

1 clementine or small orange

approximately 1/4 cup milk

1/4 cup unsalted butter, melted

1 large egg

1/2 cup plus 2 tablespoons or 5 ounces dried cranberries

12-cup muffin pan with paper baking cups

for the topping:

2 teaspoons sugar

1/2 teaspoon cinnamon

Preheat the oven to 400°F.

In a large bowl, combine the flour, baking powder, baking soda, and sugar, and grate over a generous amount of fresh nutmeg. Squeeze the orange or clementine juice into a measuring cup, then pour in milk on top till it comes up to the 2/3 cup mark. Add the melted butter and the egg, and beat to combine. Pour the liquid ingredients into the bowl of dry ingredients and stir till the ingredients are more or less combined, remembering that a lumpy batter makes light muffins. (Bearing this in mind, you could easily get the children to make up the mixture.) Last of all, lightly fold in the cranberries and fill the muffin cups. The amount of cranberries specified here makes for heavily fruited muffins; if you want them sparser, use half the amount.

Mix together the sugar and ground cinnamon and sprinkle over the tops of the muffins. Stick them in the oven and bake for 20 minutes, by which time the air should be thick with the promise of good things and the good things themselves golden brown and ready to be eaten—as they are, or broken open and spread heapingly, mouthful by mouthful, with unsalted butter and marmalade.

Makes 12.

BOXING DAY EGG-AND-BACON PIE

This recipe comes from Beryl Scoffield, the mother of one of my oldest friends, and a woman with a reputation for her pies. This one is my ideal Boxing Day supper, to be eaten on a tray with some cornichons and a glass of beer or cider, as I slump, perfectly contented and guiltless, in front of the television.

for the pastry:

1²/3 cups all-purpose flour
¼ cup vegetable shortening
¼ cup butter
3–5 tablespoons salted ice water—
or enough to bind

for the filling:

2¼ cups or 18 ounces pancetta or
bacon, chopped into small squares
1 medium onion, finely chopped
freshly ground pepper
1 green onion, finely chopped
approximately 2 tablespoons chopped
parsley
2 large eggs
8-inch pie plate

Make the pastry by freezing the fats and flour together for 10 minutes, then tip out into the food processor and blitz to a flaky rubble. Add enough ice water to bind, then form into 2 discs, cover them with plastic wrap and rest in the refrigerator for 20 minutes.

Preheat the oven to 400°F.

Cook the pancetta or bacon in a frying pan with the onion, peppering well. Beat the green onion, parsley, and eggs together, and set aside while you roll out the pastry between plastic wrap.

Using one of the discs, line the dish, leaving an overhang. Roll out the other half between plastic wrap to make a lid, and set aside for one moment. Transfer the pancetta and onion mixture to the pastry-lined pie plate and pour over the onion, parsley, and eggs. With a little cold water, dampen the edges of the pastry shell and cover with the rolled-out lid. Cut off excess pastry, and seal and pinch all around the rim. Make a hole in the lid to let out steam, put in the oven, and bake for 30 minutes.

Sit on a wire rack until slightly above room temperature, or eat cold.

Serves 6.

GAME PIE

The idea of making a raised-crust pie is a daunting one, I know, but I should tell you that a 15-year-old boy, Nick Blake, came to spend a day with us during the photo shoot for this book, and ended up making the one that you see opposite, without any earlier preparation or experience. These things, you see, are worth attempting. And the beautiful, designed-for-the-purpose pans that you can buy from most kitchen shops take a lot of the uncertainty out of it.

I love grouse so much that it's the only game I want in my pie, but venison, pheasant, wild rabbit, anything you want to use, is fine. I buy fresh veal stock, available from some butchers, specialty shops, and supermarkets.

for the filling:
7 ounces pork belly
5 ounces lean pork
5 ounces lean veal
4 ounces bacon
3 tablespoons Marsala
salt and fresh-ground pepper
1 teaspoon dry English mustard
1 teaspoon allspice
breasts from a brace of grouse or
   1/2 pound of whatever game you're
   using

for the pastry:
3/4 cup plus 2 tablespoons water

3/4 cup or 6 ounces lard
3 1/3 cups all-purpose flour
1/2 teaspoon salt
1 large egg, beaten with 1/2 teaspoon
   salt, to glaze
1 game-pie mold, 8 inches long

for the jellied stock:
2 sheets gelatin or 1/2 package
   powdered gelatin
1 cup veal stock
6 tablespoons Marsala
squeeze of lemon
1 teaspoon salt
fresh-ground pepper

Put the pork, veal, bacon, Marsala, a teaspoon of salt, a fair bit of pepper, mustard, and the allspice into the food processor and blitz to a coarse purée, then transfer to a bowl and set, covered, in the refrigerator. Chop whatever game you're using into rough chunks and set these aside, too, while you make the pastry.

In a saucepan, bring the water and lard to a boil. Then turn into a bowl containing the flour and salt. Mix everything well, creating a smooth dough. Cover the dough and leave it until it's no longer too hot to handle, but don't let it get cold. Now preheat the oven to 400°F.

Cut off a quarter of the pastry for the lid, and set it aside, covered, for a while. Roll the rest of the pastry between plastic wrap and line your beautiful, hinged game-pie mold. Push the pastry up the sides of the pan—gently, though, and making sure there are no cracks. Pack the processed filling into the pastry, adding the rough chunks of game as you go, filling right to the top. Roll out the pastry you've put aside for the lid between plastic wrap, arrange it on top, and pinch to seal. Make a central hole, with the point of a sharp knife or skewer, put in a pastry tip or similar (for ease of stock-pouring later), and decorate the pastry lid around it. I'm afraid I had no entirely appropriate cutters when I made this one here and am not talented enough to do it freehand, but I did find, to most other people's consternation, a rather fetching duck (and elephant, but I wasn't allowed to use it) in my collection. Brush the underside of your decorations with the beaten egg and stick them on the lid. Now brush all over the top with the beaten egg (and don't throw away what's left), put it in the oven for 30 minutes, and then turn the oven down to 325°F and cook for a further 1½ hours so that you can be confident that the meat is cooked through thoroughly.

Now make the jellied stock: put the gelatin sheets or powder to soak in a dish of cold water and put the veal stock and Marsala in a glass measuring cup and heat in the microwave for a couple of minutes until very hot. Squeeze in some lemon and add the salt and a vicious grating of black pepper. Taste: you do need this much more highly seasoned than you might think. Squeeze out the gelatin sheets and drop them or the softened gelatin granules into the hot stock, stirring to dissolve.

When the pie's had its time, remove it from the oven and sit it for 20 minutes before unclipping the mold. If the pastry looks pallid up the sides, brush with beaten egg and put back in the oven for 10 minutes. Otherwise, sit it on a tray (to catch spills) and pour the jellied stock through the tip-cum-funnel, going very slowly as you may well not need all of it and you don't want excess to make the crust soggy.

Refrigerate for about 24 hours before eating.

Serves 6–8.

CHRISTMAS PAVLOVA

For me, pomegranates are more essentially Christmassy than cranberries, but it's not just for seasonality that I include this receipe: I love the contrast between the crunchy, edible jewels on top and the soft, yielding cream and marshmallowy base beneath.

8 large egg whites
pinch of salt
1²/₃ cups sugar
1 tablespoon cornstarch
2 teaspoons vinegar

1 teaspoon rosewater
2 pomegranates
juice of ¹/₂ a lemon
2¹/₄ cups heavy cream
1 baking sheet and parchment paper

Preheat the oven to 350°F. Line your baking sheet with the parchment paper and draw an 8-inch circle on the paper.

Beat the egg whites and salt until satiny peaks form. Beat in the sugar, a scattered spoonful at a time, until the meringue is stiff and shiny. Sprinkle over the cornstarch, vinegar, and rosewater, and fold in lightly. Mound onto the baking tray within the circle, flatten the top and smooth the sides. Put in the oven and immediately reduce heat to 300°F. Cook for 1³/₄ hours. Turn off the oven and leave the pavlova in it to cool completely. If you've got an electric oven, however, open the oven door. When cool, you can keep it in an airtight container for a week or so.

Cut 1 of the pomegranates in half and juice it—which is easy to do if you've got an electric juicer, but manageable without. Decant the juice into a small saucepan along with the lemon juice. Bring to the boil and let bubble for a few minutes or until syrupy, then take off the heat and let cool.

Whip the heavy cream until thick but not stiff; an airy floppiness is what you're after. Invert the pavlova meringue onto a big flat-bottomed plate, peel off the baking parchment and on top of the marshmallowy whiteness pile on the cream with not too much regard for neatness or regularity. Now halve the second pomegranate and hold one half, cut side down, over the cream-peaked meringue and start bashing it with a wooden spoon, being careful not to hit the hand that's holding the pomegranate in so doing. After a while, pomegranate seeds will start slowly falling out, then faster, until the cream is beaded with pink. You might not need all of the other half, but be generous with it all the same, letting seeds fall on the rim of the plate as they will. Finally, drizzle over the puce syrup that's been waiting for this moment, and take to the table.

Serves 10–12.

CRANBERRY UPSIDE-DOWN CAKE

It's very useful around this time of year to have one or two seasonal desserts to boost a lunch or dinner otherwise made up of leftovers. Not that I wish to imply that leftovers constitute inadequate eating; indeed, they're my favorite sort of food.

I love the Christmasiness of this, all that glowing, berried redness.

scant 3/4 cup unsalted butter

1 cup sugar

3/4 cup or 6 ounces cranberries

3/4 cup self-rising cake flour

pinch of salt

1 teaspoon cinnamon

2 large eggs

1–1 1/2 tablespoons whole milk

tarte-tatin dish, cast-iron straight-sided
8-inch frying pan, or similar

Preheat the oven to 350°F, and put in a baking sheet to heat up at the same time.

Put the cast-iron frying pan—or tarte-tatin dish if you've got one—on the burner over a medium heat and melt the ¼ cup of butter. Add ½ cup of sugar, stir, then empty in the cranberries and turn to coat in the syrupy liquid. Set aside while you get on with the cake.

Put the flour, salt, cinnamon, remaining sugar, ½ cup of butter and the eggs in the processor and blitz to combine. Pulse while you add enough milk down the funnel to make a batter of a soft, dropping consistency. Pour it over the berries in the pan and transfer immediately to the heated baking sheet in the oven. Cook for 30 minutes or until the cake is bouncy, gold, and risen, and beginning to shrink back from the edges.

Take out of the oven and place a plate on top of the pan. Turn upside-down and lift the pan off. Be careful here—it's easy to burn yourself, as I prove time and time again.

Serve warm with crème fraîche or ice cream.

Serves 6.

CHRISTMAS CRÈME BRÛLÉE

I don't need to tell you how beautiful this is: you can see. It's extravagant, certainly, but it's meant to be. And it feels like a treat, breaking through that gilt-tortoiseshell crust to the voluptuous depths of eggnog-scented cream beneath.

The tip of freezing the bowl before pouring in the smooth cream-custard I culled from Simon Hopkinson, for which and for whom I am always grateful.

2¹/2 cups heavy cream
1 teaspoon orange-flower water
good grating fresh nutmeg
8 large egg yolks
3 tablespoons sugar

6 tablespoons demerara or turbinado sugar
3–4 sheets edible gold leaf, optional
pie plate approximately 8 inches in diameter
chef's blowtorch

Put the pie dish in the freezer for at least 20 minutes and half fill the sink with cold water. Put the cream, orange-flower water, and a brave grating of fresh nutmeg into a saucepan, and bring to boiling point, but do not let boil. Beat the egg yolks and granulated sugar together in a bowl, and pour the flavored cream over, still beating. Rinse and dry the pan and pour the custard mix back in. Cook over a medium heat (or low, if you're worried) until the custard thickens: about 10 minutes should do it. You do want this to be a good, voluptuous crème, so don't err on the side of runny caution. Remember you've got your sinkful of cold water to plunge the pan into should it really look as if it's about to split.

When the cream's thick enough, grate over a little more nutmeg and pour into the severely chilled pie dish. Leave to cool, then put in the refrigerator till truly cold. Sprinkle with demerara or turbinado sugar, spoonful by spoonful, and burn with a blowtorch till you have a blistered, tortoiseshell carapace on top. Dab edible gold leaf onto the hard but sticky burnt-sugar crust, using a fat pastry brush or, easier still, your fingertips. Press it gently onto the surface in a random but decorative way, smoothing it down.

Serves 8.

MONT BLANC

I think this may be my favorite dessert of all time. The chestnuts have a dizzying intensity which is a perfect foil for the fat, smooth blandness of the cream. This version is very much easier than the traditional way, which involves cooking then peeling all the chestnuts before you can get started; I know purists insist on it, but it does seem to me to be the fast route to a nervous breakdown, especially at Christmas.

This time of year demands a certain amount of vulgarity, which is why I go for the snowstorm effect with the meringue at the end. Bought meringues are fine, since you pulverize them in your hands to end up with white dust, but by all means make your own if you prefer.

**3¹/₄ cups or 25 ounces vacuum-
   packed peeled chestnuts**
1¹/₃ cups plus 2 tablespoons milk
scant teaspoon vanilla extract
4 tablespoons dark rum
³/₄ cup sugar

4 ounces best bittersweet chocolate
2¹/₂ cups heavy cream
**2–3 meringue nests or meringues
   made with 1 large egg white and
   ¹/₄ cup sugar (page 231)**
potato ricer or food mill

Put the chestnuts in a saucepan with the milk, vanilla, and 3 tablespoons of the rum. Bring to a simmer, and cook until the milk has pretty well been absorbed and the chestnuts are good and tender. This will take about 20 minutes and I find that I have to mash some of the chestnuts with a wooden spoon toward the end of the cooking time to aid the process.

Transfer the chestnut mixture to a food mill (the middle/medium disc) or push it through a sieve back into the saucepan. Stir in the sugar and the final tablespoon of rum and cook over a low to medium heat, stirring all the while for about 10 minutes or until the mixture comes together in a cohesive lump. Remove to a bowl and let cool. I sometimes do this a good couple of days in advance.

Just before you sit down for lunch, get out a huge flat round plate and put an upended cereal bowl in the center. This is to make it easier to make the mountain shape. Now push the cold chestnut purée through the potato ricer—or the food mill—to make a snakey mound over the bowl and plate. Grate the chocolate either by hand or, easier, in the food processor, and sprinkle it over the chestnuts, making sure a lot of the dark dust hits the outside rim of the plate. Then beat the cream till thick and dollop over the chestnuts to make the crowning snowy mound. Just before presenting it, smash the meringues to dust in your hands and sprinkle over. That's it.

Serves 10–12.

GALETTE DES ROIS

I should come clean about my interest in the traditions of the Epiphany: it also happens to be my birthday, and I find following French tradition by eating this cheers me more than taking down the Christmas decorations. The galette itself is simple: puff pastry covering a disc of damp frangipane, hidden within which is a china bean or charm; the person who gets this charm becomes king for the day and is crowned with the gold-paper crown that comes automatically with the cake as sold in French pâtisseries.

You can use store-bought puff pastry or my easy-puff recipe on page 83. If you're not making your own, you'll need to get the squares of puff in 1 pound packages, since the ready-to-roll kind isn't big enough to line or cover the pan. Read through the recipe calmly first, to see how easy in fact it is.

2 17- to 18-ounce packages frozen puff pastry

1³/4 cups ground almonds

1 cup plus 2 tablespoons unsalted butter, very soft indeed

³/4 cup plus 1 tablespoon sugar

¹/3 cup cake flour

1 teaspoon baking powder

¹/2 teaspoon almond extract

2 teaspoons orange-flower water

a dried lima bean or charm, such as a little china figure

gold-paper crown

10-inch springform pan

Preheat the oven to 400°F, putting a baking sheet in to heat up at the same time.

Roll out one of the packages of puff pastry till you can cut out a big enough circle to line the bottom and sides of your pan, with a generous overhang. Put in the refrigerator while you make the frangipane: put all the remaining ingredients (i.e., from ground almonds down to orange-flower water) in the processor and whizz until all's amalgamated.

Open the other package of puff pastry and roll it out till you've got enough to cut out a circle about 2 inches more than the diameter of the pan. Get the pan out of the refrigerator, dollop in the frangipane, hide the charm somewhere, level with a spatula, then place the top round to cover. Using scissors (it's easiest) snip off the overhang so that both top and bottom layers of pastry have only about 1 to 2 inches excess around the edge. Curl the edges over inward, so that you've got a tightly furled sealed rim, and then press all around with the tines of a fork. Now decorate the top of the galette: make a small hole (with the point of a small, sharp knife) in the center, and then, using the same knifepoint, draw swirly lines, like elongated Ss, coming out from the center toward the cake's rim.

Place on the hot baking sheet in the oven and bake for 30–40 minutes until the pastry is golden and well risen. Remove to a wire rack and leave for at least 20 minutes before unclipping. Adorn with crown (or not, as you wish) and present it to the person who gets the charm.

Serves 10–12.

BREAD AND YEAST

BREAD AND YEAST

Baking with yeast is the most addictive of pastimes. Once you start, you realize, first, how easy it is, and second, how almost ridiculously satisfying. Partly, this is to do with the feel, the way you sense the dough coming alive under your hands. But perhaps that's what seems spooky to some people— the thought of live yeast. That's why I am such a champion of those little packages of rapid-rise yeast: real, live, fresh cakes of yeast aren't hard to use (see below) but the packaged stuff seems more approachable at first.

The point is to get stuck in, and then you can move on to fresh cake yeast if it's available—and now that most supermarkets have in-store bakeries it tends to be. But if I'm entirely honest, I'm not sure I could detect the difference between bread that's been risen with fresh yeast cakes and bread that's been made with the packages of yeast.

The one sort of yeast I cannot, however, get on with is active dry yeast, which manufacturers of bread machines seem so keen on. To me, it tastes too intensely yeasty. And while we're here, I should say that the bread machine leaves me cold, also. Why make bread—when anyway you can buy such wonderful loaves now—if it involves no collaboration on your part? There's none of that crucial satisfaction, that warm feeling of homespun achievement. I don't want to suggest that bread baking is the province of the terminally smug—the rewards are real and stem from real activity—but it's very hard not to feel better after kneading dough. As Margaret Costa wrote in her seminal *Four Seasons Cookbook*, it does make "the baker see herself in an almost biblical light as a valiant woman whose children shall rise up and call her blessed."

It's also the case that although the bread machine does a good job of kneading the dough it does a pretty hopeless one of baking the loaf. You may disagree, but this has been my experience, and I did once spend some weeks trying one out. And when my experimental time was up, I was very, very glad to send it back.

The baking of the loaf can be a problem: domestic ovens just aren't good at producing that perfect crackly crustiness. You can try all those tricks that are meant to turn your oven into a professional baker's one—spraying the oven with water from a spritzer as you put the loaf in and regularly thereafter, slipping in underneath it a baking pan filled with ice cubes, and so on—but I have never found they work; or not enough to make the faffing about worthwhile.

But still I bake bread, and urge you to. And you can bake good bread, or I wouldn't be telling you about it. For one thing, you can concentrate on loaves that don't rely on a crackly crust; I love white bread baked with just a dusting of flour. The Finnish loaf, too, has a chewy crust, made by glazing it with melted butter the minute it comes out of the oven. True, my sourdough bread may not be quite as the San Franciscans would make it, but it's still tangy, chewy, and distinctive. I don't believe even an extremely well-appointed steam-injected oven could improve on it.

I've mentioned the kneading process earlier, and I want to return to it, just in case I've given the impression that I'm entirely of the no-pain-no-gain school: I'm not. There is a very good case for letting a mixer fitted with a dough hook do a lot of the hard work for you. But all I'd say is allow yourself just to finish it off, to do a couple of minutes' therapeutic kneading after the machine's done its efficient business. I think, probably wrongly, that the bread's better for it; certainly I feel better.

My way of baking bread is designed to make it fit more easily into the sort of lives we lead. It can be very hard to find time to leave the dough to rise for a couple of hours, and then another hour, and then bake it. What I do—and it does happen to develop and enrich the taste at the same time—is let the bread rise overnight in a cold place, even the refrigerator. This means that you can ease yourself out of the day with a little bit of bedtime kneading, and then the next morning all you need to do is let the chilly dough get to room temperature, form it into a loaf or fit it into a pan, and then leave it to get puffy and oven-ready while you get dressed or read the papers or whatever. It still means that this is more likely to be undertaken as a weekend or holiday activity, but not exclusively so.

In the recipes that follow, I specify an amount of rapid-rise yeast— i.e., yeast that doesn't need to be reconstituted. I give as an alternative double the amount of fresh yeast, and then proceed to give, unfamiliarly, exactly the same methods for using both. This is because—as I learned from a professional baker—you do not need to mix fresh yeast with liquid and then wait for it to foam; you just add it to the flour and so on as if it were the instant sort. I find cutting out this step really does erode any psychological barrier to bread making.

The quality of flour you use makes a difference. I tend to use organic bread flours from reputable mills, but not exclusively. Don't let lack of time for right-on sourcing be the excuse to stop you from immersing yourself pleasurably—if tentatively at first—in this chapter.

THE ESSENTIAL WHITE LOAF

I love homemade white bread, springy and tender crumbed, with a crust dusted with oven-caramelized flour. The best tip I can give you for making good white bread with a light crumb that lasts longer before going stale—which is ever the problem with home-made bread—is to plead with you to use old potato water as the liquid. By this, I just mean the water in which peeled potatoes have cooked. Remember, though, to check the saltiness of the water before throwing in the full amount of salt specified below. I am eccentric enough to keep the water when I drain potatoes, and then bag it up in 1½-cup quantities and stash them in the freezer to use when the bread-making urge is next upon me. Otherwise—and this works remarkably well—you can add a scant tablespoonful of instant mashed potatoes to ordinary warm water. I think it's worth doing this, and not hard to make sure you've got some instant mashed potatoes in the house, however offensive it might be to your culinary self-image.

Perhaps here is the place to try and impress upon you that all bread recipes are approximate guides; the amount of liquid that flour absorbs changes according to the flour and the weather.

3½ cups white bread flour, plus
   more for kneading
1 package (¼ ounce) rapid-rise yeast
   or 1 tablespoon fresh yeast
1 tablespoon salt

approximately 1⅓ cups warm tap or
   potato water
1 tablespoon unsalted butter, softened
1 baking sheet or 9 x 5-inch loaf pan

Put the flour, yeast, and salt in a bowl and pour in ¾ cup of the water, mixing as you do so with a wooden spoon or your hands. Be prepared to add more water, but bear in mind that you want to end up with a shaggy mess (and this of course is the technical term). Add the butter, and mix that in. Now, either start kneading, or if you've got a free-standing mixer, put in the dough hook and let it do the work. Kneading is easy to do but hard to describe. Basically, what you do is press the heel of your hand into the dough, push the dough away, and bring it back and down against the worksurface, for at least 10 minutes. You may need to add more flour as you do so; if the dough seems stickily wet, it means you do want a little more and often a lot more. When you've kneaded enough you will be able to tell the difference—it suddenly feels smoother and less sticky. It's a wonderful moment.

Form the dough into a ball and put into a large oiled or buttered bowl, turning once so the top of the dough is greased. (Most often, I wash out the bowl I've just been using, dry it out, and use it again, letting its residual warmth give a starting oomph to the yeast.) Cover with plastic wrap and put into a cold place or the refrigerator overnight, or in a warm place for an hour or two. If you're giving the bread a short warm rise, then just keep an eye on it; it's ready when it's more or less doubled in size. If you've given it a long cold rise, remove the dough from its cold storage—the next morning, later on that day, whenever—and, if it's doubled in size, punch it down, which means doing exactly what that sounds like: punch it until it deflates; I love doing this. If it doesn't look risen much, leave the bowl out at room temperature for a while (obviously, it's easiest to make bread over the weekend so you have a longer morning) and then proceed as above.

Preheat the oven to 425°F and then, after kneading the dough for a scant minute, form it into a round loaf shape (or however you want) and sit it on the baking sheet (or in the loaf pan) covered loosely with plastic wrap or a tea towel and leave for half an hour or so until puffy and again almost doubled in size. Just before you put it in the oven, remove the towel or plastic and dust with flour; as I've already said, since you can't get a truly crusty loaf from a domestic oven you might as well go for a different effect to start off with.

Bake for 35 minutes or until cooked through; the way to check is to lift up the loaf or remove it from its pan and knock with your knuckles on the underside: if it makes a hollow noise, it's cooked; if not, put it back in the oven for a few minutes. Even if it's been in a pan, do this bit unmolded. When ready, remove to a rack and let cool, if you can, before eating.

And look, I know that home-baked breads can look bulging and full of cracks and fissures—mine, for example, and see the photo on page 295, look rather like the Venus of Willendorf—but that's fine, that's because they're homemade.

MY BROWN BREAD

Everyone has a way of mixing different flours to make the breads they like, and this is one of my favorites for an everyday but highly flavored brown loaf. Follow the essential white loaf recipe, only replace the white flour with:

1 1/3 cups rye flour   **1 1/3 cups white bread flour**
1 1/3 cups whole wheat flour

Be prepared to add slightly more water—and here use ordinary, not potato, water—and bake the bread in an oven preheated to 400°F for about 45 minutes.

POTATO BREAD

This takes the potato-water idea one stage further: you're actually adding cold, cooked potatoes to the dough. This doesn't make a heavy bread, as you might suppose; the whole deal is that the starch in the potato seems to facilitate the yeast and lighten the loaf. But if this is light, it isn't airy: there is a certain chewiness about it, and an almost waxy softness, which makes it perfect for dunking into the wine-dark juices of a rich meat stew. And the toast it makes is incredible.

1 1/3 cups or 11 ounces cold or warm boiled potatoes

4 1/2–5 1/2 cups white bread flour

1 tablespoon salt

1 package (1/4 ounce) rapid-rise yeast or 1 tablespoon fresh yeast

1 tablespoon Greek yogurt

1 1/3 cups tepid potato water

1 baking sheet

Press the potatoes through a ricer into a large bowl—or just mash them once in it—and add 4 cups of the flour together with the salt and the yeast. Mix together, adding the yogurt and then the water slowly. (Even if your potato water's salty, still add the salt to the flour earlier; on cooking, the potatoes themselves tend to neutralize salinity so you have to emphasize it—though not exaggerate it—at this stage.) When you've got something approaching a dough, tip it out onto a floured surface (or keep it in the bowl and use the mixer's dough hook) and begin kneading, adding more flour as you need it. I find I can end up using another 1 1/3 cups or so.

This is damper and stickier than ordinary white bread dough, so be prepared to keep kneading for a bit longer, but when you have something that looks like it's hanging together densely (I give it about 10 minutes in my KitchenAid fitted with the dough hook, then 2 minutes by hand), form a heavy ball—it won't be very neat—put it into a buttered bowl, turn to coat well, cover with plastic wrap, and leave in a cold place overnight or a warm place for an hour or so.

When the dough's doubled in size, punch it down, letting any repressed anger joyfully out, knead for a minute, and form into a loaf of whatever shape pleases you, and preheat the oven to 425°F. Set it on the baking sheet, loosely covered with a tea towel, and after about 30 minutes, when the bread's puffy and almost doubled in size, put it in the oven for 20 minutes, before turning the temperature down to 375°F and giving it another 10 minutes or until it's cooked through. Test, as usual, by knocking on the loaf's underside: when cooked, it should give a distinctly hollow sound.

Remove from the oven and let cool on a rack.

FINNISH RYE BREAD

This is my adaptation of a wonderful loaf which comes from the equally wonderful Beatrice Ojakangas. It's dense, dark, and aromatic in an extraordinarily comforting way. I'm not Finnish, and yet I warm to this loaf as if I were brought up on it.

1¹/₂ cups rye flour

2 cups white bread flour

1 package (¹/₄-ounce) rapid-rise yeast
    or 1 tablespoon fresh yeast

1 tablespoon dark brown sugar

2 teaspoons salt

1¹/₃ cups warm water

3 tablespoons unsalted butter, melted

1 baking sheet

Put the flours, yeast, sugar, and salt into a large bowl and slowly add the water, mixing with your hands or a wooden spoon, until you've got a messy but vaguely cohesive lump of dough. Add a tablespoonful of the melted butter and mix just to incorporate it. Start kneading, either by hand or with the dough hook, until the dough comes together smoothly to form a dense ball, adding more water or flour (and I use the white bread flour, not the rye, mainly) as necessary.

Use some more of the melted butter to grease a bowl and turn the dough ball in it so that the top is oily (and won't therefore dry out), then cover the bowl with plastic wrap and leave to rise in a cold place overnight or for an hour or so somewhere warm.

When the dough's doubled in size, punch it down. This is never quite as satisfying with dense doughs as it is with white breads, but it's pleasurable all the same. Give a good few kneads, and then form into a round loaf. Set the loaf on the baking sheet, cover it with a tea towel, and leave to get puffy for about 30 minutes, during which time preheat the oven to 375°F. Bake for 45–55 minutes, or until the loaf is cooked through. It should sound hollow when you rap it on its underside with your knuckles, and an inserted skewer should come out clean.

Brush with the remaining tablespoon of melted butter and leave on a wire rack to cool.

SOURDOUGH

The reason this isn't quite a real sourdough is that it uses a teeny-weeny bit of yeast in the starter, rather than relying only on wild yeasts picked up from the atmosphere. I am not going to give an entire history and account of what a sourdough loaf is, but it helps to think of it as a bread made in three parts, with time in between for the dough to mature and acquire the characteristic tang. I know the idea of a long-drawn-out, tripartite baking process is not necessarily a welcome one, but presumably you do this because you want to, not because you are trying to find time-saving ways in the kitchen and kind of stumbled onto this by mistake.

Anyway, first you have the starter, which is really just a mixture of flour and water, with—and this is the unorthodox, not to say improper, way I do it—the addition of a drop of milk and pinch of yeast. You leave this to get good and sour and bubbly, and then you use some of it to mix the second part—the sponge—with more flour and water. Third and finally, you make the dough, which is the sponge with, again, more flour and more water. I add yeast to this; I'm not sure I should, but the American who first showed me the way of the sourdough did, so I carry on in this vein.

It is the method which is significant with sourdough; you can decide which flours you use to make it. I tend to make rye sourdough or an ordinary white sourdough loaf. I say ordinary, but it isn't at all. It's rather like—and is indeed related to—that wonderful, dense and chewy French *pain gris*. And I've made good bread by using the rye starter in a loaf otherwise made exclusively with white flour too.

The hardest thing about sourdough is not making the bread but keeping the starter alive. I always forget to feed it, which is the term used for adding flour and water to it regularly to keep it going. It dies on me. Or rather, I should say, I kill it out of neglect. To keep it alive, every time you use a cup, stir in another $1/2$ cup of water and $3/4$ cup of flour and leave out of the fridge for 4 hours. Do this once every two weeks if you can.

for the starter:
1 cup rye or white bread flour
pinch of yeast from package of rapid-rise yeast (like a small pinch of salt) or a fatter pinch of fresh yeast

1/2 teaspoon of milk
approximately 3/4 cup plus 2 tablespoons water

Combine the flour, yeast, and milk and as much water to make a mixture like a thick pancake batter, and leave, loosely covered, for 3 days.

for the sponge:

3/4 cup of starter

3/4 cup of warm water

1/2 cup rye or white bread flour

Mix all the ingredients together in a 1-cup measuring cup and leave tightly covered for 12–18 hours; longer is better but the shorter time is enough if that's all you've got.

for the dough:

2 1/4 cups whole wheat bread flour (for the rye sourdough) or 3 1/2 cups white bread flour

the rest of the package of rapid-rise yeast or 1 tablespoon fresh yeast

all of the sponge from above

1 scant tablespoon salt

1 tablespoon caraway seeds (for rye sourdough only)

1–1 1/4 cups warm water

vegetable oil for greasing bowl

1 baking sheet

Put the flour and yeast in a large bowl, then stir in the other ingredients till you've got a shaggy mess that looks like it's on its way to becoming a dough. Knead, either by hand or by machine, adding more flour as needed, to form a dense, smooth dough.

Form into a ball and put in an oiled bowl, turning once so that the top is also greased. Cover with plastic wrap and leave to double in size, either overnight in a cold place or the refrigerator, or for an hour or so somewhere warm.

When the dough's done its stuff, punch it down, knead it for 1–2 minutes, and form it into a round loaf and set it, covered with a tea towel, on a baking sheet. Preheat the oven to 400°F, and let the oven warm up while the loaf is left, for about 30 minutes, until it's puffy.

Uncover, and score the top of the loaf. For ease, you should use a razor blade or *lame* for this, but a sharp knife will do. It must be very sharp, though, because you don't want to use any pressure or the now nicely puffy loaf will deflate. I make about 5 slashes all the way over the top diagonally one way, and then the other to make a rough checkerboard design. Transfer to the oven and bake for about 45 minutes, until the loaf is cooked and sounds hollow when you rap it firmly on its underside.

NORWEGIAN MOUNTAIN LOAF

This was one of the recipes—along with the cinnamon buns on page 322—I greedily plundered from Trine Bell, a friend who's half Norwegian and is generous with her culinary birthright. As much as I love a good, British white loaf, I have a real weakness for those nubbly Northern European breads that are dense and virtuously substantial.

Because this is very easy to make, it can soon become part of a pretty painless routine. You can play around, as you like, with flours, seeds, and grains.

1 cup plus 2 tablespoons low-fat milk

1 cup plus 2 tablespoons water

2¹/4 cups whole wheat bread flour

¹/3 cup rye flour

1 package (¹/4 ounce) rapid-rise yeast or 1 tablespoon fresh yeast

¹/4 cup rolled oats (not instant)

2 tablespoons wheat germ

3 tablespoons sunflower seeds

3 tablespoons linseeds

1 tablespoon salt

non-stick loaf-shaped mold or baking sheet or ordinary well-buttered loaf pan

Mix the milk and water together in a measuring cup, and combine all the other ingredients in a large bowl. Pour the liquid into the dry ingredients, stirring all the while, to make a sticky, porridgelike mixture.

Scrape into an incredibly well-buttered loaf pan—or better still, a sturdy non-stick silicon loaf pan, which you need not prepare in any way—and put into a cold oven. Turn it on to 225°F and after 30 minutes turn it up to 350°F. Bake for 1 hour, though in some ovens it may need 10–15 minutes more. You should be able to slip it out of its pan and check by the knocking method, but with a loaf of this heaviness that's not always a reliable gauge, so do poke in a cake tester or fine skewer to make sure; if it comes out clean, the loaf's cooked. If not, you can just put it back into the oven without its pan and give it another few minutes.

MAPLE-PECAN BREAD

You won't find much in the way of flavored breads here, fashionable though they are. I don't go in for them. Bread, like a pasta, is best at conveying other flavors, not jumping about in a ra-ra skirt showing off its own. But this is an exception: it has nuts and syrup in it, but the overall effect is muted. And it stays true to its proper calling: that's to say, this is a bread that comes into its own with cheese.

3¹/₂ cups whole wheat bread flour
1 cup white bread flour
1 tablespoon salt
1 package (¹/₄ ounce) rapid-rise yeast
   or 1 tablespoon fresh yeast
1¹/₃–1²/₃ cups warm water

4 tablespoons maple syrup
¹/₄–¹/₂ cup chopped pecans
   (or walnuts)
oil (walnut oil, if you've got some) or
   butter for greasing
1 baking sheet

Combine the flours, salt, and yeast in a large bowl. Measure out 1¹/₃ cups of the warm water and stir in the maple syrup. Pour the liquid into the dry ingredients and stop when you've got a rough dough; you may need an extra ¹/₃ cup or so of water to reach this stage. Knead for a few minutes, then leave for 20 minutes.

Start kneading again, sprinkling in the nuts. It's entirely up to you how nutty to make this: with cheese I think the upper limit is fine; as an ordinary eating loaf, I'd go for the lighter amount. Carry on kneading until the dough feels smooth and elastic (though this amount of whole wheat means it won't feel that elastic) and then form into a ball.

Grease a bowl with oil, and turn the dough ball in the oil, so that the top is lightly slicked with it too. Cover the bowl with plastic wrap and leave to rise in the kitchen for 1–2 hours or until about doubled, or follow the general method for a cold, slow rise.

Punch the dough down, knead for 1 minute, and then form into a loaf. Set this loaf on a baking sheet, cover with a tea towel, preheat the oven to 425°F, and leave the dough for about 30 minutes or until puffy.

Score the loaf with a blade or sharp knife—I tend just to give three short diagonal slashes on this one—and transfer to the oven. After 15 minutes, turn the temperature down to 375°F and give a further 20 minutes or so. Check the bread's ready by rapping its bottom, then transfer to a wire rack to cool.

BAGELS

I know that making your own bagels seems like a fairly abstruse practice. I include a recipe partly because most of the bagels for sale here in London are not bagels at all, but bread rolls with a hole in the middle—real bagels should be chewy, not remotely airy, with a tightly woven crumb—but also because they're a pleasure to make. They belong here, and not in the children's chapter, though children really enjoy making them, or rather forming them. I do too.

The cooking isn't hard—though it's a dough that needs muscle power—even if it is a two-staged affair: you poach them first, and then bake them. The recipe is adapted from George Greenstein's *Secrets of a Jewish Baker*—where else should you be getting a bagel recipe?—whose tip it is to add malt to the poaching liquid to help the bagels acquire that characteristic sweet and shiny crust. Malt syrup, or extract, is sold at most health food stores and many supermarkets; but failing that, just use sugar.

6 2/3–7 cups white bread flour, plus more as necessary for kneading

1 tablespoon salt

1 package (1/4 ounce) rapid-rise yeast or 1 tablespoon fresh yeast

2 tablespoons sugar

1 tablespoon vegetable oil, plus more for greasing

2 1/4 cups warm water, plus more as needed

2 tablespoons malt or sugar, for poaching the bagels

2–3 baking sheets, oiled or greased

Combine the flour, salt, and yeast together in a large bowl. Add the sugar and oil to the water. Make a well in the dry ingredients and add the liquid, mixing to a dough with a spatula or wooden spoon.

Knead the dough either by hand or with a dough hook, trying to add more flour if you can. Often with doughs you want them as wet as you can manage; here, dry is good.

The dough will be very stiff and hard work, I know, but knead until you've got a really smooth, elastic dough; even with the dough hook and an electric mixer, this takes about 10 minutes.

Form the dough into a ball, and put it into an oiled bowl, turning once to coat all around, then cover the bowl with plastic wrap and leave it to rise for about 1 hour. It should be well risen, and, when you poke it with your finger, the impression should remain.

Now punch the dough down, really punch, and then give a good knead and divide the dough into 3 pieces. Using your hands, roll each piece into a rope, then cut each rope into 5 pieces. Roll each piece between the palms of your hands into a ball, and

then roll into another rope, curling it around to form a ring. Seal the ends by overlapping them a little and pinching them together. At about this time put on a large pan of water to boil. When it boils, add the malt or sugar.

Set the bagels on the baking sheets, cover with tea towels and leave for about 20 minutes, by which time they should be puffy. Now preheat the oven to 500°F or your maximum oven temperature.

When the malted water's boiling and your bagels are good and puffy, start poaching them. Drop a couple of bagels at a time into the boiling water and boil for 1 minute, turning them once. I use a couple of large spatulas for this (wasn't it Portnoy who always presumed spatula was a Yiddish word?).

As you poach them, put them back onto the oiled baking sheets, well spaced, then bake for 10–15 minutes or until they're shiny and golden brown.

Makes 15 bagels.

GARLIC AND PARSLEY HEARTHBREADS

These are something between garlic nan and herby focaccia: dimpled, doughy, and headily pungent. When lunch is cold and sparse—some sharp cheese, some sliced tomatoes, a green salad—these bring everything substantially, chin-drippingly together. (But please try making them once to eat with fried eggs and maybe some fried or grilled tomatoes.)

3¹/₂ cups white bread flour
1 package (¹/₄ ounce) rapid-rise yeast
  or 1 tablespoon fresh yeast
1 tablespoon salt
1¹/₃–1²/₃ cups warm water
5 tablespoons olive oil, plus more for
  greasing and for pouring over the
  garlic

3 large or 4 small heads of garlic
extra-virgin olive oil for drizzling
bunch of flat-leaf parsley
salt for sprinkling
2 baking sheets

Preheat the oven to 375°F.

Combine the flour, yeast, and salt in a bowl. Pour 1¹/₃ cups warm water into a measuring cup and stir in the olive oil. Mix the liquid with the dry ingredients to make a soft but firm dough, adding more liquid as needed, and either turn this out onto a surface and knead by hand or keep in the bowl and use a mixer fitted with the dough hook and knead until smooth, supple, and full of elastic life. Form into a ball, wash out

and dry the bowl, oil it, and turn the dough in it so it's lightly oiled all over. Cover the bowl with plastic wrap and leave to rise for an hour or so until doubled in size.

While the bread is rising, trim the tops off the heads of garlic, making sure they remain whole, sit them in some torn-off squares of foil, dribble over some oil, and wrap them loosely. That's to say, the packages should be baggy but the foil tightly sealed at the edges. Cook the garlic packages for 45 minutes; they should not be mushy by this stage but still just holding their shape. Remove from the oven, unwrap, and let cool till you can handle them. Turn the oven up to 400°F.

Tear the parsley leaves from their stems and add a good handful to the bowl of the food processor—not worrying if some stems here and there are left on—and chop. Squeeze the soft garlic cloves out of their skins and into the bowl and process again. Pour in enough extra-virgin olive oil to make a runny paste down the funnel, while still processing, and leave this pungent emulsion where it is while you get back to the bread.

When the dough's risen, punch it down and leave to rest for 10 minutes. Divide the dough in half, and get out 2 sheets of baking parchment. Sit a ball of dough on each, and roll out to form a curved rectangle or bulky oval. Then, using your hands, press out a little more. Transfer the breads on their papers to the baking sheets, cover with tea towels and leave to rise and get puffy for about 25 minutes.

Poke your fingers all over the tops of the breads to dimple them, then go back to the processor and pulse once or twice to make sure the parsley, garlic, and oil are combined and pour this green mixture all over the corrugated flatbreads.

Put the baking sheets into the oven and bake for 20 minutes or until the breads are cooked—becoming golden in parts, with the garlic flecks a darker brown, and the rims puffing up around the oily topping. Whip out of the oven and drizzle over a generous amount of good extra-virgin olive oil. Sprinkle over some salt and set down on the table for people to tear greedily at with their bare hands.

Serves 4 generously.

SCHIACCIATA WITH GORGONZOLA AND PINE NUTS

When I lived in Florence, I ate what is routinely called focaccia here but knew it as "schiacciata." This is another softer, doughier pizza, like the hearthbreads, but topped with Gorgonzola and a scattering of pine nuts. I love it as a first course with some salty-sweet Parma ham.

2¹/₄ cups white bread flour	¹/₂ cup plus 2 tablespoons, or 5
1 cup cake flour	ounces Gorgonzola
1 package (¹/₄ ounce) rapid-rise yeast	freshly ground pepper
or 1 tablespoon fresh yeast	grating fresh nutmeg
2 teaspoons salt	3–5 tablespoons extra-virgin olive oil
1¹/₃–1²/₃ cups warm water	3 tablespoons pine nuts
3 tablespoons olive oil	roasting pan, measuring approximately
	8 x 12 x 2 inches

Combine the flours, yeast, and salt in a bowl. Pour 1¹/₃ cups of the warm water into a measuring cup and stir in the 2 tablespoons of olive oil. Pour the liquid over the dry ingredients and mix to form a soft but firm dough, adding more water as necessary.

Now start kneading, treating this dough exactly as in the hearthbread recipe, only when it's risen and doubled in size, don't divide it in halves but set it in the roasting pan and press to fit, letting it rest for a few minutes if it looks as if it's never going to stretch to all four corners (it will) and then going at it again. Cover the dough with a tea towel and preheat the oven to 425°F. After 30 minutes or so, the dough should be puffy and ready for its topping.

In a bowl, with a fork, mash the cheese till soft and keep mashing while you add a generous amount of pepper and a meaner amount of nutmeg. Keep forking while you add the extra-virgin olive oil; if the 3 tablespoons aren't enough to make this a spreadable, just pourable mixture, add more.

Poke your fingers all over the dough to dimple it and then pour over the Gorgonzola mixture. Sprinkle the pine nuts on top and bake for 10 minutes. Reduce the heat to 375°F and cook for a further 15–25 minutes until the rims of the schiacciata are golden brown and the cheese is bubbling.

Remove from the oven, cut into fat, chunky slices, and let people take them straight from the pan—or transfer to a board or plate if you feel happier that way.

NIGELLAN FLATBREAD

Look, the name is meant to be a bit of joke, but what I'm talking about is a pita-like bread, glazed golden with beaten egg and sprinkled with nigella seeds. I came across a recipe rather like it in Eric Treuille and Ursula Ferrigno's inspirational *Bread* and made it, you could say, my own. (You can get the nigella seeds, usually marked "kalonji," from shops that sell Indian food, and many more besides.)

This is what I make when I'm in mezze-mode. It's not hard, and although I love some of the flatbreads you can buy (not particularly the pitas, but the doughier, softer, tear-shaped hearthbreads), it gives me more pleasure to make these, doubling the quantity and putting the flat oval loaves in the oven in batches so there's always a wooden board of warm, dippable bread on the table.

for the bread:
- **3¹/₂ cups white bread flour**
- **1 package (¹/₄ ounce) rapid-rise yeast or 1 tablespoon fresh yeast**
- **2 teaspoons salt**
- **2 tablespoons yogurt**
- **2 tablespoons olive oil, plus more for greasing**
- **approximately 1¹/₃ cups warm water**

for the glaze:
- **1 large egg**
- **1 teaspoon water**
- **1 teaspoon plain yogurt**
- **1 tablespoon nigella (kalonji) seeds**
- **2 baking sheets**

Combine the flour, yeast, and salt in a large bowl and make a well. Dollop the yogurt and oil into a measuring cup and add warm water to come up to the 1¹/₂-cup mark. Give a quick beat with a fork to combine, then pour this liquid into the dry ingredients, and mix with your hands or a wooden spoon, adding more liquid as needed, to form a firm but soft dough.

Turn out onto a floured surface (or set your mixer and dough hook to work) and start kneading. Add more flour as needed until you've got a smooth, supple, and elastic dough. Form the dough into a ball, grease a bowl, and turn the dough in it so it's lightly oiled all over. Cover the bowl with plastic wrap and leave to rise for about an hour or so, until doubled in size.

Punch the dough down, then leave to rest for 10 minutes. Preheat the oven to 425°F. Tear the dough into thirds, and then halve each piece. Form each of these 6 little pieces into an egg-shape and, one by one, roll them out to make a flat, elongated, if irregular oval. Place on baking sheets about 1¹/₂ inches apart, cover with tea towels, and leave to prove for 20 minutes, until puffy.

Using the blunt side of an ordinary kitchen knife, draw diagonal parallel lines across the loaves about ³/₄ inch apart. Do the same now the other direction, so you've got a loose crisscross.

Beat the egg with the water and yogurt and, using a pastry brush, paint this over the breads. Sprinkle on the nigella seeds and bake in the hot oven for 8–10 minutes, by which time the loaves will be golden, puffed up in places, and cooked through.

Remove them from the oven and drape immediately and for a few minutes with a tea towel so that these small, flat, breads don't dry up and get too crusty.

Makes 6.

LAHMACUN

This is one of the first things I order in Turkish restaurants—though there are variants of it in all Eastern Mediterranean cuisines —and if you haven't tried it, do so now. The simplest, if not the most appetizing, way to describe it is to say that it is a sort of Turkish pizza with a topping of finely ground lamb. Imagine discs of gold-rimmed soft-crumbed flatbread, with a smear of spiced and peppery-lemony meat daubed on top. We make these for lunch, with just a green salad and maybe some sharp goat's cheese to go with.

You can find pomegranate molasses or syrup in supermarkets these days as well as at Middle Eastern stores, but lemon juice can be substituted. It hasn't got the depth or rounded bitterness of the pomegranate molasses, but the short, sharp sourness of the citrus brings its own pleasing contrast with the sweet, spiced meat. As for that, do buy it minced if you prefer, but this is one of the few times you actually want the fine pulping that the blades of the food processor bring about.

for the dough:
1 cup bread flour
¹/2 cup all-purpose flour
1 teaspoon rapid-rise yeast or
   1 teaspoon fresh
¹/2 teaspoon salt
¹/2 cup warm water
1 tablespoon olive oil

for the topping:
1 medium onion, finely chopped
1 fat garlic clove, finely grated
2 tablespoons olive oil

9 ounces lamb, very finely chopped in
   the processor
pinch of cayenne
pinch of ground allspice
¹/2 teaspoon cumin
2 tablespoons tomato purée
2 tablespoons finely chopped flat-leaf
   parsley, plus more for serving
1 tablespoon pomegranate molasses
   (or lemon juice)
salt and pepper to taste
4 tablespoons melted butter
2 baking sheets, oiled

Combine the flours, yeast, and salt in a large bowl. Add the water and oil, and mix to a dough. Knead for 5–10 minutes, depending on whether you are using your hands or a dough hook on a mixer. You can stop kneading when the dough is smooth and elastic.

Place in an oiled bowl, turn well, and cover with plastic wrap. Let it rise in a warm place for about an hour or until it has doubled in size.

Preheat the oven to 425°F.

Meanwhile, to make the lamb paste for the top, fry the onion and garlic in the oil until soft but not colored. If you sprinkle in a pinch of salt it should help stop them browning. Add the minced or processor-pulped lamb, along with the cayenne, allspice, and cumin, and then stir in the tomato purée. Move the lamb about to break it up well, and cook for about 10 minutes until the lamb is no longer pink. Finally, add the parsley and pomegranate molasses or lemon juice and, after tasting, season with salt and pepper to taste.

Knock the dough back to get rid of the air, and divide into 8 egg-sized pieces.

Roll these out into circles of about 5 inches in diameter. Let them rest on the oiled baking sheets, with tea towels draped over them, for about 10 minutes.

Dollop about 1 tablespoon of the lamb paste onto each circle, spreading to cover the center of each one well. Paint the pizzas with melted butter, especially the edges, and cook for 8–10 minutes. When they come out of the oven, cover with a cloth—I know it will get dirty, but *tant pis*—to prevent a hard crust forming. The point about these is that they should be soft enough for you to bend them in two or roll them up to eat.

Sprinkle over more parsley, if you want, as you put them out on the table.

Makes 8 (enough for 4 people, just).

PIZZA CASARECCIA

This is the pizza as made in the Calabrian home of my own domestic goddess, Lisa Grillo. While we all struggle to produce that thin-crusted, charcoal-redolent pizzaiolo's pizza and fail, the Italians recognize that you need to go to the pizzeria for that and have instead devised a homemade alternative, doughier and with more topping, but very good in its own but different way.

I've marked the anchovies for the topping as optional, but in truth all of it is. The list that follows was how Lisa made it, but I suspect it was how Lisa made it because that was what she had in the house. And as for the cheese, don't worry if you don't have parmesan or mozzarella: Italians are mad about Cheddar on pizza.

for the dough:
1 2/3 cups cake flour
1 heaping teaspoon (1/2 package)
   yeast
1/2 teaspoon salt
approximately 1/2 cup plus
   2 tablespoons warm water
2 tablespoons extra-virgin olive oil
1 baking sheet

for the topping:
1 cup or 8 ounces canned chopped
   tomatoes
salt and pepper
2–3 pinches dried oregano
4 slices fine-cut ham
2–3 gherkins, chopped
5 anchovies, optional
fresh parmesan, mozzarella, or cheese
   of your choice

Combine the flour, yeast, and salt in a large bowl, and stir in the warm water and the olive oil, adding more water as necessary to form a dough. When you've got a shaggy mess that's on its way to being a dough, tip the contents out onto a lightly floured surface and knead for about 5 minutes (or do all this with an electric mixer's dough hook) or until the dough is smooth and bouncy, though expect this still to be on the sticky side. Put into an oiled bowl and turn it to cover it lightly with the oil. Then cover the bowl with plastic wrap and leave somewhere warm for an hour till the dough's doubled in size.

Preheat the oven to 500°F.

Knock the air out of the dough using well-oiled hands, knead a little, and press onto the baking sheet in either a rectangular or round shape. Cover with the chopped tomatoes which have been seasoned with some salt, pepper and the oregano. Put into the very hot oven for about 20 minutes or until the dough has a hollow sound when knocked.

Add the topping of your choice, then put the pizza back in the oven and cook for a further 5–10 minutes or until the cheese has melted and the base is crisp.

Serves 4 generously.

GERMAN PLUM TART

I first made this a couple of years ago now, and it was one of the recipes that drew me to yeast cookery, made me want to do more. The inspirational force is Linda Collister—you just cannot read her without wanting to put on an apron and get your hands stuck into some flour—and this comes from *Sweet Pies and Tarts*. While the two yeasted flat tarts that follow this are more suitable for long, greedy weekend breakfasts, this makes a sumptuous dessert. You could easily make the dough in the morning, set it in the refrigerator for a slow rise all day and then, with relative lack of effort, get this finished once you've got back from work, even if it's quite late. And the one thing it doesn't taste like is a hastily knocked-up little something.

for the dough:
- **½ package rapid-rise yeast (about 1½ teaspoons) or 1½ teaspoons fresh yeast**
- **about 2¼ cups white bread flour**
- **½ teaspoon salt**
- **2 tablespoons sugar**
- **¾ cup plus 2 tablespoons milk, lukewarm**
- **1 medium egg, beaten**
- **2 tablespoons unsalted butter, very soft**

for the filling:
- **1¼ pounds plums, halved and pitted**
- **3 tablespoons turbinado sugar**

for the crumble topping:
- **1 cup all-purpose flour**
- **scant ½ cup light brown sugar**
- **½ cup unsalted butter, diced**
- **1 cup walnut or pecan pieces**
- **1 large baking sheet—about 13 x 9 inch—greased or nonstick, or a roasting pan approximately 8 x 12 inches, also greased or nonstick**

To make the dough, put the yeast, flour, salt, and sugar into a mixing bowl, and slowly pour in the warm milk, stirring as you do so. Add the beaten egg and the soft butter, and stir to a soft and sticky dough. Turn out onto a floured board and knead for a good 10 minutes, or for about half that time in an electric mixer fitted with a dough hook. Don't use a food processor. The dough should be soft and satiny but not stickily wet: if you think you need to add more flour, then do; different flours absorb different amounts of liquid. Cover and let rise for 1 hour at room temperature.

To prepare the filling, toss the prepared plums with the sugar (and I sometimes use half light brown, half granulated rather than the stipulated turbinado) and set aside.

Preheat the oven to 375°F.

To make the crumble topping, combine the flour with the sugar in a mixing bowl, then work in the butter with your fingers to make pea-sized clumps of dough. Stir in the nuts and set aside.

Knock down the risen dough with your knuckles, and push out into a rectangle to cover the baking sheet or press it out in the roasting pan. (This is easier than rolling it and then transferring it, and you are not trying to produce a smooth, even finish.) Top with the plums, cut sides up, then sprinkle with the nutty crumble topping. Bake in the preheated oven for about 30 minutes until the base is golden, the fruit tender, and the topping crisp and brown.

Serve warm, with cream, crème fraîche, or ice cream—vanilla or cinnamon if you can get it.

Serves 8.

VARIATIONS

You can use whatever fruit you like here, with or without the topping or a version there-of. Cherries, messily pitted over the baking sheet so that you lose none of the juices, are wonderful, especially with almonds in place of the pecans. Apples are also good, with or without blackberries. The wonderful thing about this yeasted pastry is that it absorbs and acts as a foil to any amount of fruity juiciness.

But please, don't rule out a yeasted base for savory tarts, too. Sweat onions or leeks in butter or bacon fat and spread them out on a puffy sheet of dough made by following the recipe above, but leaving out the sugar. Grate over cheese if so wished, cut into rough squares, and eat while still warm.

APPLE KUCHEN

Kuchen, in German, just means cake. In America, it means something more specific—that yeasted, plain, but often fruit-topped, coffee cake that the German immigrants brought with them to the New World. As you might expect, it is good with coffee, and makes a fabulous breakfast if you've got people staying and you want to sit around the table eating, drinking, talking, reading the papers in an aromatic fug of apple-pie spice and buttery yeasty dough.

What I do is make the dough up before I go to bed and leave it, wrapped with plastic wrap, in the refrigerator overnight. When I get up the next morning, I turn on the oven, let the dough come back to room temperature and then I get on with the rest. It's probably ready about an hour after I've got up, which, considering how spectacular it is, is not bad going. It freezes well, too, so you can always do one batch to last you over a few weekends' worth of breakfasts.

for the dough:
2¼–3 cups white bread flour
½ teaspoon salt
2 tablespoons sugar
½ package rapid-rise yeast (1½ teaspoons) or 1½ teaspoons fresh yeast
2 large eggs
½ teaspoon vanilla extract
grated zest of ½ a lemon
good grating fresh nutmeg
½ cup milk, lukewarm
¼ cup unsalted butter, softened
Swiss-roll pan or rectangular baking dish approximately 12 x 8 inches

for the topping:
2 Granny Smith apples
1 large egg
1 tablespoon cream
grating of fresh nutmeg
1 tablespoon demerara or turbinado sugar
1 tablespoon sugar
¼ teaspoon allspice
2 tablespoons slivered almonds

for the icing:
⅓ cup confectioners' sugar, sifted
1 tablespoon hot water

Put 2¼ cups of the flour in a bowl with the salt, sugar, and yeast. Beat the eggs and add them, with the vanilla, lemon zest, and nutmeg, to the lukewarm milk. Stir the liquid ingredients into the dry ingredients, to make a medium-soft dough, being prepared to add more flour as necessary. I generally use about 2⅔ cups, but advise you to start off with the smaller amount: just add more as needed. Work in the soft butter and knead by hand for about 10 minutes or half that time by machine. When the dough is ready it will appear smoother, and springier. It suddenly seems to plump up into glossy life.

Cover with a tea towel and leave till doubled (1–1¼ hours), or leave to rise slowly in a cold place overnight. Then punch down and press to line the pan. You may think it's never going to stretch to fill, but let it rest for 10 minutes or so mid-stretch, especially if the dough had a cold rise. When it's pressed out on the pan, leave it to rise for 15–20 minutes. Preheat the oven to 400°F. Peel and core the apples and chop them finely; I use a processor but there's really no need. And you could use other apples, too, if you prefer: whatever you've got to hand; cooking apples can easily be substituted and are better if you want a pulpier covering.

When the dough's ready, beat the egg with the cream, grate over a little nutmeg and brush the top of the dough with this mixture. Cover the egg-glazed dough with the apples, then mix together the sugars and allspice and sprinkle over. Top with the flaked almonds and put in the oven for 15 minutes. Then turn down to 350°F and cook for a further 15 minutes or so, until the dough is swelling and golden at the edges and cooked within.

Remove from the oven and make a runny paste with the sifted confectioners' sugar and the hot water. Spoon or trickle over the cake.

Leave to cool for about 15 minutes, then slice it, and eat while it's still warm and juicily, stickily fragrant.

Serves 8.

RHUBARB-CRUMBLE KUCHEN

Well, this is the introduction of a very British taste to a very un-British confection and it works wonderfully—there is sometimes something to be said for melting-pot cooking.

This is a minor point, but I do think you need to drink tea, not coffee, with it.

for the dough:

2¼–3 cups white bread flour

½ teaspoon salt

3 tablespoons sugar

½ package rapid-rise yeast (about
1½ teaspoons) or 1½ teaspoon
fresh yeast

2 large eggs

½ teaspoon vanilla extract

grated zest of ½ a lemon

good grating of fresh nutmeg

½ cup milk, lukewarm

¼ cup unsalted butter, softened

Swiss-roll pan or rectangular baking
dish approximately 12 x 8 inches

for the filling:

1 large egg

1 tablespoon cream

grating of fresh nutmeg

18 ounces rhubarb (to make
12 ounces trimmed weight)

¼ cup sugar

¼ teaspoon allspice

for the crumble topping:

2 tablespoons unsalted butter, cold
and diced

scant ¼ cup self-rising flour

1 tablespoon sugar

1 tablespoon turbinado sugar

For the dough, follow the recipe for the apple kuchen.

When you've pressed the dough out in the pan, leave it to rise for 15–20 minutes. Preheat the oven to 400°F. When the dough is ready, beat the egg and cream together, grate over some nutmeg, and brush the mixture over the dough.

To make the crumble topping, rub the cold, diced butter into the flour until it becomes like oaty sand, then stir in the sugars with a fork. Chop the rhubarb finely and stir it together with the sugar and allspice. Don't do this until the last minute, though, as the sugar will make the rhubarb leach out water as it stands. Sprinkle the rhubarb-sugar mixture over the egg-washed dough, and then the crumble on top of that. Put in the oven for 15 minutes, then turn down to 350°F and cook for a further 15 minutes or so, until the dough is swelling and golden at the edges and cooked within.

Remove from the oven, and leave in the pan for about 15 minutes—if you can— then slice and eat, still warm.

Serves 8.

NORWEGIAN CINNAMON BUNS

The Northern Europeans, and especially the Scandinavians, are wonderful bakers and eating these for breakfast or tea on a cold winter's day makes one feel ours is a climate to be grateful for. But then, I've always thought that bad weather has its compensations, most of them culinary.

for the dough:

4 cups flour

¹/₃ cup sugar

¹/₂ teaspoon salt

scant 3 tablespoons (3¹/₄-ounce packages—yes, really) of rapid-rise yeast or 3 tablespoons fresh yeast

scant ¹/₂ cup butter

1²/₃ cups milk

2 eggs

for the filling:

¹/₂ cup plus 2 tablespoons soft, unsalted butter

¹/₂ cup plus 2 tablespoons sugar

1¹/₂ teaspoons cinnamon

1 egg, beaten, to glaze

roasting pan approximately 13 x 10 inches or large square pan, lined with parchment or wax paper

Preheat the oven to 450°F.

Combine the flour, sugar, salt, and yeast in a large bowl. Melt the butter and whisk it into the milk and eggs, then stir it into the flour mixture. Mix to combine and then knead the dough either by hand or using the dough hook of an electric mixer until it's smooth and springy. Form into a ball, place in an oiled bowl, cover with plastic wrap, and leave it to rise for about 25 minutes.

Take one third of the dough and roll it or stretch it to fit your pan; this will form the bottom of each bun when it has cooked. Roll out the rest of the dough on a lightly floured surface, aiming to get a rectangle of roughly 20 by 10 inches. Mix the filling ingredients in a small bowl and then spread the rectangle with the buttery cinnamon mixture. Try to get even coverage on the whole of the dough. Roll it up from the longest side until you have a giant sausage. Cut the roll into ³/₄-inch slices, which should make about 20 rounds. Set the rounds in lines on top of the dough in the pan, swirly cut-side up. Don't worry if they don't fit snugly together as they will swell and become puffy when they prove. Brush them with egg and then let them rise again for about 15 minutes to let them get duly puffy.

Put in the hot oven and cook for 20–25 minutes, by which time the buns will have risen and will be golden-brown in color. Don't worry if they catch in places—see mine in the picture. Remove them from the pan and leave to cool slightly on a rack—it's easy just to pick up the whole sheet of parchment and transfer them like that—before letting people tear them off, to eat warm.

Makes 20.

SCHNECKEN

Schnecken means "snails," which is what these German-American coiled buns resemble. They are like the Norwegian cinnamon buns, only more so. By which I mean they are stickier, puffier, gooier and generally more over the top. God, I love them.

I first came across them in one of my favorite books, *The Village Baker's Wife* by Gayle and Joe Ortiz, and I've relied heavily on their method and approach (as I do often). If you're at all keen on baking or even the idea of it, do look at this book, and its companion volume and precursor, *The Village Baker*.

for the dough:

3¹/₃ cups bread flour

3 tablespoons cup sugar

¹/₂ teaspoon salt

1 package (¹/₄ ounce) rapid-rise yeast or 1 tablespoon fresh yeast

¹/₃ cup unsalted butter

¹/₂ cup plus 2 tablespoons milk

2 large eggs

for the syrup:

¹/₂ cup plus 1 tablespoon unsalted butter

2 tablespoons turbinado sugar

4 tablespoons maple syrup

3 tablespoons light corn syrup

about 1 cup walnut or pecan pieces

for the glaze:

1 large egg

2 tablespoons milk

for the filling:

3 tablespoons sugar

¹/₂ cup demerara or turbinado sugar

1 tablespoon cinnamon

12-cup muffin pan, buttered parchment-paper-lined roasting pan or baking pan for turning the sticky buns out onto later—large enough to cover muffin pan

Combine the flour, sugar, salt, and yeast in a large bowl. Melt the butter in the milk—use a microwave and a measuring cup for ease—beat in the eggs and stir into the dry ingredients to make a dough. Knead for 10 minutes or for 5 with a dough hook. When it's springy and satiny, form it into a ball, put into an oiled bowl, turn to coat, and cover with plastic wrap. Leave in a warm place for 1 hour or until doubled in size.

Using an electric mixer, start on the syrup: beat the butter until soft and smooth and add the sugar, still beating. Beat in the syrups and then divide this mixture among the muffin cups. Top with the walnuts, about a tablespoonful in each sticky-based waiting cup.

Preheat the oven to 350°F. When the dough's ready, knock it back, knead once or twice and then roll out to a large rectangle, approximately 24 by 12 inches, with the long side nearest you. Beat the egg and add the milk. Glaze the dough, using a pastry brush to paint, or just your fingers.

Mix the filling ingredients in a little bowl and sprinkle onto the dough. Now, roll up from the long side and away from you, carefully and firmly (though not too tightly), keeping a firm sausage shape.

Cut into 12 even slices, and lie each slice spiral-swirly cut side up, on top of the nuts and syrup in the muffin cups.

Leave to rise for about 20 minutes and when they're risen and puffy, put into the oven and bake for 20–25 minutes, by which time they should be golden and cooked: crisp in parts, voluptuously gooey in others.

Place the roasting pan or baking sheet on top and turn the whole thing the other way up. (You will need oven mitts and a degree of caution for this.) Remove the muffin tray and dislodge any nuts that are still stuck in it, adding them, along with any residual syrup, to the upturned buns. Leave to cool, then apply to face—as if you needed my encouragement.

Makes 12.

VARIATION

These killer sticky buns are also wonderful (and probably more authentic) made with a half batch of processor Danish pastry—see below.

PROCESSOR DANISH PASTRY

I've mentioned Beatrice Ojakangas already in the recipe for Finnish rye bread. I came across her joyfully easy way of making Danish pastry in Dorie Greenspan's *Baking with Julia*. I've adapted it to fit my practice and prejudices, but her idea of mixing everything in the food processor is revolutionary. Truthfully, I don't think I'd even have considered making Danish pastry otherwise. It's good to know, indeed crucial, that this still produces an authentic Danish pastry. Beatrice Ojakangas helpfully writes, "Don't think you're cheating by taking the fast track—this is the way it's done these days all over Denmark."

1/4 cup warm water

1/2 cup milk, at room temperature

1 large egg, at room temperature

2 1/4 cups white bread flour

1 package (1/4 ounce) rapid-rise yeast or 1 tablespoon fresh yeast

1 teaspoon salt

1 tablespoon sugar

1 cup unsalted butter, cold, cut into thin slices

Pour the water and milk into a measuring cup and add the egg, beating with a fork to mix. Put to one side for a moment. Get out a large bowl, then put the flour, yeast, salt and sugar in the processor, and give one quick whizz just to mix. Add the cold slices of butter and process briefly so that the butter is cut up a little, though you still want visible chunks of at least 1/2 inch. Empty the contents of the food processor into the large bowl and quickly add the contents of the cup. Use your hands or a rubber spatula to fold the ingredients together, but don't overdo it: expect to have a gooey mess with some butter lumps pebbling it. Cover the bowl with plastic wrap, put in the refrigerator, and leave overnight or up to 4 days.

To turn it into pastry, take it out of the refrigerator, let it get to room temperature, and roll it out to a 20-inch square. Fold the dough square into thirds, like a business letter, turning it afterward so that the closed fold is on your left, like the spine of a book. Roll out again to a 20-inch square, repeating the steps above 3 times. Since each recipe below uses half of this, cut in half, wrap both pieces, and put each in the refrigerator for 30 minutes (you can keep them for up to 4 days, if you haven't already done so at the earlier stage), or refrigerate one to use now and put the other half in the freezer to use later.

Having made the Danish pastry, you need to know what to do with it. Obviously, the first stop is to go into making what we call Danish pastries, and they call "Vienna bread." There are two here: my all-time favorite, a cheese Danish, which you can rarely buy over here, and an almond Danish, exquisite and much better than even a good store-bought one.

ALMOND DANISH

for the pastry:

**a half quantity of processor Danish
pastry dough, rolled out and ready
to use, as above**

**2 baking sheets, oiled or lined with
parchment or wax paper**

for the filling:

**1/2 cup plus 2 tablespoons or 5 ounces
blanched almonds, toasted**

**1/3 cup plus 2 tablespoons
confectioners' sugar**

**2 tablespoons unsalted butter at room
temperature**

1/2 teaspoon almond extract

1 large egg white, beaten lightly

for the egg glaze:

1 large egg, beaten with

2 tablespoons milk

for the clear glaze:

1/3 cup sugar

1/4 cup water

for the sugar glaze:

1/2 cup confectioners' sugar

1–2 tablespoons warm water

To make the almond filling, process the almonds and confectioners' sugar together until finely ground. Add the butter, pulse again, then the almond extract and 2 tablespoons of the egg white. (This can be made in advance and kept in the fridge for a week.)

Roll out the pastry into a big square and cut into thirds horizontally. Then cut in half down the middle, giving you 6 rough squares. Take each square and put a tablespoon of the almond mixture—which you've shaped roughly into a sausage—onto the pastry at a diagonal. Bring up the opposite corners and pinch together, then flatten the pastry slightly.

Place on the baking sheets and brush with the egg glaze. Leave them to rise until they double in size, about 1¹/₂ hours; and again they should feel like marshmallow. Meanwhile, preheat the oven to 350°F.

Cook for 15 minutes or until puffy and beautifully golden brown.

Remove to a wire rack and make the two remaining glazes. To make the clear glaze, heat the granulated sugar and water in a small saucepan. Bring to the boil, then take off the heat. To make the sugar glaze, add the water to the confectioners' sugar a little at a time to make a runny icing; you should be able to ice the pastries in thin lines, running it off the prongs of a fork. So: let the Danish pastries cool slightly before brushing with the clear glaze, painting it on with a pastry brush, and then later, when they are more or less cold, zigzag the sugar glaze over them.

Makes 6.

CHEESE DANISH

for the pastry:

a half quantity of processor Danish pastry dough, rolled out, and ready to use, as above

2 baking sheets, oiled or lined with parchment or wax paper

for the filling:

1 cup ricotta cheese

6 tablespoons sugar

pinch of salt

1 tablespoon lemon zest

1 large egg, beaten

3 tablespoons unsalted butter, melted and cooled

the egg, clear, and sugar glazes:

as above

Combine the cheese, sugar, salt, lemon zest, egg, and butter to make the filling. Roll out the pastry into a big rectangle and cut it in half. Divide each half into thirds and place a tablespoon of cheese filling on each piece of dough. Fold the opposite corners up together and seal with a pinch.

Place on the baking sheets and brush with the egg glaze. Let them rise until they double in size, about 1½ hours; they should then feel like marshmallow. Meanwhile—about 30 minutes before they're ready to be cooked—preheat the oven to 350°F. Pinch the corners back together if they have become unsealed, then put them on their baking sheets into the oven and bake for 15 minutes or until puffy and golden brown.

Transfer to a wire rack and let them cool slightly before brushing with the clear glaze; then later, when they are a lot cooler, drizzle over the sugar glaze.

Makes 6.

TARTE TATIN
For Aunt Fel, 1934–2000

Tarte tatin is so overdone that I never thought I'd be including it in any book I wrote. And if tarte tatin is to be undertaken, it isn't, usually, with Danish pastry. But having made this Danish pastry, I knew instantly that it would be perfect in a tarte tatin. So I overruled myself.

I've relied a lot on my Aunt Fel's taste and judgment while working on this book, and indeed while cooking generally, and I invited her over to eat and give her comments on this. She loved it, and insofar as one can dedicate a recipe to someone's memory, I dedicate this to hers.

scant ¹/₂ cup unsalted butter

¹/₂ cup sugar

2¹/₄ pounds McIntosh or Gala apples,
peeled, quartered, and cored

half measure Danish pastry

8-inch tarte tatin dish, similar-shaped
Le Creuset or cast-iron frying pan

Preheat the oven to 400°F and put in a baking sheet at the same time.

Put the butter in the tarte tatin dish or cast-iron frying pan on the burner. Let the butter melt and add the sugar. When it foams, add the prepared apples, arranging them in a circular pattern, hump-side down, in the dish. Cook on a high heat until the buttery, sugary juices turn a glorious caramel color and the fruit has softened.

Take the pan off the heat, and leave it to stand for 10 minutes.

Roll the Danish pastry out thinly into a circle to fit the top of the dish, plus a bit of overhang. Lay it on top of the apples in the dish, tucking the edges down the sides under the apples, rather like tucking in a sheet. Transfer the dish to the baking sheet in the oven and cook for 20–30 minutes, until the pastry is golden brown and the caramel syrup is bubbling.

Take the cooked tarte out of the oven, place a large plate on top of the dish and, wearing oven mitts and with great care, turn the whole thing upside down. Remove the dish and, *voilà*, your tarte tatin, with its gloriously burnished crown of caramelized fruits. Pick up any apples that have stuck to the dish or that are otherwise out of position, and bring to the table with a small bowl of cold crème fraîche.

Serves 6.

VARIATION
You can also use quinces, either by adding just a few, in among the apples (the most harmonious way, I think), or by substituting them entirely.

THE DOMESTIC
GODDESS'S PANTRY

THE DOMESTIC GODDESS'S PANTRY

There are few things that make us feel so positively domestic as putting food in store. "Putting up," it always used to be called, the canning and preserving of the fruits and vegetables presently in glut but soon to disappear. Life's not quite like that now, but I do preserve fruits and pickle vegetables for the simple reason that I love doing it. I feel I'm putting down roots, laying down a part of the foundation for living.

But please, I'm not getting into Mrs. Bridges drag and don't suggest you do either. I'm not talking about buying bushels and pecks—whatever they may be—of produce and slaving over them for weeks on end. When I make jam, I sometimes make only one small pot at a time. For a start, it's much easier, and I suggest you begin your jam-making career just as sparsely. And few of us anyway have more than a scant shelf on which to store such things. But a few jars here and there are enough to adorn, give pleasure, and be useful. It's true that we bought the house we now live in purely because I fell in love with the pantry, had to have one, but I recognize that, in cities at any rate, certainly in any modern home, they no longer exist. A cupboard or a few inches space on a countertop or shelf is fine, though. And in fact, many of the foods in this chapter actually need to be stored in the refrigerator.

I haven't forgotten the modern world; I wanted to concentrate on jams, chutneys, curds, and pickles that were easy to make, required no expertise or experience, and didn't take days or depend upon multi-staged procedures. I know the idea of being in the kitchen faffing around with bottles and jars and hot pans might seem confining to many, but honestly, I have found it liberating. The sense of connectedness you get, with your kitchen, your home, your food, is the very opposite of constraint. Just follow one suggestion, one recipe in this chapter, and I promise you'll see what I mean.

CLEAN JARS

Before you do anything, to store jams, chutneys, glazes, jellies, etc., you need sterilized jars. I have to say, I regard a dishwasher-cleaned jar as a sterilized jar, but you do have to use it straight away, while it's still warm from the machine. Otherwise, you can sterilize the jars in the microwave by filling them a quarter full with water and microwaving them on high for 10 minutes. Drain and use while still warm.

The conventional method for rigorous sterilizing of jars involves scrubbing them well in warm soapy water, rinsing them, and then letting them dry off in a cool oven (250°F). Again, you should put the jam in them while they're still warm, so you may as well leave the jars in the oven until you need them.

VANILLA SUGAR

3³⁄₄ cups sugar   **2 vanilla beans**

Fill a canning glass jar with the sugar and the vanilla beans, each cut into thirds; after a week you will have sugar infused with the sort of domestically heady fragrance that seems as if it could only have come from the most well-stocked and well-ordered of Victorian larders. It's the aromatic equivalent of well-worn, ambrosially evocative, cream-painted tongue-and-groove paneling.

You can use it in place of ordinary sugar in cakes, pies, puddings—more or less anything sweet. You can even make this your kitchen-counter sugar pot, though have nonscented available for tea drinkers. This is good in coffee, and there's nothing nicer than mugs of vanilla-scented warm milk at bedtime.

VARIATIONS
You can go quite to town with scented sugars. In place of the vanilla beans, use cinnamon sticks, unsprayed rose petals, or dried tangerine peel, which you can find in Chinese and most Asian stores. I also keep a store of rosemary sugar, which is just granulated sugar with a few sprigs of rosemary—the needles eventually fall off of their own accord—and use, sparsely, to sweeten meat or tomato sauces for pasta and on the rosemary loaf cake on page 9.

RHUBARB SCHNAPPS

In the middle of one night, I realized that, however great my love for rhubarb, I had never drunk a liqueur made from it. This, then, is my version. Use the measurements as guidance only. As with the quince brandy below, really it comes down to choosing quantities to fit into whatever jars or bottles you have available.

approximately 2 pounds of rhubarb, to make 1 1/4 pounds trimmed weight

1 1/2 cups sugar

1 liter vodka, plus more if needed

2 1-liter jars

1-liter bottle

Chop the rhubarb and divide it between the two jars. Add ¾ cup sugar to each jar, put the lids on, and shake well. Unclip the lids and pour 2¼ cups of vodka—and I use the cheapest I can find—into each to fill. If that doesn't fill them, then pour in more. But it should; the rhubarb takes up a lot of each jar.

Close the lids, put the rhubarb somewhere cool and dark for at least 6 weeks and up to 6 months. If you remember, shake the jars every day or every other day for the first month or so.

Strain into a pitcher, then pour into a bottle. There's your rhubarb schnapps.
Makes 1 liter.

QUINCE BRANDY

To tell the truth I made this partly because I'd bought masses of quinces out of exuber-
ance and excitement because they were in season and then felt increasingly guilty because
I'd been too exhausted and busy to do anything with them. So I did this. Of course, now
I'll do it every year: it is so peachily delicious. The quinces and the aromatic spices
mellow the brandy, and their fragrances hover around just enough to let you know
they're there. Use this for the quincemeat, and indeed the Christmas pudding, on pages
265 and 256—and in anything else that you think would benefit from it.

I don't bottle this: I leave it in its beautiful jar, like something you imagine
William Morris dreaming of, and use a small, lipped ladle to spoon it out into shot
glasses after dinner.

4–6 quinces
approximately 4 bottles cheap
  brandy, or as needed to fill jar

2 large or 4 small cinnamon sticks
4 star anise
1-gallon jar or 2 1-liter jars

Wipe your quinces with kitchen towels, then cut and quarter them; but don't peel or core
them. Put them in the bottom of a large, wide-mouthed bottle or jar and pour cheap
brandy over to come to the top. Arrange the cinnamon sticks and star anise in this amber
underwater scene and fasten the lid. Leave for at least 6 weeks before drinking.

Makes approximately 2 liters.

QUINCE GLAZE

Quince jelly—which is the traditional use to which quinces are put—seems to me to involve an exhausting and masochistic procedure. Take a tree of quinces, several days' dripping through elaborately suspended cheesecloth, and what do you end up with? A bare pot's bottom of precious liquid, dotted with suicidally greedy ants and bugs.

This is the smarter alternative: if you're feeling domestically inclined you can use it to glaze fruit tarts or to sweeten and perfume apple pies and crumbles; if not, then use it as a stickily aromatic sauce over good bought ice cream (and over lemon or lemon meringue ice cream it's superb) or dribble in coral wreaths over cream-splodged meringues.

1 quince

3 cups water

2¹/₂ cups sugar

1 1-pint jar

Roughly chop the quince (a cleaver is probably the best tool for this), put the pieces—peel, seeds, and all—in a medium-sized saucepan with the water and sugar, and bring to the boil. Let it bubble away for a good hour, or until the liquid seems reduced by half, and strain into the prepared jar, in which you can keep it pretty indefinitely in the fridge.

Makes about 1 pint.

CURDS

Strictly speaking, a curd is not a pantry item because it needs to be kept in the refrigerator, but that's irrelevant to my thesis: making a fruit curd is one of the simplest ways of making yourself feel like a provider of comforting domestic bounty.

CRANBERRY CURD

There is only one word to describe the color of this fabulous, astringent but velvety curd: magenta. Well, some would say cerise, but that, of course, would convey quite the wrong culinary connotations. Either way, you get the picture.

I've given enough quantities to make quite a bit, because it occurs to me that it would make a good Christmas present.

5 cups or 1 pound cranberries	**1²/3 cups sugar**
1 cup plus 2 tablespoons water	**6 large eggs**
7 tablespoons unsalted butter	**5 ¹/2-pint jars or equivalent**

Place the cranberries and water in a saucepan, cover them, and cook on a low heat until tender and popped. Pass the cranberries through a food mill (or push through a sieve) and put the fruit purée back into a saucepan. Add the butter and sugar, melting them gently. Beat the eggs in a bowl and strain them into the saucepan. Stir the curd constantly over a medium heat until it has thickened. This requires patience as you don't want to speed things up and curdle the mixture, but that's not particularly challenging. When it has thickened, it should coat the back of a spoon. Let cool a little before pouring into the jars. Keep in the fridge.

Makes about 5 cups.

PASSIONFRUIT CURD

As wonderful as this is to eat piled on top of fresh white bread, it is exceptional sandwiching a Victoria sponge, dolloped over muffins and pancakes, or poured into a cooked and cooled pastry shell.

11 passionfruit

2 large eggs

2 large egg yolks

1/2 cup sugar

7 tablespoons unsalted butter

2 1/2-pint jars

Put the seeded pulp of 10 of the passionfruit into the processor and blitz just to loosen the seeds. Strain into a pitcher or bowl.

Beat the eggs, egg yolks, and sugar together.

Melt the butter over a low heat in a heavy-bottomed pan, and when melted stir in the sugar-egg mixture and the passionfruit juice, and keep cooking gently, stirring constantly, until thickened.

Off the heat, whisk in the pulp—seeds and all—of the remaining passionfruit, let cool slightly, then pour into the jars. Keep in the refrigerator.

Makes about 1¾ cups.

LIME CURD

Flora Woods gave me this recipe when she blessed me with her famous zucchini cake (pages 18–19). I'll pass on your thanks to her.

6 tablespoons unsalted butter

3 large eggs

1/2 cup sugar

1/2 cup lime juice (of approximately
    4 limes)

zest of 1 lime

2 1/2-pint jars

Melt the butter in a heavy-based saucepan, add all the other ingredients and whisk to a custard over a gentle heat. Let cool before filling a jar—or a cake—with it. Keep in the refrigerator.

Makes about 1¾ cups.

JAMS AND JELLIES

I know the idea of making jam can seem off-putting, but let me tell you I never, or rarely with any success, use a sugar thermometer. I put a saucer into the freezer before I start, and while cooking I take the pan off the heat and splodge teaspoons of jam onto it. If the jam wrinkles when I push at it with a finger, it's ready.

Start by making small quantities, which are easier to keep under control and are anyway more useful. Always use a big pan to make jam, preferably a preserving pan, as the jam needs room to boil rapidly without boiling over.

HANDS-FREE RASPBERRY JAM

This is the best jam to start with as it doesn't need any testing or temperature taking or indeed anything much: you just put the fruit and sugar, separately, into the oven and then, on mixing together, you've made your jam. As you'd expect, it is intensely fresh-tasting, and indeed will spoil if you don't keep it in the refrigerator. It's the best jam to use, with sweet fresh cream, to sandwich a vanilla-scented, tender-crumbed Victoria sponge.

This is another recipe that comes from the movingly hand-scrawled book that belonged to Hettie's mother, Soot.

1 cup or ½ pint raspberries   **1 8-ounce jar**
1 cup sugar

Preheat the oven to 350°F.

Put the raspberries and sugar into two separate bowls; I use pie plates, so the fruit will be spread out rather than piled up. Put the bowls into the oven for 20–25 minutes until they are really hot. Take them out of the oven carefully, and add the sugar to the raspberries. As you do so you'll find the fruit turns into a molten, ruby-red river. Pour this into the cleaned and waiting jar. Fasten it, and leave to cool before storing in the refrigerator.

Makes about 1¼ cups.

STRAWBERRY JAM

I use balsamic vinegar—which provides the darkness and really does seem to make the strawberries strawberrier—when making jam.

I use preserving sugar here instead of granulated sugar since the lemon provides enough pectin to make the jam set and the larger crystals of the preserving sugar make for a clearer, more jewel-like, jam. If you must, use ordinary granulated sugar instead.

3–3½ cups strawberries (buy 3½ cups, since you will inevitably have to discard some)

2½ cups sugar

2 tablespoons lemon juice

1 teaspoon balsamic vinegar

4 8-ounce jars or equivalent

Stick a saucer into the freezer.

Put all the ingredients into a wide saucepan and stir with a wooden spoon to make sure all the fruit is coated. I don't cut up the fruit, but you could if you wanted.

Put the pan on a low heat and, stirring every now and again, bring to the boil. Let boil for about 5–8 minutes, depending on the size of your pan, and start testing for setting point from 4 minutes, taking the pan off the heat and putting a scant teaspoon onto the saucer. Leave it to cool and then poke at it to see if it's ready (see page 346).

When you've reached this point, leave the pan to cool for 20 minutes before decanting into the cleaned, prepared jars.

Makes about 3¾ cups.

BLACKBERRY JAM

The first time I made this I used just the one ½ pint of blackberries I had in the house. It was a Saturday morning and I felt like some casual kitchen putskying. I used the same jam the next day to fill the crostata (page 105) and I urge you, when you're in the mood, to do the same.

I've given quantities for quite an uncharacteristically large amount of jam because blackberries really are the one fruit I find we do get a glut of in England. But as you can see from the ratio of ingredients, you can work out what to do with less (or more) fruit easily enough.

4 cups blackberries
3¹/₃ cups sugar

juice of 1 lemon
4 8-ounce jars or equivalent

Place your testing saucer in the freezer.

Put the fruit, sugar, and lemon juice into a preserving pan, or other large, wide pan, and let the sugar dissolve over a low heat. Turn the heat up and bring the jam to the boil. Keep the jam at a rolling boil until setting point is reached.

Makes 1 quart.

GREENGAGE JAM

If blackberries are something we often have in excess, greengage plums I can never have enough of. Nothing can match their honeyed acidity or grapey fullness. Some years I worry that I'm never going to find them at all, and I would do anything to help preserve this increasingly unavailable fruit. I've done a small, selfish bit by planting a couple of trees, but I feel that more has to be done. In the meantime, keep your eyes peeled in August.

This is what you should do with any fruit you come across that is perhaps just too sour to eat—that sourness aids the setting. But don't use hard, bitter fruits that shouldn't even have found their way to market.

3¹/₄ pounds greengage plums,
** halved and pitted**
1 cup plus 2 tablespoons water

3¹/₃ cups sugar
6 8-ounce jars or equivalent

Place a saucer in the freezer.

Get out a large pan, and gently simmer the greengages in the water for 15 minutes. Add the sugar, but don't boil until it has dissolved. Then boil until setting point is reached.

When the jam's at setting point, just, pour into warmed, cleaned jars and close. Makes about 6 cups.

SOFT-SET PEACH AND RED CURRANT JAM

Not only does this look beautiful, the coral chunks of peach suspended in crimson jelly, but the tastes of these two very different fruits seem to set each other off particularly well.

Don't use those mean, hard little unyielding peaches, as unattractive as a bony bottom, but this jam is a good way of transforming fruit that might not be juicily rewarding to eat fresh.

8 peaches, pitted and cut into chunks
2 pints red currants
4 pounds or 6 cups sugar

1 cup plus 2 tablespoons water
juice of 1/2 a lemon
7 8-ounce jars or equivalent

Put a saucer in the freezer, and get out a big pan or, ideally, a preserving pan, as the jam will need to bubble up a lot as it reduces.

Put everything in the pan, and let the sugar dissolve on a gentle heat. Then boil vigorously; it should reach setting point after about 20 minutes (and remember that this jam wants to be only just set; you need detect only the ghost of a wrinkle on the jam's surface).

Let the jam cool in the pan off the heat for 20 minutes before ladling into prepared jars and closing them.

Makes about 7 cups.

Clockwise from top left: pink-grapefruit marmalade, greengage jam (page 348) and soft-set peach and red currant jam (page 349)

PINK GRAPEFRUIT MARMALADE

Please note the easy method for making this: no funny business with suspended cheese-cloth involved.

2 pink grapefruit, weighing approximately 1³/4 pounds	**juice of 2 lemons**
2¹/4 pounds or 5 cups sugar	**4–5 8-ounce jars or equivalent**

Place a saucer in the freezer.

Put the pink grapefruit into a large saucepan, fill with enough water so that they float freely, bring to the boil and simmer for about 2 hours, by which time the grapefruit should be very soft. Add more hot water from a kettle if the liquid's boiling away.

Drain, remove the fruit to a board and slice the cooked grapefruit thinly, and then chop a bit, using the whole fruit, pith and all (though remove any large seeds). Put the grapefruit back into the saucepan, and add the sugar and lemon juice. Let the sugar dissolve over a gentle heat and then bring to the boil until setting point is reached, about 15 minutes.

Ladle into prepared jars and close the lids.

Makes just over 1 quart.

VARIATIONS

To make ordinary orange marmalade, boil the same weight of Seville oranges for the same amount of time. When they're cooked and soft, take them out of the pan, reserving the liquid, cut them in half, scoop out the seeds and put in a small pan, then chop up the oranges as finely or coarsely as you like and put them into a large pan.

Ladle some of the orange-cooking water over the seeds in the small pan and put on the heat, bring to the boil, and let boil for 5 minutes. Strain this over the chopped oranges in their pan, add the juice of 2 lemons and stir in 5–6 cups sugar. Bring to the boil gently, so that the sugar dissolves before the jam actually starts boiling and then proceed as above.

To make ginger-orange marmalade, add about 1½ inch worth of finely sliced or chopped ginger to the seeds, and then push 1 inch's worth of ginger, in batches, through a garlic press to extract the juice over the pan of chopped oranges. Taste when you've reached setting point to see if you want to add more squeezed ginger.

I also love marmalade that is dark and treacly and especially aromatic: replace half the sugar with light brown (and add 1 tablespoonful of molasses if you like this really dark) and pour in a slug of rum or bourbon, once with the chopped oranges and again after setting point is reached.

MUSCAT JELLY

This is the easiest jelly in the world. And it is more than just easy: it's pure, golden pleasure. In France, Sauternes jelly is often eaten with foie gras, and feel free to use this the same way (indeed it would make a good present to accompany some at Christmas), but I love it with most cold meats, especially ham.

1 ¹/₂ cups muscat

1 ¹/₄ cups sugar

2 teaspoons orange-flower water

hand-squeezed juice of ¹/₂ a lemon,
   with seeds

2–3 2-inch lengths orange peel

6 coriander seeds

pinch of salt

2 8-ounce jars or equivalent

Put a saucer in the freezer.

Stir together all the ingredients in a medium to small saucepan, then put on the burner over a medium to high flame and stir no longer; any stirring now will make the jelly crystallize. Bring to the boil, boil for 10 minutes, then test a little on the cold saucer. When it's reached setting point, remove it from the heat.

If you've got a jelly bag, so much the better (it's finer), otherwise just strain it through a nonmetallic sieve into a measuring cup and thence into the jars.

Makes about 1²/₃ cups.

FRUIT

FIGS IN RUM SYRUP

Preserving figs is never going to have quite the same connotations for us as it does for Italians. They have, at the end of summer, an excess of them; for us they're nearly always imported, and therefore a luxury. But I still like to make these, if only because they're at their best about 3–4 months after bottling, which means that over Christmas you can eat them, glossy with dark, aromatic syrup, with vanilla ice cream or piled onto some toasted leftover panettone.

It occurs to me, too, that bottled in beautiful jars—and I use the very beautiful one you see, centrally, in the opening pages of this chapter—these would also make wonderful Christmas presents.

2¼ pounds Black Mission figs (about 18)	⅓ cup white rum, plus 2 tablespoons and more as needed
1½ cups sugar	1 1-quart jar
2¼ cups water	

Wash the figs and wipe dry with kitchen towels—gently so as not to break the tender skin—and set aside in a colander while you get on with the syrup.

Put the sugar and water in a large pan and bring slowly to the boil, so that the sugar's dissolved before the liquid reaches boiling point.

Let the syrup bubble away for 15 minutes—not too vociferously but don't, either, let it dwindle to a simmer. Take off the heat, add the ⅓ cup of rum and, gently, the figs. Swill the pan so that the figs are more or less covered and cook at a simmer for about 1½ hours with the lid on at an angle, so that the heat doesn't build up too much, but not too much liquid evaporates. Every now and again, using wooden spatulas or some other tool that won't tear the figs' skin, turn the figs so that all parts are covered and cooked equally.

Remove the figs to the clean preserving jar, put the juices back on the heat, and let boil for 10 minutes to reduce further. Remove from the heat, add the 2 tablespoons of white rum, stir to combine and pour over the figs in the jar. If there's not enough syrup to cover them, pour in more rum.

Close the lid and leave in a dark, cool place for at least 6 weeks and not more than 6 months.

Makes enough to fill a 1-quart jar.

PICKLED PLUMS

If you go into some health-food stores or specialty shops you will find Japanese plum seasoning. It's an intensely sharp, clear pink plum (*ume*) vinegar. It seemed obvious, therefore, to use this to pickle plums. Quite apart from how good these taste, they look so beautiful—the dark red of the fruit in the tawny pink of the pickling liquid.

Bring out to eat with cold meats and use within 3–4 months, not because they'll go off but because after a while the fruit goes a bit too mushy.

2¼ cups or 16 fluid ounces Japanese red-plum seasoning

1¾ cups sugar

2 star anise

1-inch piece of fresh ginger, peeled and thinly sliced

1 tablespoon coriander seeds

2 cinnamon sticks, broken in half

3 strips of finely peeled orange zest

1 pound plums, halved and pitted

3 1-pint jars or equivalent

In a large saucepan, bring the Japanese plum seasoning to the boil with the sugar, star anise, ginger, coriander seeds, cinnamon sticks and orange zest. Stir well until all the sugar has dissolved and simmer for 15 minutes, then take off the heat and allow to cool a little.

Pack the plum halves into the sterilized jars, to come within 2 inches of the top, while the jars are still warm. Now pour the vinegar over, covering the plums by about 1 inch. Tap the jars to make sure there are no air bubbles, then insert a long skewer down the sides of the jars to double-check (this works on the swizzle-stick principle, or so I like to think). Make sure the spices and orange zest are fairly evenly shared out and arranged so as to maximize aesthetic pleasure. Seal the jars well, and store in a cool, dark place for at least a week before eating. Keep in the refrigerator once opened.

Makes 3 pints.

VARIATION

Use red-wine vinegar (or any other vinegar you want) in place of the red-plum seasoning.

Clockwise from top: pineapple chutney (page 358), spiced apple chutney and Chinese plum sauce (page 363)

CHUTNEYS AND PICKLES

Chutneys, you should know before reading further, are a breeze to make. You simply chuck everything in one pan and let it boil for about 30 minutes until you've got a pulpy mass.

SPICED APPLE CHUTNEY

Well, all chutneys contain spices, but the intense, hot flavors in this chutney are the focus. I sneered when Hettie suggested this when we had a tree full of apples that I was letting rot, but she was right. The idea of apple chutney may seem unappealing—I just thought of it as grainy mush—but the taste is out of this world. I now cannot eat a Cornish pasty without it.

1 pound cooking apples

1 medium onion

2 small red chilies such as serrano or Thai

1¼ cups demerara or turbinado sugar

1 teaspoon ground allspice

1 teaspoon ground cloves

½ teaspoon sea salt

black pepper

1 heaping tablespoon chopped or grated fresh ginger

1 teaspoon turmeric

1½ cups cider vinegar

4 8-ounce jars or equivalent

Peel and roughly chop the apples, and finely chop the onion. Seed the chilies and chop them finely (I'd advise you to put on rubber gloves for this, especially if you wear contact lenses).

Put all the ingredients in a pan, and bring to the boil. Cook over a medium heat for 30–40 minutes, until the mixture thickens. Spoon into the cleaned jars and, when cool, place them, with great and warm satisfaction, in your cupboard.

Makes 1 quart.

PINEAPPLE CHUTNEY

This is fabulous with cold ham. And you can water it down and use it to glaze hams before you've oven-blitzed them. And I adore it with cold turkey—along with some cold bread sauce and a spot of English mustard—in a Boxing-Day sandwich. Cold chicken and mayonnaise can always stand in.

1 ripe pineapple, peeled and chunked into bite-size pieces	3/4 cup demerara or turbinado sugar
juice of the pineapple (approximately 4 tablespoons)	1 cinnamon stick, broken into pieces
	3 cloves
1 medium cooking apple, peeled, cored, and finely chopped	2 star anise
	1 teaspoon mustard seeds
1/2 cup rice (or cider) vinegar	1 teaspoon turmeric
	2–3 8-ounce jars or equivalent

Put all the ingredients into a heavy-bottomed saucepan. Bring to the boil, and simmer for 45 minutes or so, until you have a rough, jammy pulp.

Cool slightly and then ladle into the washed and sterilized jars.

Makes about 2½ cups.

PARADISE CHUTNEY

In a wonderful and instructive old book, Beryl Wood's *Let's Preserve It*, which I picked up at a second-hand bookshop in Falmouth, England, I read about a marvelous-sounding jelly, made of apples, quinces, and cranberries, and called, evocatively, paradise jelly. So I thought I'd use the idea, and the name, to make something more plausible in the modern kitchen.

Since chutneys are—I think—at their best about a month after being made, it makes this perfect for adding a necessary jolt to a plateful of Christmas leftovers. For, since quinces are really only around in November, you can't make it at any other time of the year. And, you should know, it is excellent with blue cheese.

1 pound quince, peeled, cored, and cut into chunks	2¼ cups sugar
	4 cloves
3¼ cups water	2 cinnamon sticks, crumbled
1 pound cooking apples, peeled, cored, and cut into chunks	1 tablespoon English mustard powder
	juice and zest of 1 orange
1 medium onion, chopped	juice and zest of 1 lemon
8 ounces fresh cranberries	1½ cups cider vinegar
5 ounces dried cranberries	4 1-pint jars or equivalent

Save the peelings and cores from the quince, and put them into a saucepan with the water. Boil for about 10–15 minutes until you have about 1½ cups remaining.

Put all the ingredients, including the strained 1½ cups of quince-peelings liquid, in a large pan or preserving pan, and let the sugar dissolve over a low heat. Then bring it up to the boil and cook for about 1 hour. Try to keep the pan at a gentle boil, as you need everything to cook down and thicken slightly. When it's ready, all should be soft and fairly pulpy; only the pieces of quince should still be visible.

Ladle into sterilized jars.

Makes about 2 quarts.

EDITH AFIF'S LIME PICKLES

I call these lime pickles because that's what my friend Steve, who gave me this recipe of his late mother's, calls them. But think, rather, of limes, salted, rinsed, and preserved in aromatic oil. When the Edith of the title made these in her native Egypt, she dredged the limes with salt over days; only later did she adapt her method to what was then modern technology. People can get so precious about tradition that I love the proof that change and modernity can be progress: somehow, salting the limes and leaving them in the freezer—rather brilliant of her to come up with the idea—breaks down the fruit's fibers much more effectively.

You either have a sour tooth or you don't. I do, and love these pickles—with bread and cheese, aromatic stews, cold meats, anything.

10 limes
4¹/₂ cups or 2 pounds 3 ounces
  coarse salt
approximately 2¹/₄ cups olive oil
  (not extra virgin)

1 tablespoon turmeric
1 teaspoon cumin seeds
3 dried red chili peppers, crumbled
3 12-ounce preserving jars
12 x 8-inch baking tray or Pyrex dish

Cut the limes into eighths lengthways and cover the bottom of your dish with them. Cover the limes with the salt and then put in the freezer overnight or for a day (12 hours should do it, but longer won't hurt).

Remove from the freezer and thaw thoroughly. Put into a colander and rinse under the cold tap. Shake dry. Put a third into each clean, waiting jar. Decant the oil into a measuring cup and stir in the turmeric, cumin seeds, and crumbled pepper. Pour the oil to come to the very top of the jars (and if you need more than 2 cups to do this then simply add more—if the limes aren't submerged you'll get mold). Close and put away in a dark place. Leave for at least 3 weeks before eating. The longer you leave them, the more tender and exquisite they are.

Makes 3 12-ounce jars.

BROWN SAUCE

I know that the ingredients that follow hardly look like the stock constituents of brown sauce, and I should own up and say that this didn't start off life as brown sauce. It was conceived to be a rhubarb chutney, only I added too much liquid and what with one thing and another, I decided the only way to salvage it was to whizz it in the blender and turn it into a sauce. This isn't just a case of making the best of a bad lot: this is one of my favorite recipes in the whole book—for its depth of flavor, its full-toned tanginess—and a reminder that cooking is often about what you do, unplanned, in response to the here and now, not merely the careful application of culinary formulae.

2¹/4 pounds rhubarb

1 pound red onions (about 5 small ones)

2 long red chilies, deseeded

2 garlic cloves

1 medium cooking apple

1 ounce (about 1 inch) fresh ginger, minced

1 tablespoon ground ginger

1 tablespoon paprika

²/3 cup or 5 ounces golden raisins

¹/3 cup dried cherries

2¹/4 cups red-wine vinegar

1 tablespoon salt

2¹/4 pounds demerara or turbinado sugar

2 1-quart jars and 1 1-pint jar, or equivalent

Trim the rhubarb, chop it very roughly, put it into the food processor, and chop finely, but don't turn it into a mush; you may want to do this in stages, or else just cut the trimmed rhubarb into ¹/4 inch slices by hand. Tip the chopped rhubarb into a large, heavy-bottomed pan. Now process the onions, chillies, and garlic until finely chopped and transfer these to the pan with the rhubarb. Chop the apples the same way and add to the pan.

Stir in the minced fresh ginger, the ground ginger, paprika, raisins, dried cherries, red-wine vinegar, salt, and sugar.

Bring to a boil, then lower the heat and simmer until everything has turned to an undulating but still just nubbly pulp—about 45 minutes.

Take the pan off the heat, let cool for about 10 minutes, and then, a ladleful or so at a time, liquify or process until smooth. Pour into the sterilized jars, let cool, cover and store away, with joy and satisfaction in your heart.

Makes about 2¹/2 quarts.

CHINESE PLUM SAUCE

Whether people from China would call this a Chinese plum sauce I can't honestly say, but let's not quibble about details. It's wonderful with pork, with sharp Cheddar, with, well, most things. And sometimes I stir a tablespoon or two of it into a winey beef stew while I'm making it. It's very addictive, which I guess has something to do with both the sugar and the chili—and the fact that it tastes so good.

I made it last year from some plums in my garden, which was particularly satisfying, but it's certainly worth buying some expressly for this.

4¼ pounds plums, pitted and quartered

1½ pounds apples, peeled, cored, and cut into ½-inch chunks

1 medium red onion

4 cloves of garlic, minced

3 cups rice vinegar

1 pound sugar

1 pound dark brown sugar (or light if you prefer)

1-inch piece of ginger, peeled and sliced into fine splinters

2 long red chilies

2–4 dried red chilies (depending on how hot you want it), crumbled

2 teaspoons Chinese 5-spice powder

1 stick of cinnamon, broken into pieces

2 pieces dried orange peel, optional

3 1-quart jars

Use a big pan, such as a preserving pan, so that it can boil well to reduce, and put all the ingredients in it.

Cook everything at a steady boil for 1–1½ hours. When it is ready, it will still be runny—remember it is sauce—but it will become firmer; both the apples and the plums will set more on cooling. However, it should have reduced to make a jamlike mixture with no obvious signs of the fruit still apparent.

Bottle in the sterilized jars.

Makes about 2¾ quarts.

BIBLIOGRAPHY

Anderson, Pam, *The Perfect Recipe* (Houghton Mifflin, 1998)

Appel, Jennifer, and Allysa Torey, *The Magnolia Bakery Cookbook* (Simon & Schuster, 1999)

Bauer, Michael and Fran Irwin (eds), *The San Francisco Chronicle Cookbook* (Chronicle Books, 1997)

Bery, Odette J., *Another Season Cookbook* (The Globe Pequot Press, 1986)

Collister, Linda, *Sweet Pies and Tarts* (Ryland Peters & Small, 1997)

Colwin, Laurie, *Home Cooking* (HarperCollins, 2000)

Conte, Anna del, *The Gastronomy of Italy* (Bantam Press, 1987)

—— *Secrets from an Italian Kitchen* (Bantam Press, 1989)

Costa, Margaret, *Four Seasons Cookbook* (Grub Street, 1996)

Crawford-Poole, Shona, *Iced Delights* (Conran Octopus, 1986)

Farrow, Genevieve, and Diane Dreher, *The Joy of Muffins* (Golden West, 1989)

Fobel, Jim, *Jim Fobel's Old-Fashioned Baking Book: Recipes from an American Childhood* (Lake Isle Press, 1996)

Greenspan, Dorie, with Julia Child, *Baking with Julia* (William Morrow, 1996)

Greenstein, George, *Secrets of a Jewish Baker* (The Crossing Press, 1993)

Grigson, Jane, *Fruit Book* (Michael Joseph, 1982)

—— *English Food* (Ebury Press, 1992)

Kimball, Christopher, *The Yellow Farmhouse Cookbook* (Little, Brown, 1998)

Lawson, Nigella, *How to Eat* (John Wiley & Sons, 1998)

Levy Beranbaum, Rose, *The Cake Bible* (William Morrow, 1988)

Machlin, Edda Servi, *The Classic Cuisine of the Italian Jews* (Giro Press, 1981)

McNair, James, *James McNair's Cakes* (Chronicle Books, 1999)

Ojakangas, Beatrice A., *The Great Scandinavian Baking Book* (University of Minnesota Press, 1999)

Ortiz, Joe, *The Village Baker* (Ten Speed Press, 1993)

—— and Gayle Ortiz, *The Village Baker's Wife* (Ten Speed Press, 1997)

Purdy, Susan G., *The Family Baker* (Broadway Books, 1999)

Rubinstein, Helge, *The Chocolate Book* (Macdonald & Co., 1981)

Schloss, Andrew, *One-Pot Cakes* (William Morrow, 1995)
Stavroulakis, Nicolas, *The Cookbook of the Jews of Greece* (Jason Aronson Inc., 1996)

Treuille, Eric and Ursula Ferrigno, *Bread* (Dorling Kindersley, 1998)

Willan, Anne, *Real Food: Fifty Years of Good Eating* (Macmillan, 1988)
Willard, Pat, *Pie Every Day* (Algonquin Books of Chapel Hill, 1997)
Wood, Beryl, *Let's Preserve It* (Souvenir Press, 1970)

ACKNOWLEDGMENTS

There are many people who have helped, either with ingredients or equipment, in the course of this book, and to whom I owe thanks, most notably the Conran Shop, Ecko Bakeware, Graham & Greene, Kitchen Ideas, Marks & Spencer together with W. Brice and Son of Mockbeggar Farm, Michanicou Brothers, Mortimer & Bennett, Selfridges, Somerill & Bishop, Tiffany & Co., Vessel, and Wedgwood.

One wanders into the land of platitude in saying that no book is the product of only one person's effort, but it's true all the same. I am grateful to a number of people, Eugenie Boyd, Caz Hildebrand, Gail Rebuck, Alison Samuel, Petrina Tinslay, and Ed Victor chief among them.

I could not even broach the subject of my own, overwhelming gratitude without mentioning my three graces: those domestic goddesses Lisa Grillo and Kate Mellor, who have made it possible for me to work, to write, indeed to live, and Hettie Potter, who came into my life at just the right time, and without whom this book could never have been written. She has cooked with me, taken notes for me, supported me, and kept me sane.

INDEX